The Quran With Tafsir Ibn Kathir
Part 14 of 30:
Al Hijr 001 To An Nahl 128

The Quran With Tafsir Ibn Kathir
Part 14 of 30:
Al Hijr 001 To
An Nahl 128

With
Arabic Script, Transliteration of Arabic, Meaning in English
and Ibn Kathir's Abridged Tafsir (Explanation)

Muhammad Saed Abdul-Rahman

BSc, DipHE

© Muhammad Saed Abdul-Rahman, 2012
ISBN 978-1-86179-867-1

All Rights reserved

British Library Cataloguing in Publication Data. A Catalogue record for this book is available from the British Library

Designed, Typeset and produced by:
MSA Publication Limited, 4 Bello Close, Herne Hill,
London SE24 9BW
United Kingdom

Cover design: Houriyah Abdul-Rahman

TABLE OF CONTENTS

- TABLE OF CONTENTS V
- PRELUDE XIII
  - OPENING SERMAN XIII
  - OUR MISSION XIV
  - BIOGRAPHY OF HAFIZ IBN KATHIR (701 H - 774 H) XIV
    - Ibn Kathir's Teachers xiv
    - Ibn Kathir's Students xv
    - Ibn Kathir's Books xv
    - Ibn Kathir's Death xvi
- PREFACE XVII
  - ABOUT THIS BOOK XVII
  - PERFORMING PROSTRATION WHILE READING THE QUR'AN XVII
- PART 14 FULL ARABIC TEXT 1
- CHAPTER (SURAH) 15: AL-HIJR (STONELAND, ROCK CITY), VERSES 001–099 13
  - *Surah: 15 Ayah: 1, Ayah: 2 & Ayah: 3* 13
    - Tafsir Ibn Kathir 13
      - The Disbelievers will someday wish that They had been Muslims 13
  - *Surah: 15 Ayah: 4 & Ayah: 5* 14
    - Tafsir Ibn Kathir 14
      - Every Township has its allotted Time 14
  - *Surah: 15 Ayah: 6, Ayah: 7, Ayah: 8 & Ayah: 9* 15
    - Tafsir Ibn Kathir 15
      - The Accusation that the Prophet was a Madman and Demands for Him to bring down Angels 15
  - *Surah: 15 Ayah: 10, Ayah: 11, Ayah: 12 & Ayah: 13* 16
    - Tafsir Ibn Kathir 16
      - The Idolators of Every Nation made a Mockery of their Messengers 16
  - *Surah: 15 Ayah: 14 & Ayah: 15* 17
    - Tafsir Ibn Kathir 17
      - The Stubborn Disbelievers will never believe, no matter what Signs and Wonders They see 17
  - *Surah: 15 Ayah: 16, Ayah: 17, Ayah: 18, Ayah: 19 & Ayah: 20* 17
    - Tafsir Ibn Kathir 18
      - The Power of Allah and His Signs in the Heavens and on Earth 18
  - *Surah: 15 Ayah: 21, Ayah: 22, Ayah: 23, Ayah: 24 & Ayah: 25* 19
    - Tafsir Ibn Kathir 20
      - The Supplies for All Things are with Allah 20
      - Benefits of the Winds 21
      - Fresh Water is a Blessing from Allah 21

The Power of Allah to initiate and renew Creation 21
Surah: 15 Ayah: 26 & Ayah: 27... *22*
    Tafsir Ibn Kathir 22
        The Substances from which Mankind and Jinns were created 22
Surah: 15 Ayah: 28, Ayah: 29, Ayah: 30, Ayah: 31, Ayah: 32 & Ayah: 33 .... *23*
    Tafsir Ibn Kathir 24
        The creation of Adam, the Command to the Angels to prostrate to Him, and the Rebellion of Iblis 24
Surah: 15 Ayah: 34, Ayah: 35, Ayah: 36, Ayah: 37 & Ayah: 38........................... *24*
    Tafsir Ibn Kathir 25
        The Expulsion of Iblis from Jannah, and His Reprieve until the Day of Resurrection 25
Surah: 15 Ayah: 39, Ayah: 40, Ayah: 41, Ayah: 42, Ayah: 43 & Ayah: 44 .... *25*
    Tafsir Ibn Kathir 26
        The Threat of Iblis to tempt Mankind, and Allah's Promise of Hell for him 26
        The Gates of Hell are Seven 27
Surah: 15 Ayah: 45, Ayah: 46, Ayah: 47, Ayah: 48, Ayah: 49 & Ayah: 50 .... *28*
    Tafsir Ibn Kathir 29
        Description of the People of Paradise 29
Surah: 15 Ayah: 51, Ayah: 52, Ayah: 53, Ayah: 54, Ayah: 55 & Ayah: 56 .... *30*
    Tafsir Ibn Kathir 31
        The Guests of Ibrahim and their Good News of a Son for Him 31
Surah: 15 Ayah: 57, Ayah: 58, Ayah: 59 & Ayah: 60... *31*
    Tafsir Ibn Kathir 32
        The Reason why the Angels came 32
Surah: 15 Ayah: 61, Ayah: 62, Ayah: 63 & Ayah: 64... *32*
    Tafsir Ibn Kathir 33
        The Angels coming to Lut 33
Surah: 15 Ayah: 65 & Ayah: 66.. *33*
    Tafsir Ibn Kathir 34
        Lut is ordered to leave with His Family during the Night 34
Surah: 15 Ayah: 67, Ayah: 68, Ayah: 69, Ayah: 70, Ayah: 71 & Ayah: 72 .... *34*
    Tafsir Ibn Kathir 35
        The People of the City arrive upon the Angels, thinking that they are Men 35
Surah: 15 Ayah: 73, Ayah: 74, Ayah: 75, Ayah: 76 & Ayah: 77........................... *36*
    Tafsir Ibn Kathir 36
        The Destruction of the People of Lut 36
        The City of Sodom on the Highroad 37
Surah: 15 Ayah: 78 & Ayah: 79.. *37*
    Tafsir Ibn Kathir 37
        The Destruction of the Dwellers of Al-Aykah, the People of Shu`ayb 37
Surah: 15 Ayah: 80, Ayah: 81, Ayah: 82, Ayah: 83 & Ayah: 84........................... *38*
    Tafsir Ibn Kathir 38
        The Destruction of the Dwellers of Al-Hijr, Who are the People called Thamud 38
Surah: 15 Ayah: 85 & Ayah: 86.. *39*

Table of Contents

Tafsir Ibn Kathir 40
    The World has been created for some Purpose, then the Hour will come 40
Surah: 15 Ayah: 87 & Ayah: 88 41
    Tafsir Ibn Kathir 41
        A Reminder of the Blessing of the Qur'an and the Command to focus on its Message 41
Surah: 15 Ayah: 89, Ayah: 90, Ayah: 91, Ayah: 92 & Ayah: 93 43
    Tafsir Ibn Kathir 43
        The Messenger is a Plain Warner 43
        Explanation of "Al-Muqtasimin 44
Surah: 15 Ayah: 94, Ayah: 95, Ayah: 96, Ayah: 97, Ayah: 98 & Ayah: 99 45
    Tafsir Ibn Kathir 46
        The Command to proclaim the Truth openly 46
        The Command to turn away from the Idolators, and the Guarantee of Protection against
        the Mockers 47
        Encouragement to bear Difficulties, and the Command to glorify and worship Allah until
        Death 48

CHAPTER (SURAH) 16: AN-NAHL (THE BEE), VERSES 001-128 49

Surah: 16 Ayah: 1 49
    Tafsir Ibn Kathir 50
        Warning about the approach of the Hour 50
Surah: 16 Ayah: 2 51
    Tafsir Ibn Kathir 51
        Allah sends Whomever He wills with the Message of Tawhid 51
Surah: 16 Ayah: 3 & Ayah: 4 52
    Tafsir Ibn Kathir 52
        Allah is the One Who has created the Heavens, the Earth, and Man 52
Surah: 16 Ayah: 5, Ayah: 6 & Ayah: 7 53
    Tafsir Ibn Kathir 54
        The Cattle are part of the Creation of Allah and a Blessing from Him 54
Surah: 16 Ayah: 8 55
    Tafsir Ibn Kathir 55
        This refers to another category of animals that Allah has created as a blessing for His
        servants; horses, mules and donkeys, all of which He made for riding and adornment. ... 55
Surah: 16 Ayah: 9 55
    Tafsir Ibn Kathir 55
Surah: 16 Ayah: 10 & Ayah: 11 56
    Tafsir Ibn Kathir 57
        The Blessings of Rain, and explaining how it is one of the Signs 57
Surah: 16 Ayah: 12 & Ayah: 13 58
    Tafsir Ibn Kathir 58
        Signs in the Subjection of Night and Day, the Sun and the Moon, and in that which grows
        on Earth 58
Surah: 16 Ayah: 14, Ayah: 15, Ayah: 16, Ayah: 17 & Ayah: 18 59

Tafsir Ibn Kathir 60
   Signs in the Oceans, Mountains, Rivers, Roads and Stars 60
   Worship is Allah's Right 61
Surah: 16 Ayah: 19, Ayah: 20 & Ayah: 21... 61
Tafsir Ibn Kathir 61
   The gods of the Idolators are Created, they do not create 62
Surah: 16 Ayah: 22 & Ayah: 23... 62
Tafsir Ibn Kathir 62
   None is to be worshipped except Allah 62
Surah: 16 Ayah: 24 & Ayah: 25... 63
Tafsir Ibn Kathir 63
   The Destruction of the Disbelievers and Intensification of their Punishment for rejecting the Revelation 63
Surah: 16 Ayah: 26 & Ayah: 27... 65
Tafsir Ibn Kathir 65
   Discussion about what the previous Peoples did, and what was done to Them 65
Surah: 16 Ayah: 28 & Ayah: 29... 67
Tafsir Ibn Kathir 67
   The Condition of the Disbeliever during and after Death............................ 67
Surah: 16 Ayah: 30, Ayah: 31 & Ayah: 32.. 68
Tafsir Ibn Kathir 69
   What the Pious say about the Revelation, their Reward and their Condition during and after Death 69
Surah: 16 Ayah: 33 & Ayah: 34... 70
Tafsir Ibn Kathir 70
   The Disbelievers' Refrain from Faith means that They were simply awaiting Punishment 70
Surah: 16 Ayah: 35, Ayah: 36 & Ayah: 37.. 71
Tafsir Ibn Kathir 72
   The Idolators Argument that their Shirk was Divinely decreed, and the Refutation of this Claim.. 72
Surah: 16 Ayah: 38, Ayah: 39 & Ayah: 40.. 74
Tafsir Ibn Kathir 74
   The Resurrection after Death is true, there is Wisdom behind it, and it is easy for Allah. 74
Surah: 16 Ayah: 41 & Ayah: 42... 75
Tafsir Ibn Kathir 76
   The Reward of the Muhajirin... 76
Surah: 16 Ayah: 43 & Ayah: 44... 77
Tafsir Ibn Kathir 77
   Only Human Messengers have been Sent 77
Surah: 16 Ayah: 45, Ayah: 46 & Ayah: 47.. 78
Tafsir Ibn Kathir 79
   How the Guilty can feel Secure 79
Surah: 16 Ayah: 48, Ayah: 49 & Ayah: 50.. 80

Table of Contents

- Tafsir Ibn Kathir 81
  - Everything prostrates to Allah 81
- *Surah: 16 Ayah: 51, Ayah: 52, Ayah: 53, Ayah: 54 & Ayah: 55* 82
  - Tafsir Ibn Kathir 83
    - Allah Alone is Deserving of Worship 83
- *Surah: 16 Ayah: 56, Ayah: 57, Ayah: 58, Ayah: 59 & Ayah: 60* 84
  - Tafsir Ibn Kathir 85
    - Among the Behavior of the Idolators was vowing to Things that Allah had provided for Them to their gods 85
    - The Idolators' Abhorrence for Daughters 85
- *Surah: 16 Ayah: 61 & Ayah: 62* 86
  - Tafsir Ibn Kathir 87
    - Allah does not immediately punish for Disobedience 87
    - They attribute to Allah what They Themselves dislike 87
- *Surah: 16 Ayah: 63, Ayah: 64 & Ayah: 65* 88
  - Tafsir Ibn Kathir 89
    - Finding Consolation in the Reminder of Those Who came before 89
    - The Reason why the Qur'an was revealed 89
- *Surah: 16 Ayah: 66 & Ayah: 67* 89
  - Tafsir Ibn Kathir 90
    - Lessons and Blessings in Cattle and the Fruit of the Date-palm and Grapevine .. 90
- *Surah: 16 Ayah: 68 & Ayah: 69* 91
  - Tafsir Ibn Kathir 91
    - In the Bee and its Honey there is Blessing and a Lesson 91
- *Surah: 16 Ayah: 70* 93
  - Tafsir Ibn Kathir 93
    - In Man there is a Lesson 93
- *Surah: 16 Ayah: 71* 94
  - Tafsir Ibn Kathir 94
    - There is a Sign and a Blessing in Matters of People's Livelihood 94
- *Surah: 16 Ayah: 72* 95
  - Tafsir Ibn Kathir 95
    - Among His Blessings and Signs are Mates, Children and Grandchildren 95
- *Surah: 16 Ayah: 73 & Ayah: 74* 96
  - Tafsir Ibn Kathir 96
    - Denouncing the Worship of anything besides Allah 96
- *Surah: 16 Ayah: 75* 97
  - Tafsir Ibn Kathir 97
    - The Example of the Believer and the Disbeliever, or the Idol and the True God ... 97
- *Surah: 16 Ayah: 76* 98
  - Tafsir Ibn Kathir 98
    - Another Example 98
- *Surah: 16 Ayah: 77, Ayah: 78 & Ayah: 79* 98
  - Tafsir Ibn Kathir 99

    The Unseen belongs to Allah and only He has Knowledge of the Hour 99
    Among the Favors Allah has granted People are Hearing, Sight and the Heart 99
    In the Subjection of the Birds in the Sky there is a Sign 101

Surah: 16 Ayah: 80, Ayah: 81, Ayah: 82 & Ayah: 83 101
    Tafsir Ibn Kathir 102
        Homes, Furnishings and Clothing are also Blessings from Allah 102
        Shade, Places of Refuge in the Mountains, Garments and Coats of Mail are also Blessings from Allah 102
        All the Messenger has to do is convey the Message 103

Surah: 16 Ayah: 84, Ayah: 85, Ayah: 86, Ayah: 87 & Ayah: 88 103
    Tafsir Ibn Kathir 104
        The Plight of the Idolators on the Day of Judgement 104
        The gods of the Idolators will disown Them at the Time when They need them most ... 105
        Everything will surrender to Allah on the Day of Resurrection 106
        Those among the Idolators who corrupted Others will receive a Greater Punishment .. 106

Surah: 16 Ayah: 89 107
    Tafsir Ibn Kathir 107
        Every Prophet will bear Witness against his Nation on the Day of Resurrection 107
        The Qur'an explains Everything 107

Surah: 16 Ayah: 90 108
    Tafsir Ibn Kathir 109
        The Command to be Fair and Kind 109
        The Command to maintain the Ties of Kinship and the prohibition of Immoral Sins, Evil and Tyranny 109
        The Eyewitness Account of `Uthman 110

Surah: 16 Ayah: 91 & Ayah: 92 111
    Tafsir Ibn Kathir 112
        The Command to fulfill the Covenant 112

Surah: 16 Ayah: 93, Ayah: 94, Ayah: 95 & Ayah: 96 113
    Tafsir Ibn Kathir 114
        If Allah had willed, He would have made all of Humanity one Nation 114
        The Prohibition on taking an Oath for Purposes of Treachery 115
        Do not break Oaths for the sake of Worldly Gain 115

Surah: 16 Ayah: 97 116
    Tafsir Ibn Kathir 116
        Righteous Deeds and their Reward 116

Surah: 16 Ayah: 98, Ayah: 99 & Ayah: 100 116
    Tafsir Ibn Kathir 117
        The Command to seek Refuge with Allah before reciting the Qur'an 117

Surah: 16 Ayah: 101 & Ayah: 102 117
    Tafsir Ibn Kathir 118
        The Idolators' Accusation that the Prophet was a Liar since some Ayat were abrogated, and the Refutation of their Claim 118

Surah: 16 Ayah: 103 119
    Tafsir Ibn Kathir 119

The Idolators' Claim that the Qur'an was taught by a Human, and the Refutation of their Claim 119
Surah: 16 Ayah: 104 & Ayah: 105 119
Tafsir Ibn Kathir 120
Surah: 16 Ayah: 106, Ayah: 107, Ayah: 108 & Ayah: 109 120
Tafsir Ibn Kathir 121
Allah's Wrath against the Apostate, except for the One Who is forced into Disbelief 121
Surah: 16 Ayah: 110 & Ayah: 111 122
Tafsir Ibn Kathir 123
The One who is forced to renounce Islam will be forgiven if He does Righteous Deeds afterwards 123
Surah: 16 Ayah: 112 & Ayah: 113 123
Tafsir Ibn Kathir 124
The Example of Makkah 124
Surah: 16 Ayah: 114, Ayah: 115, Ayah: 116 & Ayah: 117 125
Tafsir Ibn Kathir 126
The Command to eat Lawful Provisions and to be Thankful, and an Explanation of what is Unlawful 126
Surah: 16 Ayah: 118 & Ayah: 119 127
Tafsir Ibn Kathir 128
Some Good Things were Forbidden for the Jews 128
Surah: 16 Ayah: 120, Ayah: 121, Ayah: 122 & Ayah: 123 128
Tafsir Ibn Kathir 129
He selected him, as Allah says : 129
Surah: 16 Ayah: 124 130
Tafsir Ibn Kathir 130
The Prescription of the Sabbath for the Jews 130
Surah: 16 Ayah: 125 131
Tafsir Ibn Kathir 132
The Command to invite people to Allah with Wisdom and Good Preaching 132
Surah: 16 Ayah: 126, Ayah: 127 & Ayah: 128 132
Tafsir Ibn Kathir 133
The Command for Equality in Punishment 133

PRELUDE

Opening Serman

Indeed, all praise is due to Allah. We praise Him and seek His help and forgiveness. We seek refuge with Allah from our soul's evil and our wrong doings. He whom Allah guides, no one can misguide; and he whom He misguides, no one can guide

I bear witness that there is no (true) god except Allah – alone without a partner, and I bear witness that Muhammad (peace and blessings of Allah be upon him) is His 'abd (servant) and messenger.

يَٰٓأَيُّهَا ٱلَّذِينَ ءَامَنُوا۟ ٱتَّقُوا۟ ٱللَّهَ حَقَّ تُقَاتِهِۦ وَلَا تَمُوتُنَّ إِلَّا وَأَنتُم مُّسْلِمُونَ ۝

O you who believe! Fear Allâh (by doing all that He has ordered and by abstaining from all that He has forbidden) as He should be feared. (Obey Him, be thankful to Him, and remember Him always), and die not except in a state of Islâm (as Muslims with complete submission to Allâh)).

يَٰٓأَيُّهَا ٱلنَّاسُ ٱتَّقُوا۟ رَبَّكُمُ ٱلَّذِى خَلَقَكُم مِّن نَّفْسٍ وَٰحِدَةٍ وَخَلَقَ مِنْهَا زَوْجَهَا وَبَثَّ مِنْهُمَا رِجَالًا كَثِيرًا وَنِسَآءً ۚ وَٱتَّقُوا۟ ٱللَّهَ ٱلَّذِى تَسَآءَلُونَ بِهِۦ وَٱلْأَرْحَامَ ۚ إِنَّ ٱللَّهَ كَانَ عَلَيْكُمْ رَقِيبًا ۝

O mankind! Be dutiful to your Lord, Who created you from a single person (Adam), and from him (Adam) He created his wife (Hawwâ (Eve)) and from them both He created many men and women; and fear Allâh through Whom you demand (your mutual rights), and (do not cut the relations of) the wombs (kinship). Surely, Allâh is Ever an All-Watcher over you.

يُصْلِحْ لَكُمْ أَعْمَٰلَكُمْ وَيَغْفِرْ لَكُمْ ذُنُوبَكُمْ ۗ وَمَن يُطِعِ ٱللَّهَ وَرَسُولَهُۥ فَقَدْ فَازَ فَوْزًا عَظِيمًا ۝

He will direct you to do righteous good deeds and will forgive you your sins. And whosoever obeys Allâh and His Messenger (peace be upon him), he has indeed achieved a great achievement (i.e. he will be saved from the Hell-fire and will be admitted to Paradise).

Indeed, the best speech is Allah's Book and the best guidance is Muhammad's () guidance. The worst affairs (of religion) are those innovated (by people), for every such innovation is an act of misguidance leading to the Fire

Our Mission

Our mission is to gather in one place, for the English-speaking public, all relevant information needed to make the Qur'an more understandable and easier to study. This book tries to do this by providing the following:

1. The Arabic Text for those who are able to read Arabic
2. Transliteration of the Arabic text for those who are unable to read the Arabic script. This will give them a sample of the sound of the Qur'an, which they could not otherwise comprehend from reading the English meaning.
3. The meaning of the qur'an (translated by Dr. Muhammad Taqi-ud-Din Al-Hilali, Ph.D. and Dr. Muhammad Muhsin Khan)
4. Explanation (abridged Tafsir) by Ibn Kathir (translated by Safi-ur-Rahman al-Mubarakpuri)

We hope that by doing this an ordinary English-speaker will be able to pick up a copy of this book and study and comprehend The Glorious Qur'an in a way that is acceptable to the understanding of the Rightly-guided Muslim Ummah (Community).

Biography of Hafiz Ibn Kathir (701 H - 774 H)

By the Honored Shaykh `Abdul-Qadir Al-Arna'ut, may Allah protect him.

He is the respected Imam, Abu Al-Fida', `Imad Ad-Din Isma il bin 'Umar bin Kathir Al-Qurashi Al-Busrawi - Busraian in origin; Dimashqi in training, learning and residence.

Ibn Kathir was born in the city of Busra in 701 H. His father was the Friday speaker of the village, but he died while Ibn Kathir was only four years old. Ibn Kathir's brother, Shaykh Abdul-Wahhab, reared him and taught him until he moved to Damascus in 706 H., when he was five years old.

Ibn Kathir's Teachers

Ibn Kathir studied Fiqh - Islamic jurisprudence - with Burhan Ad-Din, Ibrahim bin `Abdur-Rahman Al-Fizari, known as Ibn Al-Firkah (who died in 729 H). Ibn Kathir heard Hadiths from `Isa bin Al-Mutim, Ahmad bin Abi Talib, (Ibn Ash-Shahnah) (who died in 730 H), Ibn Al-Hajjar, (who died in 730 H), and the Hadith narrator of Ash-Sham (modern day Syria and surrounding areas); Baha Ad-Din Al-Qasim bin Muzaffar bin `Asakir (who died in 723 H), and Ibn Ash-Shirdzi, Ishaq bin Yahya Al-Ammuddi, also known as `Afif Ad-Din, the Zahiriyyah Shaykh who died in 725 H, and Muhammad bin Zarrad. He remained with Jamal Ad-Din, Yusuf bin Az-Zaki AlMizzi who died in 724 H, he benefited from his knowledge and also married his daughter. He also read with Shaykh Al-Islam, Taqi Ad-Din Ahmad bin `Abdul-Halim bin `Abdus-Salam bin Taymiyyah who died in 728 H. He also read with the Imam Hafiz and historian Shams Ad-Din, Muhammad bin Ahmad bin Uthman bin Qaymaz Adh-Dhahabi, who died in 748 H. Also, Abu Musa Al-Qarafai, Abu Al-Fath Ad-Dabbusi and

'Ali bin `Umar As-Suwani and others who gave him permission to transmit the knowledge he learned with them in Egypt.

In his book, Al-Mu jam Al-Mukhtas, Al-Hafiz Adh-Dhaliabi wrote that Ibn Kathir was, "The Imam, scholar of jurisprudence, skillful scholar of Hadith, renowned Fagih and scholar of Tafsir who wrote several beneficial books."

Further, in Ad-Durar Al-Kdminah, Al-Hafiz Ibn Hajar AlAsqalani said, "Ibn Kathir worked on the subject of the Hadith in the areas of texts and chains of narrators. He had a good memory, his books became popular during his lifetime, and people benefited from them after his death."

Also, the renowned historian Abu Al-Mahasin, Jamal Ad-Din Yusuf bin Sayf Ad-Din (Ibn Taghri Bardi), said in his book, AlManhal As-Safi, "He is the Shaykh, the Imam, the great scholar `Imad Ad-Din Abu Al-Fida'. He learned extensively and was very active in collecting knowledge and writing. He was excellent in the areas of Fiqh, Tafsfr and Hadith. He collected knowledge, authored (books), taught, narrated Hadith and wrote. He had immense knowledge in the fields of Hadith, Tafsir, Fiqh, the Arabic language, and so forth. He gave Fatawa (religious verdicts) and taught until he died, may Allah grant him mercy. He was known for his precision and vast knowledge, and as a scholar of history, Hadith and Tafsir."

Ibn Kathir's Students

Ibn Hajji was one of Ibn Kathir's students, and he described Ibn Kathir: "He had the best memory of the Hadith texts. He also had the most knowledge concerning the narrators and authenticity, his contemporaries and teachers admitted to these qualities. Every time I met him I gained some benefit from him."

Also, Ibn Al-`Imad Al-Hanbali said in his book, Shadhardt Adh-Dhahab, "He is the renowned Hafiz `Imad Ad-Din, whose memory was excellent, whose forgetfulness was miniscule, whose understanding was adequate, and who had good knowledge in the Arabic language." Also, Ibn Habib said about Ibn Kathir, "He heard knowledge and collected it and wrote various books. He brought comfort to the ears with his Fatwas and narrated Hadith and brought benefit to other people. The papers that contained his Fatwas were transmitted to the various (Islamic) provinces. Further, he was known for his precision and encompassing knowledge."

Ibn Kathir's Books

1 - One of the greatest books that Ibn Kathir wrote was his Tafsir of the Noble Qur'an, which is one of the best Tafsir that rely on narrations [of Ahadith, the Tafsir of the Companions, etc.]. The Tafsir by Ibn Kathir was printed many times and several scholars have summarized it.

2- The History Collection known as Al-Biddyah, which was printed in 14 volumes under the name Al-Bidayah wanNihdyah, and contained the stories of the Prophets and previous nations, the Prophet's Seerah (life story) and Islamic history until his time. He also added a book Al-Fitan, about the Signs of the Last Hour.

3- At-Takmil ft Ma`rifat Ath-Thiqat wa Ad-Du'afa wal Majdhil which Ibn Kathir collected from the books of his two Shaykhs Al-Mizzi and Adh-Dhahabi; Al-Kdmal and Mizan Al-Ftiddl. He added several benefits regarding the subject of Al-Jarh and AtT'adil.

4- Al-Hadi was-Sunan ft Ahadith Al-Masdnfd was-Sunan which is also known by, Jami` Al-Masdnfd. In this book, Ibn Kathir collected the narrations of Imams Ahmad bin Hanbal, Al-Bazzar, Abu Ya`la Al-Mawsili, Ibn Abi Shaybah and from the six collections of Hadith: the Two Sahihs [Al-Bukhari and Muslim] and the Four Sunan [Abu Dawud, At-Tirmidhi, AnNasa and Ibn Majah]. Ibn Kathir divided this book according to areas of Fiqh.

5-Tabaqat Ash-Shaf iyah which also contains the virtues of Imam Ash-Shafi.

6- Ibn Kathir wrote references for the Ahadith of Adillat AtTanbfh, from the Shafi school of Fiqh.

7- Ibn Kathir began an explanation of Sahih Al-Bukhari, but he did not finish it.

8- He started writing a large volume on the Ahkam (Laws), but finished only up to the Hajj rituals.

9- He summarized Al-Bayhaqi's 'Al-Madkhal. Many of these books were not printed.

10- He summarized `Ulum Al-Hadith, by Abu `Amr bin AsSalah and called it Mukhtasar `Ulum Al-Hadith. Shaykh Ahmad Shakir, the Egyptian Muhaddith, printed this book along with his commentary on it and called it Al-Ba'th Al-Hathfth fi Sharh Mukhtasar `Ulum Al-Hadith.

11- As-Sfrah An-Nabawiyyah, which is contained in his book Al-Biddyah, and both of these books are in print.

12- A research on Jihad called Al-Ijtihad ft Talabi Al-Jihad, which was printed several times.

Ibn Kathir's Death

Al-Hafiz Ibn Hajar Al-Asgalani said, "Ibn Kathir lost his sight just before his life ended. He died in Damascus in 774 H." May Allah grant mercy upon Ibn Kathir and make him among the residents of His Paradise.

PREFACE

In the name of Allah, Most Gracious, Most Merciful.

About this book

The previous publication of this book included some background information to the chapters of the Qur'an by an Islamic scholar known as Abul Ala Maududi. This information was used to shed more light on the chapters by giving a summery of why each chapter was given its name, It's period of revelation and the circumstances surrounding its revelatiom. However, some Muslims objected to the inclusion of the contributions of Maududi.

In this new publication of Tafsir Ibn Kathir, we have removed all traces of the contribution of Abul Ala Maududi. Personally, I do not know the reasons for the objections to Maududi, but this work concerns only the tafsir of Ibn Kathir, so we have not included anything from Maududi in it. We have also corrected all the typing and formatting errors found in the previous publication. We have not alter the structure of the book. The reader is still able to read the full Arabic Text of the thirty Parts of the Qur'an and follow its meanings in the English language. The transliteration of the Arabic text should also give the reader a taste of the sound of the original Arabic.

May Almighty Allah accept this effort from us, and make it a source of blessings for us in this world and in the next. I bear witness that there is none worthy of worship but Allah and I bear witness that Muhammad (may the peace and blessings of Allah be upon him) is the slave and messenger of Allah.

Performing Prostration While Reading the Qur'an

Question:

Could you please give a list of the Qur'anic verses when a prostration is recommended? What happens if we read these verses and not perform a prostration?

A. Jalil

Answer:

There are 15 verses in the Qur'an that mention prostration before God Almighty as a good action by God-fearing believers. Therefore, it is strongly recommended to perform such a prostration when we read or listen to any of these verses, whether during prayer or in any situation.

Some scholars are of the view that even if one has not performed ablution, one should prostrate oneself. These verses are given here, starting with the Arabic title of the surah which is followed by two numbers, the first indicating the surah, and the second indicating the verse,: Al-Araf 7: 206; Al-Raad 13: 15; Al-Nahl 16: 50; Al-Isra 17: 109; Maryam 19: 58; Al-Hajj 22: 18 & 22: 77; Al-Furqan 25: 60; Al-Naml 27: 26;

Al-Sajdah 32: 15; Saad 38: 25; Fussilat 41: 38; Al-Najm 53: 62; Al-Inshiqaq 84: 21 and Al-Alaq 96: 19.

If you do not perform a prostration when you read or listen to any of these verses, you have done badly because you miss out on the reward of performing a prostration for God. You incur no sin and violate no divine order.

Reference:
http://archive.arabnews.com/?page=5&section=0&article=97811&d=1&m=7&y=2007

The Glorious Qur'an Juz' 14 (Part 14): Chapter (Surah) 15: Al-Hijr (Stoneland, Rock City) 001 To Chapter (Surah) 16: An-Nahl (The Bee) 128

PART 14 FULL ARABIC TEXT

Chapter (Surah) 15: Al Hijr 001-099

بِسْمِ ٱللَّهِ ٱلرَّحْمَٰنِ ٱلرَّحِيمِ

الٓر ۚ تِلْكَ ءَايَٰتُ ٱلْكِتَٰبِ وَقُرْءَانٍ مُّبِينٍ ۝١ رُّبَمَا يَوَدُّ ٱلَّذِينَ كَفَرُوا۟ لَوْ كَانُوا۟ مُسْلِمِينَ ۝٢ ذَرْهُمْ يَأْكُلُوا۟ وَيَتَمَتَّعُوا۟ وَيُلْهِهِمُ ٱلْأَمَلُ ۖ فَسَوْفَ يَعْلَمُونَ ۝٣ وَمَآ أَهْلَكْنَا مِن قَرْيَةٍ إِلَّا وَلَهَا كِتَابٌ مَّعْلُومٌ ۝٤ مَّا تَسْبِقُ مِنْ أُمَّةٍ أَجَلَهَا وَمَا يَسْتَـْٔخِرُونَ ۝٥ وَقَالُوا۟ يَٰٓأَيُّهَا ٱلَّذِى نُزِّلَ عَلَيْهِ ٱلذِّكْرُ إِنَّكَ لَمَجْنُونٌ ۝٦ لَّوْ مَا تَأْتِينَا بِٱلْمَلَٰٓئِكَةِ إِن كُنتَ مِنَ ٱلصَّٰدِقِينَ ۝٧ مَا نُنَزِّلُ ٱلْمَلَٰٓئِكَةَ إِلَّا بِٱلْحَقِّ وَمَا كَانُوٓا۟ إِذًا مُّنظَرِينَ ۝٨ إِنَّا نَحْنُ نَزَّلْنَا ٱلذِّكْرَ وَإِنَّا لَهُۥ لَحَٰفِظُونَ ۝٩ وَلَقَدْ أَرْسَلْنَا مِن قَبْلِكَ فِى شِيَعِ ٱلْأَوَّلِينَ ۝١٠ وَمَا يَأْتِيهِم مِّن رَّسُولٍ إِلَّا كَانُوا۟ بِهِۦ يَسْتَهْزِءُونَ ۝١١ كَذَٰلِكَ نَسْلُكُهُۥ فِى قُلُوبِ ٱلْمُجْرِمِينَ ۝١٢ لَا يُؤْمِنُونَ بِهِۦ ۖ وَقَدْ خَلَتْ سُنَّةُ ٱلْأَوَّلِينَ ۝١٣ وَلَوْ فَتَحْنَا عَلَيْهِم بَابًا مِّنَ ٱلسَّمَآءِ فَظَلُّوا۟ فِيهِ يَعْرُجُونَ ۝١٤ لَقَالُوٓا۟ إِنَّمَا سُكِّرَتْ أَبْصَٰرُنَا بَلْ نَحْنُ قَوْمٌ مَّسْحُورُونَ ۝١٥ وَلَقَدْ جَعَلْنَا فِى ٱلسَّمَآءِ بُرُوجًا وَزَيَّنَّٰهَا لِلنَّٰظِرِينَ ۝١٦ وَحَفِظْنَٰهَا مِن كُلِّ شَيْطَٰنٍ رَّجِيمٍ ۝١٧ إِلَّا مَنِ ٱسْتَرَقَ ٱلسَّمْعَ فَأَتْبَعَهُۥ شِهَابٌ مُّبِينٌ ۝١٨ وَٱلْأَرْضَ مَدَدْنَٰهَا وَأَلْقَيْنَا فِيهَا رَوَٰسِىَ وَأَنۢبَتْنَا فِيهَا مِن كُلِّ شَىْءٍ مَّوْزُونٍ ۝١٩ وَجَعَلْنَا لَكُمْ فِيهَا مَعَٰيِشَ وَمَن لَّسْتُمْ لَهُۥ بِرَٰزِقِينَ ۝٢٠ وَإِن مِّن شَىْءٍ إِلَّا عِندَنَا خَزَآئِنُهُۥ وَمَا

نُنَزِّلُهُ إِلَّا بِقَدَرٍ مَّعْلُومٍ ﴿٢١﴾ وَأَرْسَلْنَا ٱلرِّيَـٰحَ لَوَٰقِحَ فَأَنزَلْنَا مِنَ ٱلسَّمَآءِ مَآءً فَأَسْقَيْنَـٰكُمُوهُ وَمَآ أَنتُمْ لَهُۥ بِخَـٰزِنِينَ ﴿٢٢﴾ وَإِنَّا لَنَحْنُ نُحْىِۦ وَنُمِيتُ وَنَحْنُ ٱلْوَٰرِثُونَ ﴿٢٣﴾ وَلَقَدْ عَلِمْنَا ٱلْمُسْتَقْدِمِينَ مِنكُمْ وَلَقَدْ عَلِمْنَا ٱلْمُسْتَـْٔخِرِينَ ﴿٢٤﴾ وَإِنَّ رَبَّكَ هُوَ يَحْشُرُهُمْ ۚ إِنَّهُۥ حَكِيمٌ عَلِيمٌ ﴿٢٥﴾ وَلَقَدْ خَلَقْنَا ٱلْإِنسَـٰنَ مِن صَلْصَـٰلٍ مِّنْ حَمَإٍ مَّسْنُونٍ ﴿٢٦﴾ وَٱلْجَآنَّ خَلَقْنَـٰهُ مِن قَبْلُ مِن نَّارِ ٱلسَّمُومِ ﴿٢٧﴾ وَإِذْ قَالَ رَبُّكَ لِلْمَلَـٰٓئِكَةِ إِنِّى خَـٰلِقٌۢ بَشَرًا مِّن صَلْصَـٰلٍ مِّنْ حَمَإٍ مَّسْنُونٍ ﴿٢٨﴾ فَإِذَا سَوَّيْتُهُۥ وَنَفَخْتُ فِيهِ مِن رُّوحِى فَقَعُوا۟ لَهُۥ سَـٰجِدِينَ ﴿٢٩﴾ فَسَجَدَ ٱلْمَلَـٰٓئِكَةُ كُلُّهُمْ أَجْمَعُونَ ﴿٣٠﴾ إِلَّآ إِبْلِيسَ أَبَىٰٓ أَن يَكُونَ مَعَ ٱلسَّـٰجِدِينَ ﴿٣١﴾ قَالَ يَـٰٓإِبْلِيسُ مَا لَكَ أَلَّا تَكُونَ مَعَ ٱلسَّـٰجِدِينَ ﴿٣٢﴾ قَالَ لَمْ أَكُن لِّأَسْجُدَ لِبَشَرٍ خَلَقْتَهُۥ مِن صَلْصَـٰلٍ مِّنْ حَمَإٍ مَّسْنُونٍ ﴿٣٣﴾ قَالَ فَٱخْرُجْ مِنْهَا فَإِنَّكَ رَجِيمٌ ﴿٣٤﴾ وَإِنَّ عَلَيْكَ ٱللَّعْنَةَ إِلَىٰ يَوْمِ ٱلدِّينِ ﴿٣٥﴾ قَالَ رَبِّ فَأَنظِرْنِىٓ إِلَىٰ يَوْمِ يُبْعَثُونَ ﴿٣٦﴾ قَالَ فَإِنَّكَ مِنَ ٱلْمُنظَرِينَ ﴿٣٧﴾ إِلَىٰ يَوْمِ ٱلْوَقْتِ ٱلْمَعْلُومِ ﴿٣٨﴾ قَالَ رَبِّ بِمَآ أَغْوَيْتَنِى لَأُزَيِّنَنَّ لَهُمْ فِى ٱلْأَرْضِ وَلَأُغْوِيَنَّهُمْ أَجْمَعِينَ ﴿٣٩﴾ إِلَّا عِبَادَكَ مِنْهُمُ ٱلْمُخْلَصِينَ ﴿٤٠﴾ قَالَ هَـٰذَا صِرَٰطٌ عَلَىَّ مُسْتَقِيمٌ ﴿٤١﴾ إِنَّ عِبَادِى لَيْسَ لَكَ عَلَيْهِمْ سُلْطَـٰنٌ إِلَّا مَنِ ٱتَّبَعَكَ مِنَ ٱلْغَاوِينَ ﴿٤٢﴾ وَإِنَّ جَهَنَّمَ لَمَوْعِدُهُمْ أَجْمَعِينَ ﴿٤٣﴾ لَهَا سَبْعَةُ أَبْوَٰبٍ لِّكُلِّ بَابٍ مِّنْهُمْ جُزْءٌ مَّقْسُومٌ ﴿٤٤﴾ إِنَّ ٱلْمُتَّقِينَ فِى جَنَّـٰتٍ وَعُيُونٍ ﴿٤٥﴾ ٱدْخُلُوهَا بِسَلَـٰمٍ ءَامِنِينَ ﴿٤٦﴾ وَنَزَعْنَا مَا فِى صُدُورِهِم مِّنْ غِلٍّ إِخْوَٰنًا عَلَىٰ سُرُرٍ مُّتَقَـٰبِلِينَ ﴿٤٧﴾ لَا يَمَسُّهُمْ فِيهَا نَصَبٌ وَمَا هُم مِّنْهَا بِمُخْرَجِينَ ﴿٤٨﴾ ۞ نَبِّئْ عِبَادِىٓ أَنِّىٓ أَنَا ٱلْغَفُورُ ٱلرَّحِيمُ ﴿٤٩﴾ وَأَنَّ عَذَابِى هُوَ ٱلْعَذَابُ ٱلْأَلِيمُ ﴿٥٠﴾ وَنَبِّئْهُمْ عَن ضَيْفِ إِبْرَٰهِيمَ ﴿٥١﴾ إِذْ دَخَلُوا۟ عَلَيْهِ فَقَالُوا۟ سَلَـٰمًا قَالَ إِنَّا مِنكُمْ وَجِلُونَ ﴿٥٢﴾ قَالُوا۟ لَا تَوْجَلْ إِنَّا نُبَشِّرُكَ

بِغُلَٰمٍ عَلِيمٍ ۝ قَالَ أَبَشَّرْتُمُونِى عَلَىٰٓ أَن مَّسَّنِىَ ٱلْكِبَرُ فَبِمَ تُبَشِّرُونَ ۝ قَالُوا۟ بَشَّرْنَٰكَ بِٱلْحَقِّ فَلَا تَكُن مِّنَ ٱلْقَٰنِطِينَ ۝ قَالَ وَمَن يَقْنَطُ مِن رَّحْمَةِ رَبِّهِۦٓ إِلَّا ٱلضَّآلُّونَ ۝ قَالَ فَمَا خَطْبُكُمْ أَيُّهَا ٱلْمُرْسَلُونَ ۝ قَالُوٓا۟ إِنَّآ أُرْسِلْنَآ إِلَىٰ قَوْمٍ مُّجْرِمِينَ ۝ إِلَّآ ءَالَ لُوطٍ إِنَّا لَمُنَجُّوهُمْ أَجْمَعِينَ ۝ إِلَّا ٱمْرَأَتَهُۥ قَدَّرْنَآ إِنَّهَا لَمِنَ ٱلْغَٰبِرِينَ ۝ فَلَمَّا جَآءَ ءَالَ لُوطٍ ٱلْمُرْسَلُونَ ۝ قَالَ إِنَّكُمْ قَوْمٌ مُّنكَرُونَ ۝ قَالُوا۟ بَلْ جِئْنَٰكَ بِمَا كَانُوا۟ فِيهِ يَمْتَرُونَ ۝ وَأَتَيْنَٰكَ بِٱلْحَقِّ وَإِنَّا لَصَٰدِقُونَ ۝ فَأَسْرِ بِأَهْلِكَ بِقِطْعٍ مِّنَ ٱلَّيْلِ وَٱتَّبِعْ أَدْبَٰرَهُمْ وَلَا يَلْتَفِتْ مِنكُمْ أَحَدٌ وَٱمْضُوا۟ حَيْثُ تُؤْمَرُونَ ۝ وَقَضَيْنَآ إِلَيْهِ ذَٰلِكَ ٱلْأَمْرَ أَنَّ دَابِرَ هَٰٓؤُلَآءِ مَقْطُوعٌ مُّصْبِحِينَ ۝ وَجَآءَ أَهْلُ ٱلْمَدِينَةِ يَسْتَبْشِرُونَ ۝ قَالَ إِنَّ هَٰٓؤُلَآءِ ضَيْفِى فَلَا تَفْضَحُونِ ۝ وَٱتَّقُوا۟ ٱللَّهَ وَلَا تُخْزُونِ ۝ قَالُوٓا۟ أَوَلَمْ نَنْهَكَ عَنِ ٱلْعَٰلَمِينَ ۝ قَالَ هَٰٓؤُلَآءِ بَنَاتِىٓ إِن كُنتُمْ فَٰعِلِينَ ۝ لَعَمْرُكَ إِنَّهُمْ لَفِى سَكْرَتِهِمْ يَعْمَهُونَ ۝ فَأَخَذَتْهُمُ ٱلصَّيْحَةُ مُشْرِقِينَ ۝ فَجَعَلْنَا عَٰلِيَهَا سَافِلَهَا وَأَمْطَرْنَا عَلَيْهِمْ حِجَارَةً مِّن سِجِّيلٍ ۝ إِنَّ فِى ذَٰلِكَ لَءَايَٰتٍ لِّلْمُتَوَسِّمِينَ ۝ وَإِنَّهَا لَبِسَبِيلٍ مُّقِيمٍ ۝ إِنَّ فِى ذَٰلِكَ لَءَايَةً لِّلْمُؤْمِنِينَ ۝ وَإِن كَانَ أَصْحَٰبُ ٱلْأَيْكَةِ لَظَٰلِمِينَ ۝ فَٱنتَقَمْنَا مِنْهُمْ وَإِنَّهُمَا لَبِإِمَامٍ مُّبِينٍ ۝ وَلَقَدْ كَذَّبَ أَصْحَٰبُ ٱلْحِجْرِ ٱلْمُرْسَلِينَ ۝ وَءَاتَيْنَٰهُمْ ءَايَٰتِنَا فَكَانُوا۟ عَنْهَا مُعْرِضِينَ ۝ وَكَانُوا۟ يَنْحِتُونَ مِنَ ٱلْجِبَالِ بُيُوتًا ءَامِنِينَ ۝ فَأَخَذَتْهُمُ ٱلصَّيْحَةُ مُصْبِحِينَ ۝ فَمَآ أَغْنَىٰ عَنْهُم مَّا كَانُوا۟ يَكْسِبُونَ ۝ وَمَا خَلَقْنَا ٱلسَّمَٰوَٰتِ وَٱلْأَرْضَ وَمَا بَيْنَهُمَآ إِلَّا بِٱلْحَقِّ وَإِنَّ ٱلسَّاعَةَ لَءَاتِيَةٌ فَٱصْفَحِ ٱلصَّفْحَ ٱلْجَمِيلَ ۝ إِنَّ رَبَّكَ هُوَ ٱلْخَلَّٰقُ ٱلْعَلِيمُ ۝ وَلَقَدْ ءَاتَيْنَٰكَ سَبْعًا مِّنَ ٱلْمَثَانِى

وَٱلْقُرْءَانَ ٱلْعَظِيمَ ۝ لَا تَمُدَّنَّ عَيْنَيْكَ إِلَىٰ مَا مَتَّعْنَا بِهِۦٓ أَزْوَٰجًا مِّنْهُمْ وَلَا تَحْزَنْ عَلَيْهِمْ وَٱخْفِضْ جَنَاحَكَ لِلْمُؤْمِنِينَ ۝ وَقُلْ إِنِّىٓ أَنَا ٱلنَّذِيرُ ٱلْمُبِينُ ۝ كَمَآ أَنزَلْنَا عَلَى ٱلْمُقْتَسِمِينَ ۝ ٱلَّذِينَ جَعَلُوا۟ ٱلْقُرْءَانَ عِضِينَ ۝ فَوَرَبِّكَ لَنَسْـَٔلَنَّهُمْ أَجْمَعِينَ ۝ عَمَّا كَانُوا۟ يَعْمَلُونَ ۝ فَٱصْدَعْ بِمَا تُؤْمَرُ وَأَعْرِضْ عَنِ ٱلْمُشْرِكِينَ ۝ إِنَّا كَفَيْنَٰكَ ٱلْمُسْتَهْزِءِينَ ۝ ٱلَّذِينَ يَجْعَلُونَ مَعَ ٱللَّهِ إِلَٰهًا ءَاخَرَ ۚ فَسَوْفَ يَعْلَمُونَ ۝ وَلَقَدْ نَعْلَمُ أَنَّكَ يَضِيقُ صَدْرُكَ بِمَا يَقُولُونَ ۝ فَسَبِّحْ بِحَمْدِ رَبِّكَ وَكُن مِّنَ ٱلسَّٰجِدِينَ ۝ وَٱعْبُدْ رَبَّكَ حَتَّىٰ يَأْتِيَكَ ٱلْيَقِينُ ۝

(Al-Hijr 001-099)

Chapter (Surah) 16: An Nahl 001-128

بِسْمِ ٱللَّهِ ٱلرَّحْمَٰنِ ٱلرَّحِيمِ

أَتَىٰٓ أَمْرُ ٱللَّهِ فَلَا تَسْتَعْجِلُوهُ ۚ سُبْحَٰنَهُۥ وَتَعَٰلَىٰ عَمَّا يُشْرِكُونَ ۝ يُنَزِّلُ ٱلْمَلَٰٓئِكَةَ بِٱلرُّوحِ مِنْ أَمْرِهِۦ عَلَىٰ مَن يَشَآءُ مِنْ عِبَادِهِۦٓ أَنْ أَنذِرُوٓا۟ أَنَّهُۥ لَآ إِلَٰهَ إِلَّآ أَنَا۠ فَٱتَّقُونِ ۝ خَلَقَ ٱلسَّمَٰوَٰتِ وَٱلْأَرْضَ بِٱلْحَقِّ ۚ تَعَٰلَىٰ عَمَّا يُشْرِكُونَ ۝ خَلَقَ ٱلْإِنسَٰنَ مِن نُّطْفَةٍ فَإِذَا هُوَ خَصِيمٌ مُّبِينٌ ۝ وَٱلْأَنْعَٰمَ خَلَقَهَا ۗ لَكُمْ فِيهَا دِفْءٌ وَمَنَٰفِعُ وَمِنْهَا تَأْكُلُونَ ۝ وَلَكُمْ فِيهَا جَمَالٌ حِينَ تُرِيحُونَ وَحِينَ تَسْرَحُونَ ۝ وَتَحْمِلُ أَثْقَالَكُمْ إِلَىٰ بَلَدٍ لَّمْ تَكُونُوا۟ بَٰلِغِيهِ إِلَّا بِشِقِّ ٱلْأَنفُسِ ۚ إِنَّ رَبَّكُمْ لَرَءُوفٌ رَّحِيمٌ ۝ وَٱلْخَيْلَ وَٱلْبِغَالَ وَٱلْحَمِيرَ لِتَرْكَبُوهَا وَزِينَةً ۚ وَيَخْلُقُ مَا لَا تَعْلَمُونَ ۝ وَعَلَى ٱللَّهِ قَصْدُ ٱلسَّبِيلِ وَمِنْهَا جَآئِرٌ ۚ وَلَوْ شَآءَ لَهَدَىٰكُمْ أَجْمَعِينَ ۝ هُوَ ٱلَّذِىٓ أَنزَلَ مِنَ ٱلسَّمَآءِ مَآءً ۖ لَّكُم مِّنْهُ شَرَابٌ وَمِنْهُ شَجَرٌ فِيهِ تُسِيمُونَ ۝ يُنۢبِتُ لَكُم بِهِ ٱلزَّرْعَ

وَالزَّيْتُونَ وَالنَّخِيلَ وَالْأَعْنَٰبَ وَمِن كُلِّ الثَّمَرَٰتِ ۗ إِنَّ فِى ذَٰلِكَ لَءَايَةً لِّقَوْمٍ يَتَفَكَّرُونَ ۝ وَسَخَّرَ لَكُمُ الَّيْلَ وَالنَّهَارَ وَالشَّمْسَ وَالْقَمَرَ ۖ وَالنُّجُومُ مُسَخَّرَٰتٌۢ بِأَمْرِهِۦٓ ۗ إِنَّ فِى ذَٰلِكَ لَءَايَٰتٍ لِّقَوْمٍ يَعْقِلُونَ ۝ وَمَا ذَرَأَ لَكُمْ فِى الْأَرْضِ مُخْتَلِفًا أَلْوَٰنُهُۥٓ ۗ إِنَّ فِى ذَٰلِكَ لَءَايَةً لِّقَوْمٍ يَذَّكَّرُونَ ۝ وَهُوَ الَّذِى سَخَّرَ الْبَحْرَ لِتَأْكُلُوا۟ مِنْهُ لَحْمًا طَرِيًّا وَتَسْتَخْرِجُوا۟ مِنْهُ حِلْيَةً تَلْبَسُونَهَا وَتَرَى الْفُلْكَ مَوَاخِرَ فِيهِ وَلِتَبْتَغُوا۟ مِن فَضْلِهِۦ وَلَعَلَّكُمْ تَشْكُرُونَ ۝ وَأَلْقَىٰ فِى الْأَرْضِ رَوَٰسِىَ أَن تَمِيدَ بِكُمْ وَأَنْهَٰرًا وَسُبُلًا لَّعَلَّكُمْ تَهْتَدُونَ ۝ وَعَلَٰمَٰتٍ ۚ وَبِالنَّجْمِ هُمْ يَهْتَدُونَ ۝ أَفَمَن يَخْلُقُ كَمَن لَّا يَخْلُقُ ۗ أَفَلَا تَذَكَّرُونَ ۝ وَإِن تَعُدُّوا۟ نِعْمَةَ اللَّهِ لَا تُحْصُوهَآ ۗ إِنَّ اللَّهَ لَغَفُورٌ رَّحِيمٌ ۝ وَاللَّهُ يَعْلَمُ مَا تُسِرُّونَ وَمَا تُعْلِنُونَ ۝ وَالَّذِينَ يَدْعُونَ مِن دُونِ اللَّهِ لَا يَخْلُقُونَ شَيْـًٔا وَهُمْ يُخْلَقُونَ ۝ أَمْوَٰتٌ غَيْرُ أَحْيَآءٍ ۖ وَمَا يَشْعُرُونَ أَيَّانَ يُبْعَثُونَ ۝ إِلَٰهُكُمْ إِلَٰهٌ وَٰحِدٌ ۚ فَالَّذِينَ لَا يُؤْمِنُونَ بِالْءَاخِرَةِ قُلُوبُهُم مُّنكِرَةٌ وَهُم مُّسْتَكْبِرُونَ ۝ لَا جَرَمَ أَنَّ اللَّهَ يَعْلَمُ مَا يُسِرُّونَ وَمَا يُعْلِنُونَ ۚ إِنَّهُۥ لَا يُحِبُّ الْمُسْتَكْبِرِينَ ۝ وَإِذَا قِيلَ لَهُم مَّاذَآ أَنزَلَ رَبُّكُمْ ۙ قَالُوٓا۟ أَسَٰطِيرُ الْأَوَّلِينَ ۝ لِيَحْمِلُوٓا۟ أَوْزَارَهُمْ كَامِلَةً يَوْمَ الْقِيَٰمَةِ ۙ وَمِنْ أَوْزَارِ الَّذِينَ يُضِلُّونَهُم بِغَيْرِ عِلْمٍ ۗ أَلَا سَآءَ مَا يَزِرُونَ ۝ قَدْ مَكَرَ الَّذِينَ مِن قَبْلِهِمْ فَأَتَى اللَّهُ بُنْيَٰنَهُم مِّنَ الْقَوَاعِدِ فَخَرَّ عَلَيْهِمُ السَّقْفُ مِن فَوْقِهِمْ وَأَتَىٰهُمُ الْعَذَابُ مِنْ حَيْثُ لَا يَشْعُرُونَ ۝ ثُمَّ يَوْمَ الْقِيَٰمَةِ يُخْزِيهِمْ وَيَقُولُ أَيْنَ شُرَكَآءِىَ الَّذِينَ كُنتُمْ تُشَٰٓقُّونَ فِيهِمْ ۚ قَالَ الَّذِينَ أُوتُوا۟ الْعِلْمَ إِنَّ الْخِزْىَ الْيَوْمَ وَالسُّوٓءَ عَلَى الْكَٰفِرِينَ ۝ الَّذِينَ تَتَوَفَّىٰهُمُ الْمَلَٰٓئِكَةُ ظَالِمِىٓ أَنفُسِهِمْ ۖ فَأَلْقَوُا۟ السَّلَمَ مَا كُنَّا نَعْمَلُ مِن سُوٓءٍ ۚ

بَلَىٰ إِنَّ ٱللَّهَ عَلِيمٌۢ بِمَا كُنتُمْ تَعْمَلُونَ ۝ فَٱدْخُلُوٓا۟ أَبْوَٰبَ جَهَنَّمَ خَٰلِدِينَ فِيهَا ۖ فَلَبِئْسَ مَثْوَى ٱلْمُتَكَبِّرِينَ ۝ ۞ وَقِيلَ لِلَّذِينَ ٱتَّقَوْا۟ مَاذَآ أَنزَلَ رَبُّكُمْ ۚ قَالُوا۟ خَيْرًا ۗ لِّلَّذِينَ أَحْسَنُوا۟ فِى هَٰذِهِ ٱلدُّنْيَا حَسَنَةٌ ۚ وَلَدَارُ ٱلْءَاخِرَةِ خَيْرٌ ۚ وَلَنِعْمَ دَارُ ٱلْمُتَّقِينَ ۝ جَنَّٰتُ عَدْنٍ يَدْخُلُونَهَا تَجْرِى مِن تَحْتِهَا ٱلْأَنْهَٰرُ ۖ لَهُمْ فِيهَا مَا يَشَآءُونَ ۚ كَذَٰلِكَ يَجْزِى ٱللَّهُ ٱلْمُتَّقِينَ ۝ ٱلَّذِينَ تَتَوَفَّىٰهُمُ ٱلْمَلَٰٓئِكَةُ طَيِّبِينَ ۙ يَقُولُونَ سَلَٰمٌ عَلَيْكُمُ ٱدْخُلُوا۟ ٱلْجَنَّةَ بِمَا كُنتُمْ تَعْمَلُونَ ۝ هَلْ يَنظُرُونَ إِلَّآ أَن تَأْتِيَهُمُ ٱلْمَلَٰٓئِكَةُ أَوْ يَأْتِىَ أَمْرُ رَبِّكَ ۚ كَذَٰلِكَ فَعَلَ ٱلَّذِينَ مِن قَبْلِهِمْ ۚ وَمَا ظَلَمَهُمُ ٱللَّهُ وَلَٰكِن كَانُوٓا۟ أَنفُسَهُمْ يَظْلِمُونَ ۝ فَأَصَابَهُمْ سَيِّـَٔاتُ مَا عَمِلُوا۟ وَحَاقَ بِهِم مَّا كَانُوا۟ بِهِۦ يَسْتَهْزِءُونَ ۝ وَقَالَ ٱلَّذِينَ أَشْرَكُوا۟ لَوْ شَآءَ ٱللَّهُ مَا عَبَدْنَا مِن دُونِهِۦ مِن شَىْءٍ نَّحْنُ وَلَآ ءَابَآؤُنَا وَلَا حَرَّمْنَا مِن دُونِهِۦ مِن شَىْءٍ ۚ كَذَٰلِكَ فَعَلَ ٱلَّذِينَ مِن قَبْلِهِمْ ۚ فَهَلْ عَلَى ٱلرُّسُلِ إِلَّا ٱلْبَلَٰغُ ٱلْمُبِينُ ۝ وَلَقَدْ بَعَثْنَا فِى كُلِّ أُمَّةٍ رَّسُولًا أَنِ ٱعْبُدُوا۟ ٱللَّهَ وَٱجْتَنِبُوا۟ ٱلطَّٰغُوتَ ۖ فَمِنْهُم مَّنْ هَدَى ٱللَّهُ وَمِنْهُم مَّنْ حَقَّتْ عَلَيْهِ ٱلضَّلَٰلَةُ ۚ فَسِيرُوا۟ فِى ٱلْأَرْضِ فَٱنظُرُوا۟ كَيْفَ كَانَ عَٰقِبَةُ ٱلْمُكَذِّبِينَ ۝ إِن تَحْرِصْ عَلَىٰ هُدَىٰهُمْ فَإِنَّ ٱللَّهَ لَا يَهْدِى مَن يُضِلُّ ۖ وَمَا لَهُم مِّن نَّٰصِرِينَ ۝ وَأَقْسَمُوا۟ بِٱللَّهِ جَهْدَ أَيْمَٰنِهِمْ ۙ لَا يَبْعَثُ ٱللَّهُ مَن يَمُوتُ ۚ بَلَىٰ وَعْدًا عَلَيْهِ حَقًّا وَلَٰكِنَّ أَكْثَرَ ٱلنَّاسِ لَا يَعْلَمُونَ ۝ لِيُبَيِّنَ لَهُمُ ٱلَّذِى يَخْتَلِفُونَ فِيهِ وَلِيَعْلَمَ ٱلَّذِينَ كَفَرُوٓا۟ أَنَّهُمْ كَانُوا۟ كَٰذِبِينَ ۝ إِنَّمَا قَوْلُنَا لِشَىْءٍ إِذَآ أَرَدْنَٰهُ أَن نَّقُولَ لَهُۥ كُن فَيَكُونُ ۝ وَٱلَّذِينَ هَاجَرُوا۟ فِى ٱللَّهِ مِنۢ بَعْدِ مَا ظُلِمُوا۟ لَنُبَوِّئَنَّهُمْ فِى ٱلدُّنْيَا حَسَنَةً ۖ وَلَأَجْرُ ٱلْءَاخِرَةِ أَكْبَرُ ۚ لَوْ كَانُوا۟ يَعْلَمُونَ ۝ ٱلَّذِينَ صَبَرُوا۟ وَعَلَىٰ رَبِّهِمْ يَتَوَكَّلُونَ ۝ وَمَآ أَرْسَلْنَا مِن قَبْلِكَ إِلَّا رِجَالًا نُّوحِىٓ إِلَيْهِمْ ۚ فَسْـَٔلُوٓا۟

أَهْلَ ٱلذِّكْرِ إِن كُنتُمْ لَا تَعْلَمُونَ ۞ بِٱلْبَيِّنَٰتِ وَٱلزُّبُرِ ۗ وَأَنزَلْنَآ إِلَيْكَ ٱلذِّكْرَ لِتُبَيِّنَ لِلنَّاسِ مَا نُزِّلَ إِلَيْهِمْ وَلَعَلَّهُمْ يَتَفَكَّرُونَ ۞ أَفَأَمِنَ ٱلَّذِينَ مَكَرُوا۟ ٱلسَّيِّـَٔاتِ أَن يَخْسِفَ ٱللَّهُ بِهِمُ ٱلْأَرْضَ أَوْ يَأْتِيَهُمُ ٱلْعَذَابُ مِنْ حَيْثُ لَا يَشْعُرُونَ ۞ أَوْ يَأْخُذَهُمْ فِى تَقَلُّبِهِمْ فَمَا هُم بِمُعْجِزِينَ ۞ أَوْ يَأْخُذَهُمْ عَلَىٰ تَخَوُّفٍ فَإِنَّ رَبَّكُمْ لَرَءُوفٌ رَّحِيمٌ ۞ أَوَلَمْ يَرَوْا۟ إِلَىٰ مَا خَلَقَ ٱللَّهُ مِن شَىْءٍ يَتَفَيَّؤُا۟ ظِلَٰلُهُۥ عَنِ ٱلْيَمِينِ وَٱلشَّمَآئِلِ سُجَّدًا لِّلَّهِ وَهُمْ دَٰخِرُونَ ۞ وَلِلَّهِ يَسْجُدُ مَا فِى ٱلسَّمَٰوَٰتِ وَمَا فِى ٱلْأَرْضِ مِن دَآبَّةٍ وَٱلْمَلَٰٓئِكَةُ وَهُمْ لَا يَسْتَكْبِرُونَ ۞ يَخَافُونَ رَبَّهُم مِّن فَوْقِهِمْ وَيَفْعَلُونَ مَا يُؤْمَرُونَ ۩ ۞ وَقَالَ ٱللَّهُ لَا تَتَّخِذُوٓا۟ إِلَٰهَيْنِ ٱثْنَيْنِ ۖ إِنَّمَا هُوَ إِلَٰهٌ وَٰحِدٌ ۖ فَإِيَّٰىَ فَٱرْهَبُونِ ۞ وَلَهُۥ مَا فِى ٱلسَّمَٰوَٰتِ وَٱلْأَرْضِ وَلَهُ ٱلدِّينُ وَاصِبًا ۚ أَفَغَيْرَ ٱللَّهِ تَتَّقُونَ ۞ وَمَا بِكُم مِّن نِّعْمَةٍ فَمِنَ ٱللَّهِ ۖ ثُمَّ إِذَا مَسَّكُمُ ٱلضُّرُّ فَإِلَيْهِ تَجْـَٔرُونَ ۞ ثُمَّ إِذَا كَشَفَ ٱلضُّرَّ عَنكُمْ إِذَا فَرِيقٌ مِّنكُم بِرَبِّهِمْ يُشْرِكُونَ ۞ لِيَكْفُرُوا۟ بِمَآ ءَاتَيْنَٰهُمْ ۚ فَتَمَتَّعُوا۟ ۖ فَسَوْفَ تَعْلَمُونَ ۞ وَيَجْعَلُونَ لِمَا لَا يَعْلَمُونَ نَصِيبًا مِّمَّا رَزَقْنَٰهُمْ ۗ تَٱللَّهِ لَتُسْـَٔلُنَّ عَمَّا كُنتُمْ تَفْتَرُونَ ۞ وَيَجْعَلُونَ لِلَّهِ ٱلْبَنَٰتِ سُبْحَٰنَهُۥ ۙ وَلَهُم مَّا يَشْتَهُونَ ۞ وَإِذَا بُشِّرَ أَحَدُهُم بِٱلْأُنثَىٰ ظَلَّ وَجْهُهُۥ مُسْوَدًّا وَهُوَ كَظِيمٌ ۞ يَتَوَٰرَىٰ مِنَ ٱلْقَوْمِ مِن سُوٓءِ مَا بُشِّرَ بِهِۦٓ ۚ أَيُمْسِكُهُۥ عَلَىٰ هُونٍ أَمْ يَدُسُّهُۥ فِى ٱلتُّرَابِ ۗ أَلَا سَآءَ مَا يَحْكُمُونَ ۞ لِلَّذِينَ لَا يُؤْمِنُونَ بِٱلْءَاخِرَةِ مَثَلُ ٱلسَّوْءِ ۖ وَلِلَّهِ ٱلْمَثَلُ ٱلْأَعْلَىٰ ۚ وَهُوَ ٱلْعَزِيزُ ٱلْحَكِيمُ ۞ وَلَوْ يُؤَاخِذُ ٱللَّهُ ٱلنَّاسَ بِظُلْمِهِم مَّا تَرَكَ عَلَيْهَا مِن دَآبَّةٍ وَلَٰكِن يُؤَخِّرُهُمْ إِلَىٰٓ أَجَلٍ مُّسَمًّى ۖ فَإِذَا جَآءَ أَجَلُهُمْ لَا يَسْتَـْٔخِرُونَ سَاعَةً ۖ وَلَا يَسْتَقْدِمُونَ ۞ وَيَجْعَلُونَ لِلَّهِ مَا يَكْرَهُونَ وَتَصِفُ أَلْسِنَتُهُمُ ٱلْكَذِبَ أَنَّ لَهُمُ ٱلْحُسْنَىٰ ۖ لَا جَرَمَ أَنَّ لَهُمُ ٱلنَّارَ وَأَنَّهُم مُّفْرَطُونَ ۞ تَٱللَّهِ لَقَدْ أَرْسَلْنَآ

إِلَىٰ أُمَمٍ مِّن قَبْلِكَ فَزَيَّنَ لَهُمُ ٱلشَّيْطَـٰنُ أَعْمَـٰلَهُمْ فَهُوَ وَلِيُّهُمُ ٱلْيَوْمَ وَلَهُمْ عَذَابٌ أَلِيمٌ ۝ وَمَآ أَنزَلْنَا عَلَيْكَ ٱلْكِتَـٰبَ إِلَّا لِتُبَيِّنَ لَهُمُ ٱلَّذِى ٱخْتَلَفُوا۟ فِيهِ ۙ وَهُدًى وَرَحْمَةً لِّقَوْمٍ يُؤْمِنُونَ ۝ وَٱللَّهُ أَنزَلَ مِنَ ٱلسَّمَآءِ مَآءً فَأَحْيَا بِهِ ٱلْأَرْضَ بَعْدَ مَوْتِهَآ ۚ إِنَّ فِى ذَٰلِكَ لَـَٔايَةً لِّقَوْمٍ يَسْمَعُونَ ۝ وَإِنَّ لَكُمْ فِى ٱلْأَنْعَـٰمِ لَعِبْرَةً ۖ نُّسْقِيكُم مِّمَّا فِى بُطُونِهِۦ مِنۢ بَيْنِ فَرْثٍ وَدَمٍ لَّبَنًا خَالِصًا سَآئِغًا لِّلشَّـٰرِبِينَ ۝ وَمِن ثَمَرَٰتِ ٱلنَّخِيلِ وَٱلْأَعْنَـٰبِ تَتَّخِذُونَ مِنْهُ سَكَرًا وَرِزْقًا حَسَنًا ۗ إِنَّ فِى ذَٰلِكَ لَـَٔايَةً لِّقَوْمٍ يَعْقِلُونَ ۝ وَأَوْحَىٰ رَبُّكَ إِلَى ٱلنَّحْلِ أَنِ ٱتَّخِذِى مِنَ ٱلْجِبَالِ بُيُوتًا وَمِنَ ٱلشَّجَرِ وَمِمَّا يَعْرِشُونَ ۝ ثُمَّ كُلِى مِن كُلِّ ٱلثَّمَرَٰتِ فَٱسْلُكِى سُبُلَ رَبِّكِ ذُلُلًا ۚ يَخْرُجُ مِنۢ بُطُونِهَا شَرَابٌ مُّخْتَلِفٌ أَلْوَٰنُهُۥ فِيهِ شِفَآءٌ لِّلنَّاسِ ۗ إِنَّ فِى ذَٰلِكَ لَـَٔايَةً لِّقَوْمٍ يَتَفَكَّرُونَ ۝ وَٱللَّهُ خَلَقَكُمْ ثُمَّ يَتَوَفَّىٰكُمْ ۚ وَمِنكُم مَّن يُرَدُّ إِلَىٰٓ أَرْذَلِ ٱلْعُمُرِ لِكَىْ لَا يَعْلَمَ بَعْدَ عِلْمٍ شَيْـًٔا ۚ إِنَّ ٱللَّهَ عَلِيمٌ قَدِيرٌ ۝ وَٱللَّهُ فَضَّلَ بَعْضَكُمْ عَلَىٰ بَعْضٍ فِى ٱلرِّزْقِ ۚ فَمَا ٱلَّذِينَ فُضِّلُوا۟ بِرَآدِّى رِزْقِهِمْ عَلَىٰ مَا مَلَكَتْ أَيْمَـٰنُهُمْ فَهُمْ فِيهِ سَوَآءٌ ۚ أَفَبِنِعْمَةِ ٱللَّهِ يَجْحَدُونَ ۝ وَٱللَّهُ جَعَلَ لَكُم مِّنْ أَنفُسِكُمْ أَزْوَٰجًا وَجَعَلَ لَكُم مِّنْ أَزْوَٰجِكُم بَنِينَ وَحَفَدَةً وَرَزَقَكُم مِّنَ ٱلطَّيِّبَـٰتِ ۚ أَفَبِٱلْبَـٰطِلِ يُؤْمِنُونَ وَبِنِعْمَتِ ٱللَّهِ هُمْ يَكْفُرُونَ ۝ وَيَعْبُدُونَ مِن دُونِ ٱللَّهِ مَا لَا يَمْلِكُ لَهُمْ رِزْقًا مِّنَ ٱلسَّمَـٰوَٰتِ وَٱلْأَرْضِ شَيْـًٔا وَلَا يَسْتَطِيعُونَ ۝ فَلَا تَضْرِبُوا۟ لِلَّهِ ٱلْأَمْثَالَ ۚ إِنَّ ٱللَّهَ يَعْلَمُ وَأَنتُمْ لَا تَعْلَمُونَ ۝ ۞ ضَرَبَ ٱللَّهُ مَثَلًا عَبْدًا مَّمْلُوكًا لَّا يَقْدِرُ عَلَىٰ شَىْءٍ وَمَن رَّزَقْنَـٰهُ مِنَّا رِزْقًا حَسَنًا فَهُوَ يُنفِقُ مِنْهُ سِرًّا وَجَهْرًا ۖ هَلْ يَسْتَوُۥنَ ۚ ٱلْحَمْدُ لِلَّهِ ۚ بَلْ أَكْثَرُهُمْ لَا يَعْلَمُونَ ۝ وَضَرَبَ ٱللَّهُ مَثَلًا رَّجُلَيْنِ أَحَدُهُمَآ أَبْكَمُ لَا يَقْدِرُ عَلَىٰ شَىْءٍ وَهُوَ كَلٌّ عَلَىٰ مَوْلَىٰهُ أَيْنَمَا يُوَجِّههُّ لَا يَأْتِ بِخَيْرٍ ۖ هَلْ يَسْتَوِى هُوَ وَمَن يَأْمُرُ بِٱلْعَدْلِ ۙ وَهُوَ عَلَىٰ

صِرَٰطٍ مُّسْتَقِيمٍ ۝ وَلِلَّهِ غَيْبُ ٱلسَّمَٰوَٰتِ وَٱلْأَرْضِ ۚ وَمَآ أَمْرُ ٱلسَّاعَةِ إِلَّا كَلَمْحِ ٱلْبَصَرِ أَوْ هُوَ أَقْرَبُ ۚ إِنَّ ٱللَّهَ عَلَىٰ كُلِّ شَىْءٍ قَدِيرٌ ۝ وَٱللَّهُ أَخْرَجَكُم مِّنۢ بُطُونِ أُمَّهَٰتِكُمْ لَا تَعْلَمُونَ شَيْـًٔا وَجَعَلَ لَكُمُ ٱلسَّمْعَ وَٱلْأَبْصَٰرَ وَٱلْأَفْـِٔدَةَ ۙ لَعَلَّكُمْ تَشْكُرُونَ ۝ أَلَمْ يَرَوْا۟ إِلَى ٱلطَّيْرِ مُسَخَّرَٰتٍ فِى جَوِّ ٱلسَّمَآءِ مَا يُمْسِكُهُنَّ إِلَّا ٱللَّهُ ۗ إِنَّ فِى ذَٰلِكَ لَءَايَٰتٍ لِّقَوْمٍ يُؤْمِنُونَ ۝ وَٱللَّهُ جَعَلَ لَكُم مِّنۢ بُيُوتِكُمْ سَكَنًا وَجَعَلَ لَكُم مِّن جُلُودِ ٱلْأَنْعَٰمِ بُيُوتًا تَسْتَخِفُّونَهَا يَوْمَ ظَعْنِكُمْ وَيَوْمَ إِقَامَتِكُمْ ۙ وَمِنْ أَصْوَافِهَا وَأَوْبَارِهَا وَأَشْعَارِهَآ أَثَٰثًا وَمَتَٰعًا إِلَىٰ حِينٍ ۝ وَٱللَّهُ جَعَلَ لَكُم مِّمَّا خَلَقَ ظِلَٰلًا وَجَعَلَ لَكُم مِّنَ ٱلْجِبَالِ أَكْنَٰنًا وَجَعَلَ لَكُمْ سَرَٰبِيلَ تَقِيكُمُ ٱلْحَرَّ وَسَرَٰبِيلَ تَقِيكُم بَأْسَكُمْ ۚ كَذَٰلِكَ يُتِمُّ نِعْمَتَهُۥ عَلَيْكُمْ لَعَلَّكُمْ تُسْلِمُونَ ۝ فَإِن تَوَلَّوْا۟ فَإِنَّمَا عَلَيْكَ ٱلْبَلَٰغُ ٱلْمُبِينُ ۝ يَعْرِفُونَ نِعْمَتَ ٱللَّهِ ثُمَّ يُنكِرُونَهَا وَأَكْثَرُهُمُ ٱلْكَٰفِرُونَ ۝ وَيَوْمَ نَبْعَثُ مِن كُلِّ أُمَّةٍ شَهِيدًا ثُمَّ لَا يُؤْذَنُ لِلَّذِينَ كَفَرُوا۟ وَلَا هُمْ يُسْتَعْتَبُونَ ۝ وَإِذَا رَءَا ٱلَّذِينَ ظَلَمُوا۟ ٱلْعَذَابَ فَلَا يُخَفَّفُ عَنْهُمْ وَلَا هُمْ يُنظَرُونَ ۝ وَإِذَا رَءَا ٱلَّذِينَ أَشْرَكُوا۟ شُرَكَآءَهُمْ قَالُوا۟ رَبَّنَا هَٰٓؤُلَآءِ شُرَكَآؤُنَا ٱلَّذِينَ كُنَّا نَدْعُوا۟ مِن دُونِكَ ۖ فَأَلْقَوْا۟ إِلَيْهِمُ ٱلْقَوْلَ إِنَّكُمْ لَكَٰذِبُونَ ۝ وَأَلْقَوْا۟ إِلَى ٱللَّهِ يَوْمَئِذٍ ٱلسَّلَمَ ۖ وَضَلَّ عَنْهُم مَّا كَانُوا۟ يَفْتَرُونَ ۝ ٱلَّذِينَ كَفَرُوا۟ وَصَدُّوا۟ عَن سَبِيلِ ٱللَّهِ زِدْنَٰهُمْ عَذَابًا فَوْقَ ٱلْعَذَابِ بِمَا كَانُوا۟ يُفْسِدُونَ ۝ وَيَوْمَ نَبْعَثُ فِى كُلِّ أُمَّةٍ شَهِيدًا عَلَيْهِم مِّنْ أَنفُسِهِمْ ۖ وَجِئْنَا بِكَ شَهِيدًا عَلَىٰ هَٰٓؤُلَآءِ ۚ وَنَزَّلْنَا عَلَيْكَ ٱلْكِتَٰبَ تِبْيَٰنًا لِّكُلِّ شَىْءٍ وَهُدًى وَرَحْمَةً وَبُشْرَىٰ لِلْمُسْلِمِينَ ۝ ۞ إِنَّ ٱللَّهَ يَأْمُرُ بِٱلْعَدْلِ وَٱلْإِحْسَٰنِ وَإِيتَآئِ ذِى ٱلْقُرْبَىٰ وَيَنْهَىٰ عَنِ ٱلْفَحْشَآءِ وَٱلْمُنكَرِ وَٱلْبَغْىِ ۚ يَعِظُكُمْ

لَعَلَّكُمْ تَذَكَّرُونَ ۝ وَأَوْفُوا بِعَهْدِ اللَّهِ إِذَا عَاهَدتُّمْ وَلَا تَنقُضُوا الْأَيْمَانَ بَعْدَ تَوْكِيدِهَا وَقَدْ جَعَلْتُمُ اللَّهَ عَلَيْكُمْ كَفِيلاً إِنَّ اللَّهَ يَعْلَمُ مَا تَفْعَلُونَ ۝ وَلَا تَكُونُوا كَالَّتِي نَقَضَتْ غَزْلَهَا مِن بَعْدِ قُوَّةٍ أَنكَاثًا تَتَّخِذُونَ أَيْمَانَكُمْ دَخَلاً بَيْنَكُمْ أَن تَكُونَ أُمَّةٌ هِيَ أَرْبَىٰ مِنْ أُمَّةٍ إِنَّمَا يَبْلُوكُمُ اللَّهُ بِهِ وَلَيُبَيِّنَنَّ لَكُمْ يَوْمَ الْقِيَامَةِ مَا كُنتُمْ فِيهِ تَخْتَلِفُونَ ۝ وَلَوْ شَاءَ اللَّهُ لَجَعَلَكُمْ أُمَّةً وَاحِدَةً وَلَٰكِن يُضِلُّ مَن يَشَاءُ وَيَهْدِي مَن يَشَاءُ وَلَتُسْأَلُنَّ عَمَّا كُنتُمْ تَعْمَلُونَ ۝ وَلَا تَتَّخِذُوا أَيْمَانَكُمْ دَخَلاً بَيْنَكُمْ فَتَزِلَّ قَدَمٌ بَعْدَ ثُبُوتِهَا وَتَذُوقُوا السُّوءَ بِمَا صَدَدتُّمْ عَن سَبِيلِ اللَّهِ وَلَكُمْ عَذَابٌ عَظِيمٌ ۝ وَلَا تَشْتَرُوا بِعَهْدِ اللَّهِ ثَمَنًا قَلِيلاً إِنَّمَا عِندَ اللَّهِ هُوَ خَيْرٌ لَّكُمْ إِن كُنتُمْ تَعْلَمُونَ ۝ مَا عِندَكُمْ يَنفَدُ وَمَا عِندَ اللَّهِ بَاقٍ وَلَنَجْزِيَنَّ الَّذِينَ صَبَرُوا أَجْرَهُم بِأَحْسَنِ مَا كَانُوا يَعْمَلُونَ ۝ مَنْ عَمِلَ صَالِحًا مِّن ذَكَرٍ أَوْ أُنثَىٰ وَهُوَ مُؤْمِنٌ فَلَنُحْيِيَنَّهُ حَيَاةً طَيِّبَةً وَلَنَجْزِيَنَّهُمْ أَجْرَهُم بِأَحْسَنِ مَا كَانُوا يَعْمَلُونَ ۝ فَإِذَا قَرَأْتَ الْقُرْآنَ فَاسْتَعِذْ بِاللَّهِ مِنَ الشَّيْطَانِ الرَّجِيمِ ۝ إِنَّهُ لَيْسَ لَهُ سُلْطَانٌ عَلَى الَّذِينَ آمَنُوا وَعَلَىٰ رَبِّهِمْ يَتَوَكَّلُونَ ۝ إِنَّمَا سُلْطَانُهُ عَلَى الَّذِينَ يَتَوَلَّوْنَهُ وَالَّذِينَ هُم بِهِ مُشْرِكُونَ ۝ وَإِذَا بَدَّلْنَا آيَةً مَّكَانَ آيَةٍ وَاللَّهُ أَعْلَمُ بِمَا يُنَزِّلُ قَالُوا إِنَّمَا أَنتَ مُفْتَرٍ بَلْ أَكْثَرُهُمْ لَا يَعْلَمُونَ ۝ قُلْ نَزَّلَهُ رُوحُ الْقُدُسِ مِن رَّبِّكَ بِالْحَقِّ لِيُثَبِّتَ الَّذِينَ آمَنُوا وَهُدًى وَبُشْرَىٰ لِلْمُسْلِمِينَ ۝ وَلَقَدْ نَعْلَمُ أَنَّهُمْ يَقُولُونَ إِنَّمَا يُعَلِّمُهُ بَشَرٌ لِّسَانُ الَّذِي يُلْحِدُونَ إِلَيْهِ أَعْجَمِيٌّ وَهَٰذَا لِسَانٌ عَرَبِيٌّ مُّبِينٌ ۝ إِنَّ الَّذِينَ لَا يُؤْمِنُونَ بِآيَاتِ اللَّهِ لَا يَهْدِيهِمُ اللَّهُ وَلَهُمْ عَذَابٌ أَلِيمٌ ۝ إِنَّمَا يَفْتَرِي الْكَذِبَ الَّذِينَ لَا يُؤْمِنُونَ بِآيَاتِ اللَّهِ

وَأُوْلَٰٓئِكَ هُمُ ٱلْكَٰذِبُونَ ۝ مَن كَفَرَ بِٱللَّهِ مِنۢ بَعْدِ إِيمَٰنِهِۦٓ إِلَّا مَنْ أُكْرِهَ وَقَلْبُهُۥ مُطْمَئِنٌّۢ بِٱلْإِيمَٰنِ وَلَٰكِن مَّن شَرَحَ بِٱلْكُفْرِ صَدْرًا فَعَلَيْهِمْ غَضَبٌ مِّنَ ٱللَّهِ وَلَهُمْ عَذَابٌ عَظِيمٌ ۝ ذَٰلِكَ بِأَنَّهُمُ ٱسْتَحَبُّوا۟ ٱلْحَيَوٰةَ ٱلدُّنْيَا عَلَى ٱلْءَاخِرَةِ وَأَنَّ ٱللَّهَ لَا يَهْدِى ٱلْقَوْمَ ٱلْكَٰفِرِينَ ۝ أُو۟لَٰٓئِكَ ٱلَّذِينَ طَبَعَ ٱللَّهُ عَلَىٰ قُلُوبِهِمْ وَسَمْعِهِمْ وَأَبْصَٰرِهِمْ وَأُو۟لَٰٓئِكَ هُمُ ٱلْغَٰفِلُونَ ۝ لَا جَرَمَ أَنَّهُمْ فِى ٱلْءَاخِرَةِ هُمُ ٱلْخَٰسِرُونَ ۝ ثُمَّ إِنَّ رَبَّكَ لِلَّذِينَ هَاجَرُوا۟ مِنۢ بَعْدِ مَا فُتِنُوا۟ ثُمَّ جَٰهَدُوا۟ وَصَبَرُوٓا۟ إِنَّ رَبَّكَ مِنۢ بَعْدِهَا لَغَفُورٌ رَّحِيمٌ ۝ ۞ يَوْمَ تَأْتِى كُلُّ نَفْسٍ تُجَٰدِلُ عَن نَّفْسِهَا وَتُوَفَّىٰ كُلُّ نَفْسٍ مَّا عَمِلَتْ وَهُمْ لَا يُظْلَمُونَ ۝ وَضَرَبَ ٱللَّهُ مَثَلًا قَرْيَةً كَانَتْ ءَامِنَةً مُّطْمَئِنَّةً يَأْتِيهَا رِزْقُهَا رَغَدًا مِّن كُلِّ مَكَانٍ فَكَفَرَتْ بِأَنْعُمِ ٱللَّهِ فَأَذَٰقَهَا ٱللَّهُ لِبَاسَ ٱلْجُوعِ وَٱلْخَوْفِ بِمَا كَانُوا۟ يَصْنَعُونَ ۝ وَلَقَدْ جَآءَهُمْ رَسُولٌ مِّنْهُمْ فَكَذَّبُوهُ فَأَخَذَهُمُ ٱلْعَذَابُ وَهُمْ ظَٰلِمُونَ ۝ فَكُلُوا۟ مِمَّا رَزَقَكُمُ ٱللَّهُ حَلَٰلًا طَيِّبًا وَٱشْكُرُوا۟ نِعْمَتَ ٱللَّهِ إِن كُنتُمْ إِيَّاهُ تَعْبُدُونَ ۝ إِنَّمَا حَرَّمَ عَلَيْكُمُ ٱلْمَيْتَةَ وَٱلدَّمَ وَلَحْمَ ٱلْخِنزِيرِ وَمَآ أُهِلَّ لِغَيْرِ ٱللَّهِ بِهِۦ فَمَنِ ٱضْطُرَّ غَيْرَ بَاغٍ وَلَا عَادٍ فَإِنَّ ٱللَّهَ غَفُورٌ رَّحِيمٌ ۝ وَلَا تَقُولُوا۟ لِمَا تَصِفُ أَلْسِنَتُكُمُ ٱلْكَذِبَ هَٰذَا حَلَٰلٌ وَهَٰذَا حَرَامٌ لِّتَفْتَرُوا۟ عَلَى ٱللَّهِ ٱلْكَذِبَ إِنَّ ٱلَّذِينَ يَفْتَرُونَ عَلَى ٱللَّهِ ٱلْكَذِبَ لَا يُفْلِحُونَ ۝ مَتَٰعٌ قَلِيلٌ وَلَهُمْ عَذَابٌ أَلِيمٌ ۝ وَعَلَى ٱلَّذِينَ هَادُوا۟ حَرَّمْنَا مَا قَصَصْنَا عَلَيْكَ مِن قَبْلُ وَمَا ظَلَمْنَٰهُمْ وَلَٰكِن كَانُوٓا۟ أَنفُسَهُمْ يَظْلِمُونَ ۝ ثُمَّ إِنَّ رَبَّكَ لِلَّذِينَ عَمِلُوا۟ ٱلسُّوٓءَ بِجَهَٰلَةٍ ثُمَّ تَابُوا۟ مِنۢ بَعْدِ ذَٰلِكَ وَأَصْلَحُوٓا۟ إِنَّ رَبَّكَ مِنۢ بَعْدِهَا لَغَفُورٌ رَّحِيمٌ ۝ إِنَّ إِبْرَٰهِيمَ كَانَ أُمَّةً قَانِتًا لِّلَّهِ حَنِيفًا وَلَمْ يَكُ مِنَ ٱلْمُشْرِكِينَ ۝ شَاكِرًا

لِأَنْعُمِهِ ۚ اجْتَبَىٰهُ وَهَدَىٰهُ إِلَىٰ صِرَٰطٍ مُّسْتَقِيمٍ ۝ وَءَاتَيْنَٰهُ فِى ٱلدُّنْيَا حَسَنَةً ۖ وَإِنَّهُۥ فِى ٱلْءَاخِرَةِ لَمِنَ ٱلصَّٰلِحِينَ ۝ ثُمَّ أَوْحَيْنَآ إِلَيْكَ أَنِ ٱتَّبِعْ مِلَّةَ إِبْرَٰهِيمَ حَنِيفًا ۖ وَمَا كَانَ مِنَ ٱلْمُشْرِكِينَ ۝ إِنَّمَا جُعِلَ ٱلسَّبْتُ عَلَى ٱلَّذِينَ ٱخْتَلَفُوا۟ فِيهِ ۚ وَإِنَّ رَبَّكَ لَيَحْكُمُ بَيْنَهُمْ يَوْمَ ٱلْقِيَٰمَةِ فِيمَا كَانُوا۟ فِيهِ يَخْتَلِفُونَ ۝ ٱدْعُ إِلَىٰ سَبِيلِ رَبِّكَ بِٱلْحِكْمَةِ وَٱلْمَوْعِظَةِ ٱلْحَسَنَةِ ۖ وَجَٰدِلْهُم بِٱلَّتِى هِىَ أَحْسَنُ ۚ إِنَّ رَبَّكَ هُوَ أَعْلَمُ بِمَن ضَلَّ عَن سَبِيلِهِۦ ۖ وَهُوَ أَعْلَمُ بِٱلْمُهْتَدِينَ ۝ وَإِنْ عَاقَبْتُمْ فَعَاقِبُوا۟ بِمِثْلِ مَا عُوقِبْتُم بِهِۦ ۖ وَلَئِن صَبَرْتُمْ لَهُوَ خَيْرٌ لِّلصَّٰبِرِينَ ۝ وَٱصْبِرْ وَمَا صَبْرُكَ إِلَّا بِٱللَّهِ ۚ وَلَا تَحْزَنْ عَلَيْهِمْ وَلَا تَكُ فِى ضَيْقٍ مِّمَّا يَمْكُرُونَ ۝ إِنَّ ٱللَّهَ مَعَ ٱلَّذِينَ ٱتَّقَوا۟ وَّٱلَّذِينَ هُم مُّحْسِنُونَ ۝

(An-Nahl 001-128)

CHAPTER (SURAH) 15: AL-HIJR (STONELAND, ROCK CITY), VERSES 001–099

(بِسْمِ اللَّهِ الرَّحْمَنِ الرَّحِيمِ)

In the Name of Allah, the Most Gracious, the Most Merciful.

Surah: 15 Ayah: 1, Ayah: 2 & Ayah: 3

﴿ الٓر تِلْكَ ءَايَٰتُ ٱلْكِتَٰبِ وَقُرْءَانٍ مُّبِينٍ ۝ ﴾

1. Alif-Lâm-Râ. (These letters are one of the miracles of the Qur'ân, and none but Allâh (Alone) knows their meanings). These are the Verses of the Book, and a plain Qur'ân.

﴿ رُّبَمَا يَوَدُّ ٱلَّذِينَ كَفَرُواْ لَوْ كَانُواْ مُسْلِمِينَ ۝ ﴾

2. How much will those who disbelieved desire that they were Muslims (those who have submitted themselves to Allâh's Will in Islâm Islâmic Monotheism - this will be on the Day of Resurrection when they will see the disbelievers going to Hell and the Muslims going to Paradise).

﴿ ذَرْهُمْ يَأْكُلُواْ وَيَتَمَتَّعُواْ وَيُلْهِهِمُ ٱلْأَمَلُ فَسَوْفَ يَعْلَمُونَ ۝ ﴾

3. Leave them to eat and enjoy, and let them be preoccupied with (false) hope. They will come to know!

Transliteration

1. Alif-lam-ra tilka ayatu alkitabi waqur-anin mubeenin   2. Rubama yawaddu allatheena kafaroo law kanoo muslimeena   3. Tharhum ya/kuloo wayatamattaAAoo wayulhihimu al-amalu fasawfa yaAAlamoona

Tafsir Ibn Kathir

The Disbelievers will someday wish that They had been Muslims

We have already discussed the letters which appear at the beginning of some Surahs. Allah said:

(How much would those who disbelieved wish) Here Allah tells us that they will regret having lived in disbelief, and will wish that they had been Muslims in this world. Regarding Allah's saying,

(How much would those who disbelieved wish that they had been Muslims.) Sufyan Ath-Thawri reported from Salamah bin Kuhayl, who reported from Abi Az-Za`ra', from `Abdullah, who said: "This is about the Jahannamiyyun (the sinners among the believers who will stay in Hell for some time), when they (the disbelievers) see them being brought out of Hell."

(How much would those who disbelieved wish that they had been Muslims.) Ibn Jarir reported that Ibn `Abbas and Anas bin Malik explained that this Ayah refers to the Day when Allah will detain the sinful Muslims in Hell along with the idolators. He said: "The idolators will say to them, `What you used to worship on earth has not helped you.' Then by virtue of His mercy, Allah will be angry for their sake, and He will remove them (from it). That is when

(How much would those who disbelieved wish that they had been Muslims)."

(Leave them to eat and enjoy) this is a stern and definitive threat for them, like His saying,

(Say: "Enjoy your brief life! But certainly, your destination is the Fire!") (14:30)

((O disbelievers!) Eat and enjoy yourselves (in this worldly life) for a little while. Verily, you are the guilty.)(77:46) Allah says:

(let them be preoccupied with false hope.) i.e., distracted from repentance and turning to Allah, for

(They will soon come to know!) that is, their punishment.

Surah: 15 Ayah: 4 & Ayah: 5

﴿ وَمَآ أَهْلَكْنَا مِن قَرْيَةٍ إِلَّا وَلَهَا كِتَابٌ مَّعْلُومٌ ﴾

4. And never did We destroy a township but there was a known decree for it.

﴿ مَّا تَسْبِقُ مِنْ أُمَّةٍ أَجَلَهَا وَمَا يَسْتَـْٔخِرُونَ ﴾

5. No nation can advance its term, nor delay it.

Transliteration

4. Wama ahlakna min qaryatin illa walaha kitabun maAAloomun 5. Ma tasbiqu min ommatin ajalaha wama yasta/khiroona

Tafsir Ibn Kathir

Every Township has its allotted Time

Allah is informing us that He never destroys a township until He has established evidences for it and its allotted time has ended. When the time for a nation's destruction has come, He never delays it, and He never moves its appointed time forward. This was a message and a warning to the people of Makkah, telling them to give up their Shirk, their stubbornness and disbelief for which they deserved to be destroyed.

Surah: 15 Ayah: 6, Ayah: 7, Ayah: 8 & Ayah: 9

﴿ وَقَالُوا۟ يَـٰٓأَيُّهَا ٱلَّذِى نُزِّلَ عَلَيْهِ ٱلذِّكْرُ إِنَّكَ لَمَجْنُونٌ ۝ ﴾

6. And they say: "O you (Muhammad (peace be upon him)) to whom the Dhikr (the Qur'ân) has been sent down! Verily, you are a mad man!

﴿ لَّوْ مَا تَأْتِينَا بِٱلْمَلَـٰٓئِكَةِ إِن كُنتَ مِنَ ٱلصَّـٰدِقِينَ ۝ ﴾

7. "Why do you not bring angels to us if you are of the truthful?"

﴿ مَا نُنَزِّلُ ٱلْمَلَـٰٓئِكَةَ إِلَّا بِٱلْحَقِّ وَمَا كَانُوٓا۟ إِذًا مُّنظَرِينَ ۝ ﴾

8. We send not the angels down except with the truth (i.e. for torment), and in that case, they (the disbelievers) would have no respite!

﴿ إِنَّا نَحْنُ نَزَّلْنَا ٱلذِّكْرَ وَإِنَّا لَهُۥ لَحَـٰفِظُونَ ۝ ﴾

9. Verily We, it is We Who have sent down the Dhikr (i.e. the Qur'ân) and surely, We will guard it (from corruption).

Transliteration

6. Waqaloo ya ayyuha allathee nuzzila AAalayhi alththikru innaka lamajnoonun 7. Law ma ta/teena bialmala-ikati in kunta mina alssadiqeena 8. Ma nunazzilu almala-ikata illa bialhaqqi wama kanoo ithan munthareena 9. Inna nahnu nazzalna alththikra wa-inna lahu lahafithoona

Tafsir Ibn Kathir

The Accusation that the Prophet was a Madman and Demands for Him to bring down Angels

Allah tells us about the disbelief, arrogance and stubbornness of the disbelievers as reflected in their words:

(O you (Muhammad) to whom the Dhikr (the Qur'an) has been revealed!) i.e., the one who claims to receive it.

(Verily, you are a mad man!) i.e., by your invitation to us to follow you and leave the way of our forefathers.

(Why do you not bring angels to us) i.e., to bear witness to the accuracy of what you have brought to us is true, if you are really telling the truth This is similar to what Pharaoh said:

(Why then are not golden bracelets bestowed on him, or angels sent along with him)(43:53). And Allah said:

(And those who do not expect a meeting with Us (i. e., those who deny the Day of Resurrection and the life of the Hereafter), say: "Why are not the angels sent down to us, or why do we not see our Lord" Indeed they think too highly of themselves, and are scornful with great pride. On the Day that they do see the angels - there will be no good news given on that day to the guilty. And they (angels) will say: "All kinds of glad tidings are forbidden for you.") (25:21-22) For this reason Allah said:

(We do not send the angels down except with the truth, and in that case, they (the disbelievers) would have no respite!) Mujahid said in this Ayah:

(We do not send the angels down except with the truth) "(i.e.,) with the Message and the punishment." Then Allah, may He be exalted, stated that He is the One Who revealed the Dhikr to him, which is the Qur'an, and He is protecting it from being changed or altered.

Surah: 15 Ayah: 10, Ayah: 11, Ayah: 12 & Ayah: 13

﴿ وَلَقَدْ أَرْسَلْنَا مِن قَبْلِكَ فِي شِيَعِ ٱلْأَوَّلِينَ ۝ ﴾

10. Indeed, We sent Messengers before you (O Muhammad (peace be upon him)) amongst the sects (communities) of old.

﴿ وَمَا يَأْتِيهِم مِّن رَّسُولٍ إِلَّا كَانُوا بِهِ يَسْتَهْزِءُونَ ۝ ﴾

11. And never came a Messenger to them but they did mock him.

﴿ كَذَٰلِكَ نَسْلُكُهُ فِي قُلُوبِ ٱلْمُجْرِمِينَ ۝ ﴾

12. Thus do We let it (polytheism and disbelief) enter the hearts of the Mujrimûn (criminals, polytheists, pagans (because of their mocking at the Messengers))

﴿ لَا يُؤْمِنُونَ بِهِ وَقَدْ خَلَتْ سُنَّةُ ٱلْأَوَّلِينَ ۝ ﴾

13. They would not believe in it (the Qur'ân); and already the example of (Allâh's punishment of) the ancients (who disbelieved) has gone forth.

Transliteration

10. Walaqad arsalna min qablika fee shiyaAAi al-awwaleena 11. Wama ya/teehim min rasoolin illa kanoo bihi yastahzi-oona   12. Kathalika naslukuhu fee quloobi almujrimeena 13. La yu/minoona bihi waqad khalat sunnatu al-awwaleena

Tafsir Ibn Kathir

The Idolators of Every Nation made a Mockery of their Messengers

Consoling His Messenger for the rejection of the disbelieving Quraysh, Allah says that He has sent Messengers before him to the nations of the past, and no Messenger came to a nation but they rejected him and mocked him. Then He tells him that He lets disbelief enter the hearts of those sinners who are too stubborn and too arrogant to follow His guidance.

(Thus We allow it to enter the hearts of the guilty.) Anas and Al-Hasan Al-Basri said that this referred to Shirk.

(and already the example of the ancients has gone forth.) meaning the destruction wrought by Allah on those who rejected His Messengers, and how He saved His Prophets and their followers in this world and in the Hereafter, is well known.

Surah: 15 Ayah: 14 & Ayah: 15

﴿ وَلَوْ فَتَحْنَا عَلَيْهِم بَابًا مِّنَ ٱلسَّمَآءِ فَظَلُّوا۟ فِيهِ يَعْرُجُونَ ۝ ﴾

14. And even if We opened to them a gate from the heaven and they were to continue ascending thereto (all the day long)

﴿ لَقَالُوٓا۟ إِنَّمَا سُكِّرَتْ أَبْصَـٰرُنَا بَلْ نَحْنُ قَوْمٌ مَّسْحُورُونَ ۝ ﴾

15. They would surely say: "Our eyes have been (as if) dazzled. Nay, we are a people bewitched."

Transliteration

14. Walaw fatahna AAalayhim baban mina alssama-i fathalloo feehi yaAArujoona 15. Laqaloo innama sukkirat absaruna bal nahnu qawmun mashooroona

Tafsir Ibn Kathir

The Stubborn Disbelievers will never believe, no matter what Signs and Wonders They see

Allah explains the extent of their disbelief and stubborn resistance to the truth by stating that even if a door to heaven were to be opened for them, and they were to be taken up through it, they would still not believe. Rather, they would say:

(Our eyes have been (as if) dazzled.) Mujahid, Ibn Kathir and Ad-Dahhak said, "(this means) our vision has been blocked." Qatadah narrated that Ibn `Abbas said, "(this means) our eyesight has been taken away." Al-`Awfi reported that Ibn `Abbas said, "(this means) we were confused and put under a spell."

(Our eyes have been (as if) dazzled.) Ibn Zayd said: "The one who is dazzled (lit. intoxicated) is the one who cannot reason."

Surah: 15 Ayah: 16, Ayah: 17, Ayah: 18, Ayah: 19 & Ayah: 20

﴿ وَلَقَدْ جَعَلْنَا فِى ٱلسَّمَآءِ بُرُوجًا وَزَيَّنَّـٰهَا لِلنَّـٰظِرِينَ ۝ ﴾

16. And indeed, We have put the big stars in the heaven and We beautified it for the beholders.

﴿ وَحَفِظْنَٰهَا مِن كُلِّ شَيْطَٰنٍ رَّجِيمٍ ۝ ﴾

17. And We have guarded it (near heaven) from every outcast Shaitân (devil).

﴿ إِلَّا مَنِ ٱسْتَرَقَ ٱلسَّمْعَ فَأَتْبَعَهُۥ شِهَابٌ مُّبِينٌ ۝ ﴾

18. Except him (devil) who steals the hearing then he is pursued by a clear flaming fire.

﴿ وَٱلْأَرْضَ مَدَدْنَٰهَا وَأَلْقَيْنَا فِيهَا رَوَٰسِىَ وَأَنۢبَتْنَا فِيهَا مِن كُلِّ شَىْءٍ مَّوْزُونٍ ۝ ﴾

19. And the earth We have spread out, and have placed therein firm mountains, and caused to grow therein all kinds of things in due proportion.

﴿ وَجَعَلْنَا لَكُمْ فِيهَا مَعَٰيِشَ وَمَن لَّسْتُمْ لَهُۥ بِرَٰزِقِينَ ۝ ﴾

20. And We have provided therein means of living, for you and for those whom you provide not (moving (living) creatures, cattle, beasts, and other animals).

Transliteration

16. Walaqad jaAAalna fee alssama-i buroojan wazayyannaha lilnnathireena 17. Wahafithnaha min kulli shaytanin rajeemin 18. Illa mani istaraqa alssamAAa faatbaAAahu shihabun mubeenun 19. Waal-arda madadnaha waalqayna feeha rawasiya waanbatna feeha min kulli shay-in mawzoonin 20. WajaAAalna lakum feeha maAAayisha waman lastum lahu biraziqeena

Tafsir Ibn Kathir

The Power of Allah and His Signs in the Heavens and on Earth

To those who ponder, and look repeatedly at the dazzling signs and wonders that are to be seen in the creation, Allah mentions His creation of the heavens, with their immense height, and both the fixed and moving heavenly bodies with which He has adorned it. Here, Mujahid and Qatadah said that Buruj (big stars) refers to the heavenly bodies. (I say): This is like the Ayah :

(Blessed be He Who has placed the big stars in the heavens.) (25:61) `Atiyah Al-`Awfi said: "Buruj here refers to sentinel fortresses." He made the "shooting stars" to guard it against the evil devils who try to listen to information conveyed at the highest heights. If any devil breaches it and advances hoping to listen, a clear "shooting star" comes to him and destroys him. He may already have passed on whatever he heard before the fire hit him, to another devil below him; the latter will then take it to his friends (among humans), as is stated in the Sahih. Explaining this Ayah, Al-Bukhari reported from Abu Hurayrah that the Prophet said:

> «إِذَا قَضَى اللَّهُ الْأَمْرَ فِي السَّمَاءِ ضَرَبَتِ الْمَلَائِكَةُ بِأَجْنِحَتِهَا خُضْعَانًا لِقَوْلِهِ كَأَنَّهُ سِلْسِلَةٌ عَلَى صَفْوَانٍ»

(When Allah decrees any matter in heaven, the angels beat their wings in submission to His Word, (with a sound like) a chain (beating) on a smooth rock.") (`Ali and other subnarrators said, "The sound reaches them.") "When the fright leaves their (angels') hearts, they (angels) are asked: `What did your Lord say' They respond: "The truth. And He is the Most High, the Most Great.' So those who hope to hear something listen, and they are standing one above the other." Sufyan (the narrator) described them with a gesture, spreading the fingers of his right hand and holding it in such a way that the fingers were above one another. "Sometimes the flaming fire hits one of these listeners before he is able to convey what he has heard to the one who is beneath him, and he is burned up, or sometimes the fire does not hit him until he has pit on to the one beneath him, so he brings it to the earth." Perhaps Sufyan said: "...until it reaches the earth and he puts it into the mouth of the sorcerer or fortune-teller, so that after telling a hundred lies he gets something right, and the people say, `Did he not tell us that on such and such a day such and such would happen, and we found it to be the truth among the statements which were heard from heaven.'" Then Allah mentions His creation of the earth and how He spread it out, and the firm mountains, valleys, lands and sands that he has placed in it, and the plants and fruits that He causes to grow in their appropriate locations.

(all kinds of things in due proportion.) Ibn `Abbas said that this means with their predetermined proportions. This was also the opinion of Sa`id bin Jubayr, `Ikrimah, Abu Malik, Mujahid, Al-Hakim bin `Utaybah, Al-Hasan bin Muhammad, Abu Salih and Qatadah.

(And We have provided therein means of living, for you) Here Allah mentions that He created the earth with different means of provisions and livelihood of all kinds.

(and for those whom you provide not.) Mujahid said, "This refers to the riding animals and the cattle." Ibn Jarir said, "They are slaves, men and women, as well as the animals and the cattle. The meaning is that Allah, may He be exalted, is reminding them of the ways of earning provision that He has made easy for them, and of the animals that He has subjugated for them to ride and to eat, and the slaves from whom they benefit, but the provision of all of these comes from Allah alone."

Surah: 15 Ayah: 21, Ayah: 22, Ayah: 23, Ayah: 24 & Ayah: 25

﴿ وَإِن مِّن شَيْءٍ إِلَّا عِندَنَا خَزَائِنُهُ وَمَا نُنَزِّلُهُ إِلَّا بِقَدَرٍ مَّعْلُومٍ ﴾

21. And there is not a thing, but with Us are the stores thereof. And We send it not down except in a known measure.

$$\text{﴿ وَأَرْسَلْنَا ٱلرِّيَـٰحَ لَوَٰقِحَ فَأَنزَلْنَا مِنَ ٱلسَّمَآءِ مَآءً فَأَسْقَيْنَـٰكُمُوهُ وَمَآ أَنتُمْ لَهُۥ بِخَـٰزِنِينَ ﴾}$$

22. And We send the winds fertilizing (to fill heavily the clouds with water), then caused the water (rain) to descend from the sky, and We gave it to you to drink, and it is not you who are the owners of its stores (i.e. to give water to whom you like or to withhold it from whom you like).

$$\text{﴿ وَإِنَّا لَنَحْنُ نُحْىِۦ وَنُمِيتُ وَنَحْنُ ٱلْوَٰرِثُونَ ﴾}$$

23. And certainly We! We it is Who give life, and cause death, and We are the Inheritors.

$$\text{﴿ وَلَقَدْ عَلِمْنَا ٱلْمُسْتَقْدِمِينَ مِنكُمْ وَلَقَدْ عَلِمْنَا ٱلْمُسْتَـْٔخِرِينَ ﴾}$$

24. And indeed, We know the first generations of you who had passed away, and indeed, We know the present generations of you (mankind), and also those who will come afterwards.

$$\text{﴿ وَإِنَّ رَبَّكَ هُوَ يَحْشُرُهُمْ إِنَّهُۥ حَكِيمٌ عَلِيمٌ ﴾}$$

25. And verily, your Lord will gather them together. Truly, He is All-Wise, All-Knowing.

Transliteration

21. Wa-in min shay-in illa AAindana khaza-inuhu wama nunazziluhu illa biqadarin maAAloomin   22. Waarsalna alrriyaha lawaqiha faanzalna mina alssama-i maan faasqaynakumoohu wama antum lahu bikhazineena   23. Wa-inna lanahnu nuhyee wanumeetu wanahnu alwarithoona 24. Walaqad AAalimna almustaqdimeena minkum walaqad AAalimna almusta/khireena   25. Wa-inna rabbaka huwa yahshuruhum innahu hakeemun AAaleemun

Tafsir Ibn Kathir

The Supplies for All Things are with Allah

Allah tells us that He is the Owner of all things, and that everything is easy for Him. He has the supplies for all things with Him.

(and We do not send it down but in a known measure.) meaning, as He wills and as He wants. Doing so out of His great wisdom and mercy towards His servants, in a way that He is under no obligation to do. But He has decreed mercy for Himself. Yazid bin Abi Ziyad reported from Abu Juhayfah that `Abdullah said: "No year has more rain than another, but Allah divides the rain between them as He wills, it rains here a year and there a year. Then he recited:

(And there is not a thing, but the supplies for it are with Us...) Reported by Ibn Jarir.

Benefits of the Winds

(And We send the winds fertilizing.) i.e., fertilizing the clouds so that they give rain, and fertilizing the trees so that they open their leaves and blossoms. These winds are mentioned here in the plural form because they give results, unlike the barren wind (Ar-Rih Al-'Aqim, see Adh-Dhariyat 51:41), which is mentioned in the singular and described as barren since it does not produce anything; because results can only be produced when there are two or more things.

(And We sent the winds fertilizing.) `Abdullah bin Mas`ud said, "The wind is sent bearing water from the sky, then it fertilizes the clouds until rain begins to generously fall, just as the milk of the pregnant camel flows generously." This was also the opinion of Ibn `Abbas, Ibrahim An-Nakha`i and Qatadah. Ad-Dahhak said: "Allah sends it to the clouds and it gets fertilized and becomes full of water." `Ubayd bin `Umayr Al-Laythi said: "Allah sends the wind which stirs up the earth, then Allah sends the wind which raises clouds, then Allah sends the wind which forms clouds, then Allah sends the fertilizing wind which pollinates the trees. Then he recited,

(And We sent the winds fertilizing,)

Fresh Water is a Blessing from Allah

(and We give it to you to drink,) This means, "and We send it down to you fresh and sweet, so that you can drink it; if We had wished, We could have made it salty (and undrinkable)", as Allah points out in another Ayah in Surat Al-Waqi`ah, where He says:

(Tell Me! The water that you drink, is it you who cause it to come down from the rain clouds, or are We the cause of it coming down. If We willed, We verily could make it salty (and undrinkable), why then do you not give thanks (to Allah)) (56:68-70). And Allah says:

(He it is Who sends water down from the sky; from it you drink and from it (grows) the vegetation on which you send your cattle to pasture.) (16:10)

(and it is not you who are the owners of its supply.) The meaning is, "You are not taking care of it; rather We send it down and take care of it for you, making springs and wells flourish on the earth. " If Allah so willed, He could make it disappear, but by His mercy He sends it down and makes it fresh and sweet, maintaining the springs, wells, rivers and so on, so that they may drink from it all year long, water their livestock and irrigate their crops.

The Power of Allah to initiate and renew Creation

(And certainly We! We it is Who give life, and cause death,) Here Allah tells us of His power to initiate creation and renew it. He is the One Who brings life to creatures out of nothingness, then He causes them to die, then He will resurrect all of them on the Day when He will gather them together. He also tells us that He will inherit the earth and everyone on it, and then it is to Him that they will return. Then He tells us about His perfect knowledge of them, the first and the last of them. He says

(And indeed, We know the first generations of you who had passed away...). Ibn `Abbas said, "The first generations are all those who have passed away since the time of Adam. The present generations and those who will come afterward refer to those who are alive now and who are yet to come, until the Day of Resurrection." Something similar was narrated from `Ikrimah, Mujahid, Ad-Dahhak, Qatadah, Muhammad bin Ka`b, Ash-Sha`bi and others. Ibn Jarir reported from Muhammad bin Abi Ma`shar, from his father, that he heard `Awn bin `Abdullah discussing the following Ayah with Muhammad bin Ka`b:

(And indeed, We know the first generations of you who had passed away, and indeed, We know the present generations of you (mankind), and also those who will come afterwards), and it was stated that it refers to the rows for prayer. Muhammad bin Ka`b said, "This is not the case.

(And indeed, We know the first generations of you who had passed away) it refers to those who are dead or have been killed, and;

(and also those who will come afterwards) meaning those who have yet to be created.

(And verily your Lord will gather them together. Truly, He is Most Wise, (and) Knowing)." `Awn bin `Abdullah said, "May Allah help you and reward you with good."

Surah: 15 Ayah: 26 & Ayah: 27

﴿ وَلَقَدْ خَلَقْنَا ٱلْإِنسَـٰنَ مِن صَلْصَـٰلٍ مِّنْ حَمَإٍ مَّسْنُونٍ ۝ ﴾

26. And indeed, We created man from dried (sounding) clay of altered mud.

﴿ وَٱلْجَآنَّ خَلَقْنَـٰهُ مِن قَبْلُ مِن نَّارِ ٱلسَّمُومِ ۝ ﴾

27. And the jinn, We created aforetime from the smokeless flame of fire.

Transliteration

26. Walaqad khalaqna al-insana min salsalin min hama-in masnoonin 27. Waaljanna khalaqnahu min qablu min nari alssamoomi

Tafsir Ibn Kathir

The Substances from which Mankind and Jinns were created

Ibn `Abbas, Mujahid and Qatadah said that Salsal means dry mud. The apparent meaning is similar to the Ayah:

(He created man (Adam) from sounding clay like the potter's clay, And He created the Jinns from a smokeless flame of fire.) (55:14-15) It was also reported from Mujahid that,

(dried (sounding) clay) means "putrid", but it is more appropriate to interpret an Ayah with another Ayah.

(of altered mud) means the dried clay that comes from mud, which is soil. "Altered" here means smooth.

(And the Jinn, We created earlier) means before creating humans.

(from the smokeless flame of fire.) Ibn `Abbas said, "It is the smokeless flame that kills." Abu Dawud At-Tayalisi said that Shu`bah narrated to them from Abu Ishaq, who said: "I visited `Umar Al-Asamm when he was sick, and he said: `Shall I not tell you a Hadith that I heard from `Abdullah bin Mas`ud He said: `This smokeless flame is one of the seventy parts of the smokeless fire from which the Jinn where created. Then he recited,

(And the Jinn, We created earlier from the smokeless flame of fire).'" The following is found in the Sahih,

»خُلِقَتِ الْمَلَائِكَةُ مِنْ نُورٍ، وَخُلِقَتِ الْجَانُّ مِنْ مَارِجٍ مِنْ نَارٍ، وَخُلِقَ آدَمُ مِمَّا وُصِفَ لَكُم«

(The angels were created from light, the Jinn were created from a smokeless flame of fire, and Adam was created from that which has been described to you.) The Ayah is intended to point out the noble nature, good essence and pure origin of Adam.

Surah: 15 Ayah: 28, Ayah: 29, Ayah: 30, Ayah: 31, Ayah: 32 & Ayah: 33

﴿ وَإِذْ قَالَ رَبُّكَ لِلْمَلَٰٓئِكَةِ إِنِّى خَٰلِقٌۢ بَشَرًا مِّن صَلْصَٰلٍ مِّنْ حَمَإٍ مَّسْنُونٍ ۝ ﴾

28. And (remember) when your Lord said to the angels: "I am going to create a man (Adam) from dried (sounding) clay of altered mud.

﴿ فَإِذَا سَوَّيْتُهُۥ وَنَفَخْتُ فِيهِ مِن رُّوحِى فَقَعُوا۟ لَهُۥ سَٰجِدِينَ ۝ ﴾

29. "So, when I have fashioned him completely and breathed into him (Adam) the soul which I created for him, then fall (you) down prostrating yourselves unto him."

﴿ فَسَجَدَ ٱلْمَلَٰٓئِكَةُ كُلُّهُمْ أَجْمَعُونَ ۝ ﴾

30. So, the angels prostrated themselves, all of them together.

﴿ إِلَّآ إِبْلِيسَ أَبَىٰٓ أَن يَكُونَ مَعَ ٱلسَّٰجِدِينَ ۝ ﴾

31. Except Iblîs (Satan) - he refused to be among the prostrators.

﴿ قَالَ يَٰٓإِبْلِيسُ مَا لَكَ أَلَّا تَكُونَ مَعَ ٱلسَّٰجِدِينَ ۝ ﴾

32. (Allâh) said: "O Iblîs (Satan)! What is your reason for not being among the prostrators?"

﴿ قَالَ لَمْ أَكُن لِّأَسْجُدَ لِبَشَرٍ خَلَقْتَهُ مِن صَلْصَـٰلٍ مِّنْ حَمَإٍ مَّسْنُونٍ ۝ ﴾

33. (Iblîs (Satan)) said: "I am not the one to prostrate myself to a human being, whom You created from dried (sounding) clay of altered mud."

Transliteration

28. Wa-ith qala rabbuka lilmala-ikati innee khaliqun basharan min salsalin min hama-in masnoonin 29. Fa-itha sawwaytuhu wanafakhtu feehi min roohee faqaAAoo lahu sajideena 30. Fasajada almala-ikatu kulluhum ajmaAAoona 31. Illa ibleesa aba an yakoona maAAa alssajideena 32. Qala ya ibleesu ma laka alla takoona maAAa alssajideena 33. Qala lam akun li-asjuda libasharin khalaqtahu min salsalin min hama-in masnoonin

Tafsir Ibn Kathir

The creation of Adam, the Command to the Angels to prostrate to Him, and the Rebellion of Iblis

Allah informs us of how He mentioned Adam to His angels before He created him, and how He honored him by commanding the angels to prostrate to him. He mentions how His enemy Iblis, amidst all the angels, refused to prostrate to him out of envy, disbelief, stubbornness, arrogance, and false pride. This is why Iblis said:

(I am not one to prostrate myself to a human, whom You created from dried (sounding) clay of altered mud.) this is like when he said,

(I am better than him (Adam), You created me from Fire and him You created from clay.)(7:12) and

("Do you see this one whom You have honored above me...") (17:62)

Surah: 15 Ayah: 34, Ayah: 35, Ayah: 36, Ayah: 37 & Ayah: 38

﴿ قَالَ فَٱخْرُجْ مِنْهَا فَإِنَّكَ رَجِيمٌ ۝ ﴾

34. (Allâh) said: "Then, get out from here, for verily, you are Rajîm (an outcast or a cursed one)." (Tafsîr At-Tabarî)

﴿ وَإِنَّ عَلَيْكَ ٱللَّعْنَةَ إِلَىٰ يَوْمِ ٱلدِّينِ ۝ ﴾

35. "And verily, the curse shall be upon you till the Day of Recompense (i.e. the Day of Resurrection)."

﴿ قَالَ رَبِّ فَأَنظِرْنِىٓ إِلَىٰ يَوْمِ يُبْعَثُونَ ۝ ﴾

36. (Iblîs (Satan)) said: "O my Lord! Give me then respite till the Day they (the dead) will be resurrected."

﴿ قَالَ فَإِنَّكَ مِنَ ٱلْمُنظَرِينَ ۝ ﴾

37. Allâh said: "Then, verily, you are of those reprieved,

﴿ إِلَىٰ يَوْمِ ٱلْوَقْتِ ٱلْمَعْلُومِ ۝ ﴾

38. "Till the Day of the time appointed."

Transliteration

34. Qala faokhruj minha fa-innaka rajeemun 35. Wa-inna AAalayka allaAAnata ila yawmi alddeeni 36. Qala rabbi faanthirnee ila yawmi yubAAathoona 37. Qala fa-innaka mina almunthareena 38. Ila yawmi alwaqti almaAAloomi

Tafsir Ibn Kathir

The Expulsion of Iblis from Jannah, and His Reprieve until the Day of Resurrection

Allah tells us how He issued an unconditional command to Iblis to leave the position he held among the highest of heights. He told him that he was an outcast, i.e., cursed, and that he would be followed by a curse that would hound him until the Day of Resurrection. It was reported that Sa`id bin Jubayr said: "When Allah cursed Iblis, his image into something different from that of the angels, and he made a sound like a bell. Every bell that rings on this earth until the Day of Resurrection is part of that. This was reported by Ibn Abi Hatim.

Surah: 15 Ayah: 39, Ayah: 40, Ayah: 41, Ayah: 42, Ayah: 43 & Ayah: 44

﴿ قَالَ رَبِّ بِمَآ أَغْوَيْتَنِى لَأُزَيِّنَنَّ لَهُمْ فِى ٱلْأَرْضِ وَلَأُغْوِيَنَّهُمْ أَجْمَعِينَ ۝ ﴾

39. (Iblîs (Satan)) said: "O my Lord! Because you misled me, I shall indeed adorn the path of error for them (mankind) on the earth, and I shall mislead them all.

﴿ إِلَّا عِبَادَكَ مِنْهُمُ ٱلْمُخْلَصِينَ ۝ ﴾

40. "Except Your chosen, (guided) slaves among them."

﴿ قَالَ هَـٰذَا صِرَٰطٌ عَلَىَّ مُسْتَقِيمٌ ۝ ﴾

41. (Allâh) said: "This is the Way which will lead straight to Me."

﴿ إِنَّ عِبَادِى لَيْسَ لَكَ عَلَيْهِمْ سُلْطَـٰنٌ إِلَّا مَنِ ٱتَّبَعَكَ مِنَ ٱلْغَاوِينَ ۝ ﴾

42. "Certainly, you shall have no authority over My slaves, except those who follow you of the Ghâwûn (Mushrikûn and those who go astray, criminals, polytheists, and evil-doers).

﴿ وَإِنَّ جَهَنَّمَ لَمَوْعِدُهُمْ أَجْمَعِينَ ۝ ﴾

43. "And surely, Hell is the promised place for them all.

﴿ لَهَا سَبْعَةُ أَبْوَابٍ لِّكُلِّ بَابٍ مِّنْهُمْ جُزْءٌ مَّقْسُومٌ ۝ ﴾

44. "It (Hell) has seven gates, for each of those gates is a (special) class (of sinners) assigned.

Transliteration

39. Qala rabbi bima aghwaytanee laozayyinanna lahum fee al-ardi walaoghwiyannahum ajmaAAeena 40. Illa AAibadaka minhumu almukhlaseena 41. Qala hatha siratun AAalayya mustaqeemun 42. Inna AAibadee laysa laka AAalayhim sultanun illa mani ittabaAAaka mina alghaweena 43. Wa-inna jahannama lamawAAiduhum ajmaAAeena 44. Laha sabAAatu abwabin likulli babin minhum juz-on maqsoomun

Tafsir Ibn Kathir

The Threat of Iblis to tempt Mankind, and Allah's Promise of Hell for him

Allah informed about the rebellion and arrogance of Iblis, in that he said to the Lord:

(Because You misled me,) i.e., because You misled me and misguided me.

(I shall indeed adorn the path of error for them) meaning, for the progeny of Adam.

(on the earth,) meaning - I will make sin dear to them, and will encourage, provoke and harass them to commit sin.

(and I shall mislead them all.) meaning - just as You have misled me and have ordained that for me.

(Except Your chosen, (guided) servants among them.) This is like the Ayah:

("Do you see this one whom You have honored above me, if You give me respite until the Day of Resurrection, I will surely seize and mislead his offspring, all but a few!") (17:62).

((Allah) said), i.e., threatening and warning Iblis.

(This is the way which will lead straight to Me.) means, `all of you will return to Me, and I will reward or punish you according to your deeds: if they are good then I will reward you, and if they are bad then I will punish you.' This is like the Ayah:

(Verily, your Lord is ever watchful.) (89:14) and

Chapter 15: Al-Hijr (Stoneland, Rock City), Verses 001-099   27

(And it is up to Allah to show the right way.) (16:9)

(Certainly, you shall have no authority over My servants) meaning, `you will have no way to reach those for whom I have decreed guidance.'

(except those of the astray who follow you.) Ibn Jarir mentioned that Yazid bin Qusayt said: "The Prophets used to have Masjids outside their cities, and if a Prophet wanted to consult with his Lord about something, he would go out to his place of worship and pray as Allah decreed. Then he would ask Him about whatever was concerning him. Once while a Prophet was in his place of worship, the enemy of Allah - meaning Iblis - came and sat between him and the Qiblah (direction of prayer). The Prophet said, `I seek refuge with Allah from the accursed Shaytan.' (The enemy of Allah said, `Do you know who you are seeking refuge from? Here he is!' The Prophet said, `I seek refuge with Allah from the accursed Shaytan'), and he repeated that three times. Then the enemy of Allah said, `Tell me about anything in which you will be saved from me.' The Prophet twice said, `No, you tell me about something in which you can overpower the son of Adam?' Each of them was insisting that the other answer first, then the Prophet said, Allah says,

(Certainly, you shall have no authority over My servants, except those of the astray who follow you.) The enemy of Allah said, `I heard this before you were even born.' The Prophet said, `And Allah says,

(And if an evil whisper comes to you from Shaytan then seek refuge with Allah. Verily, He is All-Hearing, All-Knowing) (7: 200). By Allah, I never sense that you are near but I seek refuge with Allah from you.' The enemy of Allah said, `You have spoken the truth. In this way you will be saved from me.' The Prophet said, `Tell me in what ways you overpower the son of Adam.' He said, `I seize him at times of anger and times of desire.'

(And surely, Hell is the place promised for them all.) meaning, Hell is the abode designated for all those who follow Iblis, as Allah says in the Qur'an:

(but those of the sects (Jews, Christians and all the other non-Muslim nations) that reject it (the Qur'an), the Fire will be their promised meeting place.)(11:17)

The Gates of Hell are Seven

Then Allah tells us that Hell has seven gates:

(for each of those gates is a (special) class (of sinners) assigned.) means, for each gate a portion of the followers of Iblis have been decreed, and they will have no choice in the matter. May Allah save us from that. Each one will enter a gate according to his deeds, and will settle in a level of Hell according to his deeds. Ibn Abi Hatim recorded that Samurah bin Jundub reported from the Prophet about,

(for each of those gates is a class assigned.) He said,

》إِنَّ مِنْ أَهْلِ النَّارِ مَنْ تَأْخُذُهُ النَّارُ إِلَى كَعْبَيْهِ، وَإِنَّ مِنْهُمْ مَنْ تَأْخُذُهُ النَّارُ إِلَى حُجْزَتِهِ، وَمِنْهُمْ مَنْ تَأْخُذُهُ النَّارُ إِلَى تَرَاقِيهِ《

(Among the people of Hell are those whom the Fire will swallow up to the ankles, and those whom it will swallow up to the waist, and those whom it will swallow up to the collarbone.) The degree of which will depend upon their deeds. This is like the Ayah;

(for each of those gates is a class assigned.)

Surah: 15 Ayah: 45, Ayah: 46, Ayah: 47, Ayah: 48, Ayah: 49 & Ayah: 50

﴿ إِنَّ ٱلْمُتَّقِينَ فِى جَنَّـٰتٍ وَعُيُونٍ ۝ ﴾

45. "Truly! The Muttaqûn (pious and righteous persons - see V.2:2) will be amidst Gardens and water-springs (Paradise).

﴿ ٱدْخُلُوهَا بِسَلَـٰمٍ ءَامِنِينَ ۝ ﴾

46. "(It will be said to them): 'Enter therein (Paradise), in peace and security.'

﴿ وَنَزَعْنَا مَا فِى صُدُورِهِم مِّنْ غِلٍّ إِخْوَٰنًا عَلَىٰ سُرُرٍ مُّتَقَـٰبِلِينَ ۝ ﴾

47. "And We shall remove from their breasts any deep feeling of bitterness (that they may have). (So they will be like) brothers facing each other on thrones.

﴿ لَا يَمَسُّهُمْ فِيهَا نَصَبٌ وَمَا هُم مِّنْهَا بِمُخْرَجِينَ ۝ ﴾

48. "No sense of fatigue shall touch them, nor shall they (ever) be asked to leave it."

﴿ ۞ نَبِّئْ عِبَادِى أَنِّى أَنَا ٱلْغَفُورُ ٱلرَّحِيمُ ۝ ﴾

49. Declare (O Muhammad (peace be upon him)) unto My slaves, that truly, I am the Oft-Forgiving, the Most-Merciful.

﴿ وَأَنَّ عَذَابِى هُوَ ٱلْعَذَابُ ٱلْأَلِيمُ ۝ ﴾

50. And that My Torment is indeed the most painful torment.

Transliteration

45. Inna almuttaqeena fee jannatin waAAuyoonin 46. Odkhulooha bisalamin amineena 47. WanazaAAna ma fee sudoorihim min ghillin ikhwanan AAala sururin mutaqabileena 48. La yamassuhum feeha nasabun wama hum minha bimukhrajeena 49. Nabbi/ AAibadee annee ana alghafooru alrraheemu 50. Waanna AAathabee huwa alAAathabu al-aleemu

Tafsir Ibn Kathir

Description of the People of Paradise

Since Allah mentioned the condition of the people of Hell, He followed that by mentioning the people of Paradise. He tells us that they will dwell in Gardens and water springs.

(Enter it in peace) meaning free of all problems.

(and security.) meaning free from all fear and concern. They will not have any fear of expulsion, nor will they fear that their condition will be disrupted or end.

(And We shall remove any deep feeling of bitterness from their breasts. (So they will be like) brothers facing each other on thrones.) Al-Qasim narrated that Abu Umamah said: "The people of Paradise will enter Paradise with whatever enmity is left in their hearts from this world. Then, when they come together, Allah will remove whatever hatred the world has left in their hearts." Then he recited:

(And We shall remove any deep feeling of bitterness from their breasts.) This is how it was narrated in this report, but Al-Qasim bin `Abdur-Rahman is weak in his reports from Abu Umamah. However, this is in accord with the report in the Sahih where Qatadah says, "Abu Al-Mutawakkil An-Naji told us that Abu Sa`id Al-Khudri told them that the Messenger of Allah said:

»يَخْلُصُ الْمُؤْمِنُونَ مِنَ النَّارِ، فَيُحْبَسُونَ عَلَى قَنْطَرَةٍ بَيْنَ الْجَنَّةِ وَالنَّارِ. فَيُقْتَصُّ لِبَعْضِهِمْ مِنْ بَعْضٍ مَظَالِمُ كَانَتْ بَيْنَهُمْ فِي الدُّنْيَا حَتَّى إِذَا هُذِّبُوا وَنُقُّوا، أَذِنَ لَهُمْ فِي دُخُولِ الْجَنَّةِ«

(The believers will be removed from the Fire, and they will be detained on a bridge between Paradise and Hell. Then judgment will be passed between them concerning any wrong they have committed in this world against one another, until they are cleansed and purified. Then permission will be given to them to enter Paradise.)"

(No sense of fatigue shall touch them) meaning no harm or hardship, as was reported in the Sahihs:

»أَنَّ اللهَ أَمَرَنِي أَنْ أُبَشِّرَ خَدِيجَةَ بِبَيْتٍ فِي الْجَنَّةِ مِنْ قَصَبٍ لَا صَخَبَ فِيهِ وَلَا نَصَبَ«

(Allah commanded me to tell Khadijah the good news of a jeweled palace in Paradise in which there will be no toil and no fatigue.)

(nor shall they (ever) be asked to leave it.) As was reported in the Hadith:

«يُقَالُ: يَا أَهْلَ الْجَنَّةِ إِنَّ لَكُمْ أَنْ تَصِحُّوا فَلَا تَمْرَضُوا أَبَدًا، وَإِنَّ لَكُمْ أَنْ تَعِيشُوا فَلَا تَمُوتُوا أَبَدًا، وَإِنَّ لَكُمْ أَنْ تَشِبُّوا فَلَا تَهْرَمُوا أَبَدًا، وَإِنَّ لَكُمْ أَنْ تُقِيمُوا فَلَا تَظْعُنُوا أَبَدًا»

(It will be said, O dwellers of Paradise! You will be healthy and never fall sick; you will live and never die; you will be young and never grow old; you will stay here and never leave.) Allah says:

(Wherein they shall dwell (forever). They will have no desire to be removed from it.) (18:108)

(Declare to My servants, that I am truly the Oft-Forgiving, the Most Merciful. And that My torment is indeed the most painful torment.) meaning, `O Muhammad, tell My servants that I am the source of mercy and I am the source of punishment.' Similar Ayat to this have already been quoted above, which indicate that we must always be in a state between hope (for Allah's mercy) and fear (of His punishment).

Surah: 15 Ayah: 51, Ayah: 52, Ayah: 53, Ayah: 54, Ayah: 55 & Ayah: 56

﴿ وَنَبِّئْهُمْ عَن ضَيْفِ إِبْرَاهِيمَ ۞ ﴾

51. And tell them about the guests (the angels) of Ibrâhîm (Abraham).

﴿ إِذْ دَخَلُواْ عَلَيْهِ فَقَالُواْ سَلَـٰمًا قَالَ إِنَّا مِنكُمْ وَجِلُونَ ۞ ﴾

52. When they entered unto him, and said: Salâm (peace)! (Ibrâhîm (Abraham)) said: "Indeed! We are afraid of you."

﴿ قَالُواْ لَا تَوْجَلْ إِنَّا نُبَشِّرُكَ بِغُلَـٰمٍ عَلِيمٍ ۞ ﴾

53. They (the angels) said: "Do not be afraid! We give you glad tidings of a boy (son) possessing much knowledge and wisdom."

﴿ قَالَ أَبَشَّرْتُمُونِى عَلَىٰ أَن مَّسَّنِىَ ٱلْكِبَرُ فَبِمَ تُبَشِّرُونَ ۞ ﴾

54. (Ibrâhîm (Abraham)) said: "Do you give me glad tidings (of a son) when old age has overtaken me? Of what then is your news?"

﴿ قَالُواْ بَشَّرْنَـٰكَ بِٱلْحَقِّ فَلَا تَكُن مِّنَ ٱلْقَـٰنِطِينَ ۞ ﴾

Chapter 15: Al-Hijr (Stoneland, Rock City), Verses 001-099

55. They (the angels) said: "We give you glad tidings in truth. So be not of the despairing."

﴿ قَالَ وَمَن يَقْنَطُ مِن رَّحْمَةِ رَبِّهِ إِلَّا ٱلضَّآلُّونَ ۝ ﴾

56. (Ibrâhîm (Abraham)) said: "And who despairs of the Mercy of his Lord except those who are astray?"

Transliteration

51. Wanabbi/hum AAan dayfi ibraheema 52. Ith dakhaloo AAalayhi faqaloo salaman qala inna minkum wajiloona 53. Qaloo la tawjal inna nubashshiruka bighulamin AAaleemin 54. Qala abashshartumoonee AAala an massaniya alkibaru fabima tubashshirooni 55. Qaloo bashsharnaka bialhaqqi fala takun mina alqaniteena 56. Qala waman yaqnatu min rahmati rabbihi illa alddalloona

Tafsir Ibn Kathir

The Guests of Ibrahim and their Good News of a Son for Him

Allah is saying: `Tell them, O Muhammad, about the story of

(the guests of Ibrahim.)'

(they entered upon him, and said: "Salaman (peace!)." He said: "Indeed we are frightened of you.") meaning that they were scared. The reason for their fear has been mentioned previously, which is that they noticed that these guests did not eat of the food that was offered, which was a fattened calf.

(They said: "Do not be afraid!...") meaning, do not be scared.

(We bring you the good news of a boy possessing much knowledge and wisdom.) this refers to Ishaq, as was previously mentioned in Surat Hud. Then

(He said) meaning he spoke with wonder and astonishment, asking for confirmation, because he was old and his wife was old:

(Do you give me this good news while old age has overtaken me Of what then is your news about) They responded by confirming the good news they had brought, good news after good news:

(They said: "We give you good news in truth. So do not be of those who despair.")

Surah: 15 Ayah: 57, Ayah: 58, Ayah: 59 & Ayah: 60

﴿ قَالَ فَمَا خَطْبُكُمْ أَيُّهَا ٱلْمُرْسَلُونَ ۝ ﴾

57. (Ibrâhîm (Abraham) again) said: "What then is the business on which you have come, O Messengers?"

﴿ قَالُوٓا۟ إِنَّآ أُرْسِلْنَآ إِلَىٰ قَوْمٍ مُّجْرِمِينَ ۝ ﴾

58. They (the angels) said: "We have been sent to a people who are Mujrimûn (criminals, disbelievers, polytheists, sinners).

﴿ إِلَّآ ءَالَ لُوطٍ إِنَّا لَمُنَجُّوهُمْ أَجْمَعِينَ ۝ ﴾

59. "(All) except the family of Lût (Lot). Them all we are surely going to save (from destruction).

﴿ إِلَّا ٱمْرَأَتَهُۥ قَدَّرْنَآ إِنَّهَا لَمِنَ ٱلْغَٰبِرِينَ ۝ ﴾

60. "Except his wife, of whom We have decreed that she shall be of those who remain behind (i.e. she will be destroyed)."

Transliteration

57. Qala fama khatbukum ayyuha almursaloona 58. Qaloo inna orsilna ila qawmin mujrimeena 59. Illa ala lootin inna lamunajjoohum ajmaAAeena 60. Illa imraatahu qaddarna innaha lamina alghabireena

Tafsir Ibn Kathir

The Reason why the Angels came

Allah tells us that after Ibrahim had calmed down from the excitement of this good news, he started to ask them why they had come to him. They said,

(We have been sent to a guilty people.) meaning the people of Lut. They told him that they were going to save the family of Lut from among those people, except for his wife, because she was one of those who were doomed. Thus it was said,

(Except for his wife, of whom We have decreed that she shall be of those who remain behind.) i.e., she was one of those who would be left behind and will be destroyed.

Surah: 15 Ayah: 61, Ayah: 62, Ayah: 63 & Ayah: 64

﴿ فَلَمَّا جَآءَ ءَالَ لُوطٍ ٱلْمُرْسَلُونَ ۝ ﴾

61. Then, when the Messengers (the angels) came unto the family of Lût (Lot).

﴿ قَالَ إِنَّكُمْ قَوْمٌ مُّنكَرُونَ ۝ ﴾

62. He said: "Verily! You are people unknown to me."

﴿ قَالُوٓا۟ بَلْ جِئْنَٰكَ بِمَا كَانُوا۟ فِيهِ يَمْتَرُونَ ۝ ﴾

63. They said: "Nay, we have come to you with that (torment) which they have been doubting.

﴿ وَأَتَيْنَاكَ بِالْحَقِّ وَإِنَّا لَصَادِقُونَ ۝ ﴾

64. "And we have brought to you the truth (the news of the destruction of your nation) and certainly, we tell the truth.

Transliteration

61. Falamma jaa ala lootin almursaloona 62. Qala innakum qawmun munkaroona 63. Qaloo bal ji/naka bima kanoo feehi yamtaroona 64. Waataynaka bialhaqqi wa-inna lasadiqoona

Tafsir Ibn Kathir

The Angels coming to Lut

Allah tells us about when the angels came to Lut in the form of young men with handsome faces. When they entered his home, he said:

("Verily, you are people unknown to me." They said: "Nay, we have come to you with that (torment) which they have been doubting.") meaning that they were bringing the punishment and destruction that the people doubted they would ever suffer from.

(And we have brought you the truth) is like the Ayah,

(We do not send the angels down except with the truth) (15:8) and

(and certainly, we tell the truth.) They said this in affirmation of the news that they brought him, that he would be saved and his people would be destroyed.

Surah: 15 Ayah: 65 & Ayah: 66

﴿ فَأَسْرِ بِأَهْلِكَ بِقِطْعٍ مِّنَ الَّيْلِ وَاتَّبِعْ أَدْبَارَهُمْ وَلَا يَلْتَفِتْ مِنكُمْ أَحَدٌ وَامْضُوا حَيْثُ تُؤْمَرُونَ ۝ ﴾

65. "Then travel in a part of the night with your family, and you go behind them in the rear, and let no one amongst you look back, but go on to where you are ordered."

﴿ وَقَضَيْنَا إِلَيْهِ ذَلِكَ الْأَمْرَ أَنَّ دَابِرَ هَؤُلَاءِ مَقْطُوعٌ مُّصْبِحِينَ ۝ ﴾

66. And We made known this decree to him, that the root of those (sinners) was to be cut off in the early morning.

Transliteration

65. Faasri bi-ahlika biqitAAin mina allayli waittabiAA adbarahum wala yaltafit minkum ahadun waimdoo haythu tu/maroona 66. Waqadayna ilayhi thalika al-amra anna dabira haola-i maqtooAAun musbiheena

Tafsir Ibn Kathir

Lut is ordered to leave with His Family during the Night

Allah tells us that His angels ordered Lut to set out after part of the night had passed. They told him to walk behind them, to protect them. Similarly, the Messenger of Allah would walk in the rear of the army on military campaigns, in order to help the weak and carry those who had no means of transport.

(and let no one amongst you look back,) meaning - when you hear the people screaming from their torment, do not turn around to look at them; leave them to face whatever punishment and vengeance is coming to them.

(but go on to where you are ordered.) - it is as if they had a guide with them to show them the way.

(And We made this decree known to him) meaning - We already told him about that.

(that those (sinners) would be rooted out in the early morning.) meaning in the morning, as in another Ayah:

(Indeed, morning is their appointed time. Is not the morning near) (11:81)

Surah: 15 Ayah: 67, Ayah: 68, Ayah: 69, Ayah: 70, Ayah: 71 & Ayah: 72

﴿ وَجَآءَ أَهْلُ ٱلْمَدِينَةِ يَسْتَبْشِرُونَ ﴾

67. And the inhabitants of the city came rejoicing (at the news of the young men's arrival).

﴿ قَالَ إِنَّ هَـٰٓؤُلَآءِ ضَيْفِى فَلَا تَفْضَحُونِ ﴾

68. (Lût (Lot)) said: "Verily! these are my guests, so shame me not.

﴿ وَٱتَّقُوا۟ ٱللَّهَ وَلَا تُخْزُونِ ﴾

69. "And fear Allâh and disgrace me not."

﴿ قَالُوٓا۟ أَوَلَمْ نَنْهَكَ عَنِ ٱلْعَـٰلَمِينَ ﴾

70. They (people of the city) said: "Did we not forbid you from entertaining (or protecting) any of the 'Alamîn (people, foreigners, strangers from us)?"

﴿ قَالَ هَـٰٓؤُلَآءِ بَنَاتِىٓ إِن كُنتُمْ فَـٰعِلِينَ ﴾

71. (Lût (Lot)) said: "These (the girls of the nation) are my daughters (to marry lawfully), if you must act (so)."

﴿ لَعَمْرُكَ إِنَّهُمْ لَفِى سَكْرَتِهِمْ يَعْمَهُونَ ۝ ﴾

72. Verily, by your life (O Muhammad (peace be upon him)) in their wild intoxication, they were wandering blindly.

Transliteration

67. Wajaa ahlu almadeenati yastabshiroona 68. Qala inna haola-i dayfee fala tafdahooni 69. Waittaqoo Allaha wala tukhzooni 70. Qaloo awa lam nanhaka AAani alAAalameena 71. Qala haola-i banatee in kuntum faAAileena 72. LaAAamruka innahum lafee sakratihim yaAAmahoona

Tafsir Ibn Kathir

The People of the City arrive upon the Angels, thinking that they are Men

Allah tells us about how Lut's people came to him when they found out about his handsome guests, and they came happily rejoicing about them.

((Lut) said: "Verily, these are my guests, so do not shame me. And have Taqwa of Allah, and do not disgrace me.") This is what Lut said to them before he knew that his guests were messengers from Allah, as mentioned in Surat Hud, but here (in this Surah), we have already been told that they are messengers from Allah, and this is followed by an account of Lut's people coming and his exchange with them. However, here the conjunction (wa, meaning "and") does not imply the sequence of events, especially since there is something to indicate that this is not the case. They said answering him,

(Did we not forbid you from entertaining (or protecting) any of the `Alamin) meaning, `did we not tell you that you should not have anyone as a guest' He reminded them about their womenfolk and what their Lord had created for them in the women of permissible sexual relationships. This issue has already been explained and is no need to repeat the discussion here. All of this happened while they were still unaware of the inevitable calamity and punishment that was about to befall them the following morning. Hence Allah, may He be exalted, said to Muhammad ,

(Verily, by your life, in their wild intoxication, they were wandering blindly.) Allah swore by the life of His Prophet , which is an immense honor reflecting his high rank and noble status. `Amr bin Malik An-Nakari reported from Abu Al-Jawza' that Ibn `Abbas said: "Allah has never created or made or formed any soul that is dearer to him than Muhammad . I never heard that Allah swore by the life of anyone else. Allah says,

(Verily, by your life, in their wild intoxication, they were wandering blindly.) meaning, by your life and the length of your stay in this world,

(in their wild intoxication, they were wandering blindly.) This was reported by Ibn Jarir. Qatadah said:

(in their wild intoxication) "It means - in their misguided state;

(they were wandering blindly) means - they were playing. " `Ali bin Abi Talhah reported that Ibn `Abbas said:

(Verily, by your life) means by your life, and

(in their wild intoxication, they were wandering blindly.) means that they were confused."

Surah: 15 Ayah: 73, Ayah: 74, Ayah: 75, Ayah: 76 & Ayah: 77

﴿ فَأَخَذَتْهُمُ ٱلصَّيْحَةُ مُشْرِقِينَ ﴾

73. So As-Saihah (torment - awful cry) overtook them at the time of sunrise.

﴿ فَجَعَلْنَا عَٰلِيَهَا سَافِلَهَا وَأَمْطَرْنَا عَلَيْهِمْ حِجَارَةً مِّن سِجِّيلٍ ﴾

74. And We turned (the towns of Sodom in Palestine) upside down and rained down on them stones of baked clay.

﴿ إِنَّ فِى ذَٰلِكَ لَءَايَٰتٍ لِّلْمُتَوَسِّمِينَ ﴾

75. Surely! In this are signs for those who see (or understand or learn the lessons from the Signs of Allâh).

﴿ وَإِنَّهَا لَبِسَبِيلٍ مُّقِيمٍ ﴾

76. And verily! They (the cities) were right on the highroad (from Makkah to Syria i.e. the place where the Dead Sea is now).

﴿ إِنَّ فِى ذَٰلِكَ لَءَايَةً لِّلْمُؤْمِنِينَ ﴾

77. Surely! Therein is indeed a sign for the believers.

Transliteration

73. Faakhathat-humu alssayhatu mushriqeena 74. FajaAAalna AAaliyaha safilaha waamtarna AAalayhim hijaratan min sijjeelin 75. Inna fee thalika laayatin lilmutawassimeena 76. Wa-innaha labisabeelin muqeemin 77. Inna fee thalika laayatan lilmu/mineena

Tafsir Ibn Kathir

The Destruction of the People of Lut

Allah said;

(So the Sayhah overtook them) This is the piercing sound that came to them when the sun rose, which was accompanied by the city being flipped upside down, and stones of baked clay (As-Sijjil) raining down upon them. The discussion of As-Sijjil in Surah Hud is a sufficient explanation. Allah said:

(Surely, in this are signs for those who see.) meaning that the traces of the destruction of that city are easily visible to any one who ponder about it, whether they look at it with physical eyesight or mental and spiritual insight, as Mujahid said concerning the phrase,

(those who see) he said, "those who have insight and discernment." It was reported from Ibn `Abbas and Ad-Dahhak that it referred to those who look. Qatadah said: "those who learn lessons".

(those who see) therefore the meaning is "those who ponder".

The City of Sodom on the Highroad

(And verily, they were right on the highroad.) meaning that the city of Sodom, which was physically and spiritually turned upside down, and pelted with stones until it became a foul smelling lake (the Dead Sea), is on a route that is easily accessible until the present day. This is like the Ayah,

(Verily, you pass by them in the morning, and at night. Will you not then reflect) (37:137-138).

(Surely, there is indeed a sign in that for the believers.) meaning, `All that We did to the people of Lut, from the destruction and the vengeance, to how We saved Lut and his family, these are clear signs to those who believe in Allah and His Messengers.'

Surah: 15 Ayah: 78 & Ayah: 79

﴿ وَإِن كَانَ أَصْحَـٰبُ ٱلْأَيْكَةِ لَظَـٰلِمِينَ ۝ ﴾

78. And the Dwellers in the Wood (i.e. the people of Madyan (Midian) to whom Prophet Shu'aib (peace be upon him) was sent by Allâh), were also Zâlimûn (polytheists and wrong-doers).

﴿ فَٱنتَقَمْنَا مِنْهُمْ وَإِنَّهُمَا لَبِإِمَامٍ مُّبِينٍ ۝ ﴾

79. So, We took vengeance on them. They are both on an open highway, plain to see.

Transliteration

78. Wa-in kana as-habu al-aykati lathalimeena 79. Faintaqamna minhum wa-innahuma labi-imamin mubeenin

Tafsir Ibn Kathir

The Destruction of the Dwellers of Al-Aykah, the People of Shu`ayb

The Dwellers of Al-Aykah, were the people of Shu`ayb. Ad-Dahhak, Qatadah and others said that Al-Aykah refers to intertwined trees. Their evildoing included associating partners with Allah (Shirk), banditry and cheating in weights and measures. Allah punished them with the Sayhah (the awful cry or torment), the earthquake, and the torment of the Day of Shadow. They lived near the people of Lut, but at a later time, and the people of Lut were known to them, which is why Allah says,

(They are both on an open route, plain to see.) Ibn `Abbas, Mujahid, Ad-Dahhak and others said, "a visible route." This is why, when Shu`ayb warned his people, he said to them,

(And the people of Lut are not far off from you!) (11:89)

Surah: 15 Ayah: 80, Ayah: 81, Ayah: 82, Ayah: 83 & Ayah: 84

﴿ وَلَقَدْ كَذَّبَ أَصْحَـٰبُ ٱلْحِجْرِ ٱلْمُرْسَلِينَ ۞ ﴾

80. And verily, the dwellers of Al-Hijr (the rocky tract) denied the Messengers.

﴿ وَءَاتَيْنَـٰهُمْ ءَايَـٰتِنَا فَكَانُوا۟ عَنْهَا مُعْرِضِينَ ۞ ﴾

81. And We gave them Our Signs, but they were averse to them.

﴿ وَكَانُوا۟ يَنْحِتُونَ مِنَ ٱلْجِبَالِ بُيُوتًا ءَامِنِينَ ۞ ﴾

82. And they used to hew out dwellings from the mountains (feeling themselves) secure.

﴿ فَأَخَذَتْهُمُ ٱلصَّيْحَةُ مُصْبِحِينَ ۞ ﴾

83. But As-Saihah (torment - awful cry) overtook them in the early morning (of the fourth day of their promised punishment days).

﴿ فَمَآ أَغْنَىٰ عَنْهُم مَّا كَانُوا۟ يَكْسِبُونَ ۞ ﴾

84. And all that which they used to earn availed them not.

Transliteration

80. Walaqad kaththaba as-habu alhijri almursaleena 81. Waataynahum ayatina fakanoo AAanha muAArideena 82. Wakanoo yanhitoona mina aljibali buyootan amineena 83. Faakhathat-humu alssayhatu musbiheena 84. Fama aghna AAanhum ma kanoo yaksiboona

Tafsir Ibn Kathir

The Destruction of the Dwellers of Al-Hijr, Who are the People called Thamud

The Dwellers of the Al Hijr were the people of Thamud who rejected their Prophet, Salih. Whoever denies even one Messenger, then he has disbelieved in all of the Messengers, thus they are described as rejecting "the Messengers". Allah tells us that he (Salih) brought them signs to prove that what he was telling them was true, such

Chapter 15: Al-Hijr (Stoneland, Rock City), Verses 001-099

as the she-camel which Allah created for them out of a solid rock in response to the supplication of Salih. This she-camel was grazing on their lands, and the people and the camel took water on alternate days that were well-known. When they rebelled and killed it, he said to them,

("Enjoy yourselves in your homes for three days. This is a promise which will not be belied.") (11:65) Allah said:

(And as for Thamud, We showed them and made the path of truth clear but they preferred blindness to guidance.) (41:17) Allâh tells us that,

(And they used to hew out dwellings from the mountains, (feeling) secure.) meaning, they were without fear and they had no real need for those houses; it was merely a form of extravagance and work without a purpose. This could be seen from their work in the houses in the Al-Hijr through which the Messenger of Allah passed on his way to Tabuk. He covered his head and urged his camel to go faster, saying to his Companions:

»لَا تَدْخُلُوا بُيُوتَ الْقَوْمِ الْمُعَذَّبِينَ إِلَّا أَنْ تَكُونُوا بَاكِينَ، فَإِنْ لَمْ تَبْكُوا فَتَبَاكَوْا خَشْيَةَ أَنْ يُصِيبَكُمْ مَا أَصَابَهُمْ«

(Do not enter the dwellings of those who were punished unless you are weeping, and if you do not weep then make yourself weep out of fear that perhaps what struck them may also strike you.)

(But the Sayhah (torment - awful cry) overtook them in the early morning.) meaning in the morning of the fourth day.

(And all that they used to earn availed them not.) meaning all of the benefits that they used to gain from their crops and fruits, and the water which they did not want to share with the she-camel that they killed so that it would not reduce their share of the water - all of that wealth would not protect them or help them when the command of their Lord came to pass.

Surah: 15 Ayah: 85 & Ayah: 86

﴿ وَمَا خَلَقْنَا ٱلسَّمَٰوَٰتِ وَٱلْأَرْضَ وَمَا بَيْنَهُمَآ إِلَّا بِٱلْحَقِّ وَإِنَّ ٱلسَّاعَةَ لَأَتِيَةٌ فَٱصْفَحِ ٱلصَّفْحَ ٱلْجَمِيلَ ۝ ﴾

85. And We created not the heavens and the earth and all that is between them except with truth, and the Hour is surely coming, so overlook (O Muhammad (peace be upon him)) their faults with gracious forgiveness. (This was before the ordainment of Jihâd - holy fighting in Allâh's cause).

86. Verily, your Lord is the All-Knowing Creator.

Transliteration

85. Wama khalaqna alssamawati waal-arda wama baynahuma illa bialhaqqi wa-inna alssaAAata laatiyatun faisfahi alssafha aljameela   86. Inna rabbaka huwa alkhallaqu alAAaleemu

Tafsir Ibn Kathir

The World has been created for some Purpose, then the Hour will come

Allah says,

(And We did not create the heavens and the earth and all that is between them except with the truth, and the Hour is surely coming), i.e., with justice to -

(requite those who do evil with that which they have done) (53:31) Allah says,

(And We did not create the heaven and the earth, and all that is between them without purpose! That is what those who disbelieve think! Then let those who disbelieve be warned of the Fire!)(38:27)

("Did you think that We created you in play, and that you would not be brought back to Us" So exalted be Allah, the Truth, the King, none has the right to be worshipped but He, the Lord of the Honored Throne!)(23:115-116). Then Allah informed His Prophet about the Hour, and that it will be the faults of the idolators when they insult him and reject the Message that he brings to them. This is like the Ayah,

(So turn away from them, and say: "Salam (Peace!)." But they will come to know) (43:89). Mujahid, Qatadah and others said: "This was before fighting was prescribed". It is as they said, because this Surah was revealed in Makkah and fighting was prescribed after the Hijrah.

(Verily, your Lord is the Knowing Creator)(15:86). This is a confirmation of the Day of Resurrection and that Allah, may He be exalted, is able to bring the Hour to pass. He is the Creator and nothing is beyond Him. He is the Knowing, Who knows what has been dispersed from people's bodies and scattered throughout the regions of the earth, as He says:

(Is not He, Who created the heavens and the earth able to create the like of them Yes, indeed! He is the Knowing, Creator. Verily, His command, when He intends a thing, is only that He says to it, "Be!" - and it is! So glorified and exalted is He above all that they associate with Him, and in whose Hands is the dominion of all things, and to Him you shall return.)(36:81-83).

Surah: 15 Ayah: 87 & Ayah: 88

﴿ وَلَقَدْ ءَاتَيْنَٰكَ سَبْعًا مِّنَ ٱلْمَثَانِى وَٱلْقُرْءَانَ ٱلْعَظِيمَ ۞ ﴾

87. And indeed, We have bestowed upon you seven of Al-Mathâni (the seven repeatedly recited Verses), (i.e. Sûrat Al-Fâtiha) and the Grand Qur'ân.

﴿ لَا تَمُدَّنَّ عَيْنَيْكَ إِلَىٰ مَا مَتَّعْنَا بِهِۦٓ أَزْوَٰجًا مِّنْهُمْ وَلَا تَحْزَنْ عَلَيْهِمْ وَٱخْفِضْ جَنَاحَكَ لِلْمُؤْمِنِينَ ۞ ﴾

88. Look not with your eyes ambitiously at what We have bestowed on certain classes of them (the disbelievers), nor grieve over them. And lower your wings for the believers (be courteous to the fellow-believers).

Transliteration

87. Walaqad ataynaka sabAAan mina almathanee waalqur-ana alAAatheema 88. La tamuddanna AAaynayka ila ma mattaAAna bihi azwajan minhum wala tahzan AAalayhim waikhfid janahaka lilmu/mineena

Tafsir Ibn Kathir

A Reminder of the Blessing of the Qur'an and the Command to focus on its Message

Allah is saying to His Prophet : Since We have given you the Grand Qur'an, then do not look at this world and its attractions, or the transient delights that we have given to its people in order to test them. Do not envy what they have in this world, and do not upset yourself with regret for their rejection of you and their opposition to your religion.

(And lower your wings to the believers who follow you) (26:215) meaning - be gentle with them, like the Ayah,

(Verily, there has come unto you a Messenger from among yourselves. It grieves him that you should receive any injury or difficulty. He is anxious for you, for the believers - he is full of pity, kind and merciful)(9:128). There were some differences among the scholars over the meaning of "seven of the Mathani". Ibn Mas`ud, Ibn `Umar, Ibn `Abbas, Mujahid, Sa`id bin Jubayr, Ad-Dahhak and others said that they are the seven long (Surahs), meaning Al-Baqarah, Al-`Imran, An-Nisa', Al-Ma'idah, Al-An`am, Al-A`raf and Yunus. There are texts to this effect reported from Ibn `Abbas and Sa`id bin Jubayr. Sa`id said: "In them, Allah explains the obligations, the Hudud (legal limits), stories and rulings." Ibn `Abbas said, "He explains the parables, stories and lessons." The second opinion is that they (the seven of the Mathani) are Al-Fatihah, which is composed of seven Ayat. This was reported from `Ali, `Umar, Ibn Mas`ud and Ibn `Abbas. Ibn `Abbas said: "The Bismillah, is completing seven Ayah, which Allah has given exclusively to you (Muslims)." This is also the opinion of Ibrahim An-Nakha`i, `Abdullah bin `Umayr, Ibn Abi Mulaykah, Shahr bin Hawshab, Al-Hasan Al-Basri and Mujahid. Al-Bukhari, may Allah have mercy on him, recorded two Hadiths on this topic. (The first) was recorded from Abu Sa`id bin Al-Mu`alla, who said: "The Prophet passed by me while I was praying. He called out for me but I did not come until I finished my prayer. Then I came to him, and He asked,

》مَا مَنَعَكَ أَنْ تَأْتِيَنِي؟《

(What stopped you from coming to me) I said, `I was praying'. He said,

》أَلَمْ يَقُلِ اللهُ《

(Did not Allah say)

(يَأَيُّهَا الَّذِينَ ءَامَنُواْ اسْتَجِيبُواْ لِلَّهِ وَلِلرَّسُولِ إِذَا دَعَاكُمْ)

(O you who believe! Answer Allah (by obeying Him) and (His) Messenger when he calls you...) (8:24)

》أَلَا أُعَلِّمُكَ أَعْظَمَ سُورَةٍ فِي الْقُرْآنِ قَبْلَ أَنْ أَخْرُجَ مِنَ الْمَسْجِدِ《

(Shall I not teach you the most magnificent Surah before I leave the Masjid) Then the Prophet went to leave the Masjid, and I reminded him, so he said,

(الْحَمْدُ لِلَّهِ رَبِّ الْعَالَمِينَ)

("Al-Hamdu Lillahi Rabbil-'Alamin (All praises and thanks be to Allah, the Lord of all that exists))(1:2).

》هِيَ السَّبْعُ الْمَثَانِي وَالْقُرْآنُ الَّذِي أُوتِيتُهُ《

(This is the seven of the Mathani and the Qur'an which I have been given.)" (The second Hadith) was reported from Abu Hurayrah who said that the Messenger of Allah said:

》أُمُّ الْقُرْآنِ هِيَ السَّبْعُ الْمَثَانِي وَالْقُرْآنُ الْعَظِيمُ《

(Umm Al-Qur'an (the Mother or the Essence of the Qur'an,) is the seven Mathani, and the Grand Qur'an.) This means that Al-Fatihah is the seven Mathani and the Grand Qur'an, but this does not contradict the statement that the seven Mathani are the seven long Surahs, because they also share these attributes, as does the whole Qur'an. As Allah says,

(Allah has sent down the best statement, a Book (this Qur'an), its parts resembling each other in goodness and truth, oft-recited) (39:23). So it is oft-recited in one way, and its parts resemble one another in another way, and this is also the Grand Qur'an.

(Look not with your eyes ambitiously at what We have given to certain classes of them) (20: 131) meaning, be content with the Grand Qur'an that Allah has given to you, and do not long for the luxuries and transient delights that they have.

(Look not with your eyes ambitiously) Al-`Awfi reported that Ibn `Abbas said: "He (in this Ayah) forbade a man to wish for what his companion has."

(at what We have given to certain classes of them,) Mujahid said: "This refers to the rich."

Surah: 15 Ayah: 89, Ayah: 90, Ayah: 91, Ayah: 92 & Ayah: 93

﴿ وَقُلْ إِنِّى أَنَا ٱلنَّذِيرُ ٱلْمُبِينُ ۝ ﴾

89. And say (O Muhammad (peace be upon him)) "I am indeed a plain warner."

﴿ كَمَا أَنزَلْنَا عَلَى ٱلْمُقْتَسِمِينَ ۝ ﴾

90. As We have sent down on the dividers, (Quraish pagans or Jews and Christians).

﴿ ٱلَّذِينَ جَعَلُوا ٱلْقُرْءَانَ عِضِينَ ۝ ﴾

91. Who have made the Qur'ân into parts. (i.e. believed in one part and disbelieved in the other). (Tafsir Al-Tabari)

﴿ فَوَرَبِّكَ لَنَسْـَٔلَنَّهُمْ أَجْمَعِينَ ۝ ﴾

92. So, by your Lord (O Muhammad (peace be upon him)) We shall certainly call all of them to account.

﴿ عَمَّا كَانُوا يَعْمَلُونَ ۝ ﴾

93. For all that they used to do.

Transliteration

89. Waqul innee ana alnnatheeru almubeenu 90. Kama anzalna AAala almuqtasimeena 91. Allatheena jaAAaloo alqur-ana AAideena 92. Fawarabbika lanas-alannahum ajmaAAeena 93. AAamma kanoo yaAAmaloona

Tafsir Ibn Kathir

The Messenger is a Plain Warner

Allah commanded His Prophet to tell the people:

(I am indeed a plain warner) coming to warn the people of a severe punishment that they will suffer if they reject him, as happened to those nations before them who disbelieved in their Messengers, upon whom Allah sent His punishment and vengeance. In the two Sahihs it is reported from Abu Musa that the Prophet said:

»إِنَّمَا مَثَلِي وَمَثَلُ مَا بَعَثَنِي اللهُ بِهِ كَمَثَلِ رَجُلٍ أَتَى قَوْمَهُ فَقَالَ: يَا قَوْمِ إِنِّي رَأَيْتُ الْجَيْشَ بِعَيْنَيَّ، وَإِنِّي أَنَا النَّذِيرُ الْعُرْيَانُ فَالنَّجَاءَ النَّجَاءَ، فَأَطَاعَهُ طَائِفَةٌ مِنْ قَوْمِهِ فَأَدْلَجُوا وَانْطَلَقُوا عَلَى مُهْلِهِمْ فَنَجَوْا، وَكَذَّبَهُ طَائِفَةٌ مِنْهُمْ فَأَصْبَحُوا مَكَانَهُمْ، فَصَبَّحَهُمُ الْجَيْشُ فَأَهْلَكَهُمْ وَاجْتَاحَهُمْ، فَذَلِكَ مَثَلُ مَنْ أَطَاعَنِي وَاتَّبَعَ مَا جِئْتُ بِهِ وَمَثَلُ مَنْ عَصَانِي وَكَذَّبَ مَا جِئْتُ بِهِ مِنَ الْحَقِّ«

(The parable of myself and that with which Allah has sent me is that of a man who came to his people and said, `O people! I have seen the (invading) army with my own eyes, and I am a naked warner, so escape, escape!' Some of his people obeyed him and set out at nightfall, setting off at a slow pace and managing to escape. Others did not believe him and stayed where they were until the next morning when the (invading) army overtook them and destroyed them, wiping them out. This is the parable of the one who obeys me and follows what I have brought, and the example of the one who disobeys me and rejects the truth that I have brought.)

Explanation of "Al-Muqtasimin

(the Muqtasimin) refers to those who had made a pact to oppose, deny, and insult the Prophets. Similarly, Allah tells us about the people of Salih:

(They said, "Swear to one another (Taqasamu) by Allah that we shall make a secret night attack on him and his household") (27:49) i.e., they plotted to kill him at night. Mujahid said "Taqasamu means they swore an oath."

(And they swear by Allah with their strongest oaths, that Allah will not raise up one who dies)(16:38).

((It will be said): "Did you not before swear that you would not leave (the world for the Hereafter)) (14:44)

(Are they those, of whom you swore that Allah would never show them mercy)(7:49) It is as if they took an oath for every single thing that they denied in this world, so they are called the Muqtasimin.

(Who have made the Qur'an into parts.) meaning, they have split up the Books that were revealed to them, believing in parts of them and rejecting parts of them. Al-Bukhari reported that Ibn `Abbas said,

Chapter 15: Al-Hijr (Stoneland, Rock City), Verses 001-099   *45*

(Who have made the Qur'an into parts.) "They are the People of the Book, who divided the Book into parts, believing in some of it, and rejecting some of it." Some have said that Al-Mutaqasimin refers to the Quraysh, that the Qur'an means this Qur'an (as opposed to the Scriptures of the People of the Book), and that "made it into parts" referred to what `Ata' said that some of them said that he (the Prophet ) was a sorcerer, some said he was crazy, or a soothsayer. These various allegations were the parts. This opinion was also reported from Ad-Dahhak and others. Muhammad bin Ishaq reported from Ibn `Abbas that Al-Walid bin Al-Mughirah - holding a noble position among the people - rallied a group of Quraysh behind him when Al-Mawsim (the time for pilgrims to meet in Makkah for Hajj) had come. He said to them, "O people of Quraysh! The time of Al-Mawsim has come, and delegations of Arabs will come to you during this time. They will have heard some things about this companion of yours (meaning the Prophet), so agree on one opinion, let there be no contradicting or denials of each other's sayings". They said, "And you, O Abu `Abd Shams, give us an opinion and we will say that." He said, "No, you make the suggestions and I will listen." They said, "We say he is a soothsayer." He said, "He is not a soothsayer." They said, "We say he is crazy." He said, "He is not crazy." They said, "We say he is a poet." He said, "He is not a poet." They said, "We say he is a sorcerer." He said, "He is not a sorcerer." They said, "So what should we say" He said, "By Allah, what he says is as palatable (to the average person) as something sweet, so you cannot say anything against it without it being obviously false. Therefore the most appropriate thing you can say is that he is a sorcerer." So they left having agreed upon that, and Allah revealed concerning them:

(Who have made the Qur'an into parts.) meaning, of different types, and

(So, by your Lord, We shall certainly call all of them to account. For all that they used to do) Those were the group who said that about the Messenger of Allah ."

(So, by your Lord, We shall certainly call all of them to account. For all that they used to do.) Abu Ja`far reported from Ar-Rabi` that Abu Al-`Aliyah said, "All the people will be asked about two things on the Day of Resurrection: what they used to worship, and what their response was to the Messengers." `Ali bin Abi Talhah repor- ted that Ibn `Abbas said,

(So, by your Lord, We shall certainly call all of them to account. For all that they used to do.) then he said:

(So on that Day no question will be asked of man or Jinn as to his sin) (55:39). He said, "They will not be asked, `Did you do such and such' Because Allah knows better than they do about that. But He will say, `Why did you do such and such'"

Surah: 15 Ayah: 94, Ayah: 95, Ayah: 96, Ayah: 97, Ayah: 98 & Ayah: 99

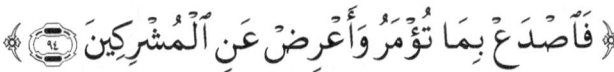

94. Therefore proclaim openly (Allâh's Message - Islâmic Monotheism) that which you are commanded, and turn away from Al-Mushrikûn (polytheists, idolaters, and disbelievers - see V.2:105).

﴿ إِنَّا كَفَيْنَاكَ ٱلْمُسْتَهْزِءِينَ ۝ ﴾

95. Truly! We will suffice you against the scoffers,

﴿ ٱلَّذِينَ يَجْعَلُونَ مَعَ ٱللَّهِ إِلَٰهًا ءَاخَرَ فَسَوْفَ يَعْلَمُونَ ۝ ﴾

96. Who set up along with Allâh another ilâh (god); but they will come to know.

﴿ وَلَقَدْ نَعْلَمُ أَنَّكَ يَضِيقُ صَدْرُكَ بِمَا يَقُولُونَ ۝ ﴾

97. Indeed, We know that your breast is straitened at what they say.

﴿ فَسَبِّحْ بِحَمْدِ رَبِّكَ وَكُن مِّنَ ٱلسَّٰجِدِينَ ۝ ﴾

98. So glorify the praises of your Lord and be of those who prostrate themselves (to Him).

﴿ وَٱعْبُدْ رَبَّكَ حَتَّىٰ يَأْتِيَكَ ٱلْيَقِينُ ۝ ﴾

99. And worship your Lord until there comes unto you the certainty (i.e. death).

Transliteration

94. FaisdaAA bima tu/maru waaAArid AAani almushrikeena 95. Inna kafaynaka almustahzi-eena 96. Who set up along with Allâh another ilâh (god), they will come to know. 97. Walaqad naAAlamu annaka yadeequ sadruka bima yaqooloona 98. Fasabbih bihamdi rabbika wakun mina alssajideena 99. WaoAAbud rabbaka hatta ya/tiyaka alyaqeenu

Tafsir Ibn Kathir

The Command to proclaim the Truth openly

Allah commanded His Messenger to convey what He sent him with, to proclaim and spread the Message, which means confronting the idolators with it. Ibn `Abbas said that the Ayah,

(Therefore openly proclaim that what you have been commanded,) means, "Go ahead with it." According to another report it means, "Therefore proclaim that which you are commanded." Mujahid said, "It is reciting the Qur'an aloud during prayer." Abu `Ubaydah reported that `Abdullah bin Mas`ud said, "The Prophet was still practicing and preaching Islam secretly until this Ayah was revealed:

(Therefore openly proclaim that which you are commanded) then he and his Companions came out into the open."

Chapter 15: Al-Hijr (Stoneland, Rock City), Verses 001-099

The Command to turn away from the Idolators, and the Guarantee of Protection against the Mockers

Allah's statement,

(and turn away from idolators. Truly, We will suffice you against the mockers.) meaning - convey that which has been revealed to you by your Lord, and do not pay attention to the idolators who want to turn you away from the signs of Allah.

(They wish that you should compromise for them, so that they would compromise for you) (68:9). Do not fear them because Allah will suffice you against them, and He will protect you from them. This is like the Ayah:

(O Messenger! Proclaim that which has been revealed to you from your Lord. And if you do not do it, then you have not conveyed His Message. Allah will protect you from mankind.) (5:67) Muhammad bin Ishaq said: "The great ones of the mockers were five people, who were elders and noblemen among their people. From Bani Asad bin `Abd Al-`Uzza bin Qusayy there was Al-Aswad bin Al-Muttalib Abu Zam`ah. According to what I heard, the Messenger of Allah () had supplicated against him because of the pain and mockery he had suffered at his hands. He had said,

«اللَّهُمَّ أَعِمْ بَصَرَهُ، وَأَثْكِلْهُ وَلَدَه»

(O Allah, make him blind and take (the life of) his son.) From Bani Zahrah there was Al-Aswad bin `Abd Yaghuth bin Wahb bin `Abd Manaf bin Zahrah. From Bani Makhzum there was Al-Walid bin Al-Mughirah bin `Abdullah bin `Umar bin Makhzum. From Bani Sahm bin `Amr bin Husays bin Ka`b bin Lu'ayy there was Al-`As bin Wa'il bin Hisham bin Sa`id bin Sa`d. From Khuza`ah there was Al-Harith bin At-Talatilah bin `Amr bin Al-Harith bin `Abd `Amr bin Malkan. When their evil went to extremes and their mockery of the Messenger of Allah went too far, Allah revealed:

(Therefore openly proclaim that which you are commanded, and turn away from the idolators. Truly, We will suffice you against the mockers, who make another god along with Allah; but they will come to know.) Ibn Ishaq said: Yazid bin Ruman told me that `Urwah bin Az-Zubayr or one of the other scholars said that Jibril came to the Messenger of Allah when he was performing Tawaf around the House (the Ka`bah). He stood and the Messenger of Allah stood next to him. Al-Aswad Ibn Al-Mutalib passed by, and he threw a green leaf in his face, and he became blind. Al-Aswad bin `Abd Yaghuth passed by, and he pointed to his stomach, which swelled up and he died (of dropsy). Al-Walid bin Al-Mughirah passed by, and he pointed at a wound on lower of his ankle, which he got two years earlier when He once was trailing his garment and he passed by a man who was feathering his arrows. One of the arrows got caught in his garment and scratched his foot. It was an insignificant wound, but now it opened again and he died of it. Al-`As bin Wa'il passed by, and he pointed to the instep of his foot. He (Al-`As) set off on his donkey, heading for At-Ta'if. He rested by a thorny tree, a thorn pierced his foot and he died from it. Al-Harith bin At-Talatilah passed by and he pointed at his head. It filled with pus and killed him."

(Who make another god along with Allah; but they will come to know.) This is a strong warning and grave threat against those who have other deities along with Allah.

Encouragement to bear Difficulties, and the Command to glorify and worship Allah until Death

Allah said,

(Indeed, We know that your breast becomes tight because of what they say. So glorify the praises of your Lord and be of those who prostrate themselves (to Him).) meaning 'We know, O Muhammad, that you are distressed by their insults towards you, but do not let that weaken your resolve or cause you to give up conveying the Message of Allah. Put your trust in Him, for He will suffice you and will support you against them. Keep yourself busy with remembering Allah, praising Him, glorifying Him, and worshipping Him (which means Salah, or prayer)' Hence Allah says:

(So glorify the praises of your Lord and be of those who prostrate themselves (to Him)) Imam Ahmad reported from Nu`aym bin Hammar that he heard the Messenger of Allah say:

«قَالَ اللهُ تَعَالَى يَا ابْنَ آدَمَ لَا تَعْجَزْ عَنْ أَرْبَعِ رَكَعَاتٍ مِنْ أَوَّلِ النَّهَارِ أَكْفِكَ آخِرَه»

(Allah said, "O son of Adam! It is not too difficult for you to perform four Rak'at at the beginning of the day, (and if you do them,) I will take care of you until the end of it.")

(And worship your Lord until the certainty comes to you) (15: 99). Al-Bukhari said: "Salim said, `(This means) death.'" This Salim is Salim bin `Abdullah bin `Umar. Ibn Jarir also recorded from Salim bin `Abdullah,

(And worship your Lord until the Yaqin comes to you.) He said, "Death." It is reported in the Sahih from Umm Al-`Ala'- one of the women of the Ansar - that when the Messenger of Allah entered upon `Uthman bin Maz`un after he had died, Umm Al-`Ala' said, "May the mercy of Allah be upon you, Abu As-Sa`ib. My testimony over you is that Allah has honored you." The Messenger of Allah said,

«وَمَا يُدْرِيكِ أَنَّ اللهَ أَكْرَمَهُ؟»

(How do you know that Allah has honored him) I said, "May my father and mother be sacrificed for you, O Messenger of Allah! If not him, then who else" He said,

«أَمَّا هُوَ فَقَدْ جَاءَهُ الْيَقِينُ، وَإِنِّي لَأَرْجُو لَهُ الْخَيْرَ»

(As far as he is concerned, the death has come to him, and I hope for good for him.) This is evidence that the meaning of this Ayah,

(And worship your Lord until the certainty comes to you.) is that acts of worship, such as prayer and the like, are obligatory on man so long as his mind is sound, so he should pray according to his best ability. It was reported in Sahih Al-Bukhari from `Imran bin Husayn that the Messenger of Allah said:

«صَلِّ قَائِمًا، فَإِنْ لَمْ تَسْتَطِعْ فَقَاعِدًا، فَإِنْ لَمْ تَسْتَطِعْ فَعَلَى جَنْبٍ»

(Pray standing, and if you cannot, then sitting, and if you cannot, then on your side.) From this we may understand that it is a mistake to interpret Yaqin (the certainty) as Ma`rifah ("spiritual knowing") as some of the Sufis do. According to them, when one of them attains the level of Ma`rifah, they consider him to be free of these obligations. This is disbelief, misguidance and ignorance. The Prophets - peace be upon them - and their companions, were the most knowledgeable of people about Allah, about His rights, His attributes, and the glorification that He deserves. But at the same time, they were the people who worshipped Him the most, continuing in good deeds until the time they died. Therefore, what is meant by Yaqin here is death, as we have stated above. To Allah be praise and thanks. Praise be to Allah for His guidance. It is to Him that we turn for help and it is in Him that we put our trust. He is the One Whom we ask to help us to reach the best of circumstances, for He is the Most Generous and Kind. This is the end of the Tafsir of Surat Al-Hijr. Praise be to Allah, the Lord of all that exists.

CHAPTER (SURAH) 16: AN-NAHL (THE BEE), VERSES 001-128

(بِسْمِ اللَّهِ الرَّحْمَنِ الرَّحِيمِ)

In the Name of Allah, the Most Gracious, the Most Merciful.

Surah: 16 Ayah: 1

﴿أَتَىٰ أَمْرُ ٱللَّهِ فَلَا تَسْتَعْجِلُوهُ سُبْحَٰنَهُۥ وَتَعَٰلَىٰ عَمَّا يُشْرِكُونَ ۝﴾

1. The Event (the Hour or the punishment of disbelievers and polytheists or the Islâmic laws or commandments) ordained by Allâh will come to pass, so seek not to hasten it. Glorified and Exalted be He above all that they associate as partners with Him.

Transliteration

1. Ata amru Allahi fala tastaAAjiloohu subhanahu wataAAala AAamma yushrikoona

Tafsir Ibn Kathir

Warning about the approach of the Hour

Allah is informing about the approach of the Hour in the past tense (in Arabic) in order to confirm that it will undoubtedly come to pass. This is like the following Ayat, in which the verbs appear in the past tense in Arabic:

(Mankind's reckoning has drawn near them, while they turn away in heedlessness.)(21:1)

(The Hour has drawn near, and the moon has been cleft.) (54:1)

(so do not seek to hasten it.) means, what was far is now near, so do not try to rush it. As Allah said,

(And they ask you to hasten the torment (for them), and had it not been for a term appointed, the torment would certainly have come to them. And surely, it will come upon them suddenly while they are unaware! They ask you to hasten on the torment. And verily! Hell, of a surety, will encompass the disbelievers) (29:53-54). Ibn Abi Hatim reported from `Uqbah bin `Amir that the Messenger of Allah said:

«تَطْلُعُ عَلَيْكُمْ عِنْدَ السَّاعَةِ سَحَابَةٌ سَوْدَاءُ مِنَ الْمَغْرِبِ مِثْلَ التُّرْسِ، فَمَا تَزَالُ تَرْتَفِعُ فِي السَّمَاءِ ثُمَّ يُنَادِي مُنَادٍ فِيهَا: يَا أَيُّهَا النَّاسُ فَيُقْبِلُ النَّاسُ بَعْضُهُمْ عَلَى بَعْضٍ: هَلْ سَمِعْتُمْ، فَمِنْهُمْ مَنْ يَقُولُ: نَعَمْ، وَمِنْهُمْ مَنْ يَشُكُّ، ثُمَّ يُنَادِي الثَّانِيَةَ: يَا أَيُّهَا النَّاسُ فَيَقُولُ النَّاسُ بَعْضُهُمْ لِبَعْضٍ: هَلْ سَمِعْتُمْ، فَيَقُولُونَ: نَعَمْ، ثُمَّ يُنَادِي الثَّالِثَةَ: يَا أَيُّهَا النَّاسُ أَتَى أَمْرُ اللهِ فَلَا تَسْتَعْجِلُوهُ»

(When the Hour approaches, a black cloud resembling a shield will emerge upon from the west. It will continue rising in the sky, then a voice will call out, `O mankind!' The people will say to one another, `Did you hear that' Some will say, `yes', but others will doubt it. Then a second call will come, `O mankind!' The people will say to one another, `Did you hear that' And they will say, `Yes.' Then a third call will come, `O mankind!' The Event ordained by Allah has indeed come, so do not seek to hasten it.') The Messenger of Allah said:

«فَوَ الَّذِي نَفْسِي بِيَدِهِ، إِنَّ الرَّجُلَيْنِ لَيَنْشُرَانِ الثَّوْبَ فَمَا يَطْوِيَانِهِ أَبَدًا، وَإِنَّ الرَّجُلَ لَيَمُدَّنَّ حَوْضَهُ فَمَا يَسْقِي فِيهِ شَيْئًا أَبَدًا، وَإِنَّ الرَّجُلَ لَيَحْلُبُ نَاقَتَهُ فَمَا يَشْرِبُهُ أَبَدًا قَالَ وَيَشْتَغِلُ النَّاسُ»

(By the One in Whose Hand is my soul, two men will spread out a cloth, but will never refold it; a man will prepare his trough, but will never water his animals from it; and a man will milk his camel, but will never drink the milk." Then he said, "The people will be distracted.") Then Allah tells us that He is free from their allegations of partners to their worship of idols, and making equals for Him. Glorified and exalted be He far above that. These are the people who deny the Hour, so He says:

(Glorified and Exalted be He above all that they associate as partners with Him.)

Surah: 16 Ayah: 2

﴿ يُنَزِّلُ ٱلْمَلَٰٓئِكَةَ بِٱلرُّوحِ مِنْ أَمْرِهِۦ عَلَىٰ مَن يَشَآءُ مِنْ عِبَادِهِۦٓ أَنْ أَنذِرُوٓاْ أَنَّهُۥ لَآ إِلَٰهَ إِلَّآ أَنَا۠ فَٱتَّقُونِ ۝ ﴾

2. He sends down the angels with the Rûh (revelation) of His Command to whom of His slaves He wills (saying): "Warn mankind that Lâ ilâha illa Ana (none has the right to be worshipped but I), so fear Me (by abstaining from sins and evil deeds).

Transliteration

2. Yunazzilu almala-ikata bialrroohi min amrihi AAala man yashao min AAibadihi an anthiroo annahu la ilaha illa ana faittaqooni

Tafsir Ibn Kathir

Allah sends Whomever He wills with the Message of Tawhid

(He sends down the angels with the Ruh) refers to the revelation. This is like the Ayat:

(And thus We have sent to you a Ruh (revelation) by Our command. You knew not what is the Book, nor what is the faith. But We have made it a light by which We guide whomever We will among Our servants.) (43:52)

(to those servants of His whom He wills) meaning the Prophets, as Allah says:

(Allah best knows where to place His Message.) (6:124)

(Allah chooses Messengers from angels and from men.) (22:75)

(He sends the Ruh (revelation) by His command to whoever among His servants He wills to, that he may warn of the Day of Meeting. The Day when they will (all) come out, nothing about them will be hidden from Allah. Whose is the kingdom this Day: It is Allah's, the One, the Irresistible!) (40:15-16)

((saying): "Warn...") meaning that they should alert them.

(that none has the right to be worshipped but I, so have Taqwa of Me.) means, `fear My punishment, if you go against My commands and worship anything other than Me.'

Surah: 16 Ayah: 3 & Ayah: 4

﴿ خَلَقَ ٱلسَّمَٰوَٰتِ وَٱلۡأَرۡضَ بِٱلۡحَقِّ تَعَٰلَىٰ عَمَّا يُشۡرِكُونَ ۝ ﴾

3. He has created the heavens and the earth with truth. High is He, Exalted above all they associate as partners with Him.

﴿ خَلَقَ ٱلۡإِنسَٰنَ مِن نُّطۡفَةٍ فَإِذَا هُوَ خَصِيمٌ مُّبِينٌ ۝ ﴾

4. He has created man from Nutfah (mixed drops of male and female sexual discharge), then behold, this same (man) becomes an open opponent.

Transliteration

3. Khalaqa alssamawati waal-arda bialhaqqi taAAala AAamma yushrikoona 4. Khalaqa al-insana min nutfatin fa-itha huwa khaseemun mubeenun

Tafsir Ibn Kathir

Allah is the One Who has created the Heavens, the Earth, and Man

Allah tells us about His creation of the upper realm, which is the heavens, and the lower realm, which is the earth, and everything in them. They have been created for a true purpose, not in vain, so that

(He may requite those who do evil with that which they have done (i.e. punish them in Hell), and reward those who do good, with what is best (i.e. Paradise).) (53:31) Then He declares Himself to be above the Shirk of those who worship others besides Him. He is independent of His creation, alone with no partner or associate. For this reason He deserves to be worshipped Alone, without partners. Then He mentions how man has been created from a Nutfah, i.e., something that is insignificant, weak and has no value - but when man becomes independent and is able to fend for himself - then he begins to dispute with his Lord, may He be exalted, and disbelieves in Him and fights His Messengers. But man was created to be a servant, not an opponent, as Allah says:

(And it is He Who has created man from water, and gave him descendants, and made Him kindred by marriage, and your Lord is capable (of all things). And they worship besides Allah, that which can neither profit them nor harm them; and the disbeliever is ever a helper (of Shaytan) against his Lord) (25: 54-55). And;

Chapter 16: An-Nahl (The Bee), Verses 001-128

(Does not man see that We have created him from Nutfah. Yet, behold he stands as an open opponent. And he puts forth for Us a parable, and forgets his own creation. He says: "Who will give life to these bones after they are rotten and have become dust" Say: "He will give life to them Who created them the first time! And He is the knower of every creature!") (36:77-79). Imam Ahmad and Ibn Majah reported that Busr bin Jahhash said: "The Messenger of Allah spat in his palm, then he said,

«يَقُولُ اللهُ تَعَالَى: ابْنَ آدَمَ أَنَّى تُعْجِزُنِي وَقَدْ خَلَقْتُكَ مِنْ مِثْلِ هَذِهِ، حَتَّى إِذَا سَوَّيْتُكَ فَعَدَلْتُكَ مَشَيْتَ بَيْنَ بُرْدَيْكَ وَلِلْأَرْضِ مِنْكَ وَئِيدٌ، فَجَمَعْتَ وَمَنَعْتَ حَتَّى إِذَا بَلَغَتِ الْحُلْقُومَ قُلْتَ: أَتَصَدَّقُ، وَأَنَّى أَوَانُ الصَّدَقَةِ»

(Allah, may He be exalted, says: "O son of Adam, how could you be more powerful than I when I have created you from something like this, and when I have fashioned you perfectly and made you complete, you walk wearing your two garments and the earth makes a sound (beneath your feet). You collect money but do not give anything to anyone, then when the soul of a dying person reaches the throat, you say, `I want to give in charity', but it is too late for charity.")

Surah: 16 Ayah: 5, Ayah: 6 & Ayah: 7

﴿ وَٱلۡأَنۡعَٰمَ خَلَقَهَاۖ لَكُمۡ فِيهَا دِفۡءٌ وَمَنَٰفِعُ وَمِنۡهَا تَأۡكُلُونَ ۝ ﴾

5. And the cattle, He has created them for you; in them there is warmth (warm clothing), and numerous benefits, and of them you eat.

﴿ وَلَكُمۡ فِيهَا جَمَالٌ حِينَ تُرِيحُونَ وَحِينَ تَسۡرَحُونَ ۝ ﴾

6. And wherein is beauty for you, when you bring them home in the evening, and as you lead them forth to pasture in the morning.

﴿ وَتَحۡمِلُ أَثۡقَالَكُمۡ إِلَىٰ بَلَدٍ لَّمۡ تَكُونُواْ بَٰلِغِيهِ إِلَّا بِشِقِّ ٱلۡأَنفُسِۚ إِنَّ رَبَّكُمۡ لَرَءُوفٌ رَّحِيمٌ ۝ ﴾

7. And they carry your loads to a land that you could not reach except with great trouble to yourselves. Truly, your Lord is full of Kindness, Most Merciful.

Transliteration

5. Waal-anAAama khalaqaha lakum feeha dif-on wamanafiAAu waminha ta-kuloona
6. Walakum feeha jamalun heena tureehoona waheena tasrahoona   7. Watahmilu athqalakum ila baladin lam takoonoo baligheehi illa bishiqqi al-anfusi inna rabbakum laraoofun raheemun

Tafsir Ibn Kathir

The Cattle are part of the Creation of Allah and a Blessing from Him

Allah reminds His servants of the blessing in His creation of An`am, this term includes camels, cows and sheep, as was explained in detail in Surat Al-An`am where the "eight pairs" are mentioned. The blessings include the benefits derived from their wool and hair, from which clothes and furnishings are made, from their milk which is drunk, and their young which are eaten. Their beauty is a kind of adornment, thus Allah says,

(And there is beauty in them for you, when you bring them home in the evening.) which is when they are brought back from the pasture in the evening. This is a reference to how their flanks become fat, their udders fill with milk and their humps become bigger.

(and as you lead them forth to pasture (in the morning).) meaning when you send them out to the pasture in the morning.

(And they carry your loads) meaning the heavy burdens that you cannot move or carry by yourselves

(to a land that you could not reach except with great trouble to yourselves) meaning journeys for Hajj, `Umrah, military campaigns, and journeys for the purpose of trading, and so on. They use these animals for all kinds of purposes, for riding and for carrying loads, as Allah says:

(And verily, there is indeed a lesson for you in the An'am (cattle). We give you to drink (milk) of that which is in their bellies. And there are numerous (other) benefits in them for you. Of them you eat, and on them and on ships you are carried.) (23:21-22)

(Allah, it is He Who has made cattle for you, so that some you may ride, and some you may eat. And you find (many other) benefits in them; you may reach by their means a desire that is in your breasts (i.e. carry your goods, loads), and on them and on ships you are carried. And He shows you His Ayat. Which, then of the Ayat of Allah do you deny) (40:79-81). Thus here Allah says, after enumerating these blessings,

(Truly, your Lord is full of kindness, Most Merciful.) meaning, your Lord is the One Who has subjugated the An`am (cattle) to you. This is like the Ayat:

(Do they not see, that of what Our Hands have created, We created the An'am (cattle) for them, so that they may own them, and We subdued them so that they may ride some and they may eat some.)(36:71-72).

(And He made mounts for you out of ships and cattle. In order that you may ride on their backs, and may then remember the favor of your Lord when you mount upon them, and say: "Glory be to the One Who subjected this to us, and we could never have it (by our efforts). And verily, to Our Lord we indeed are to return!") (43:12-14) Ibn `Abbas said,

(In them there is warmth) refers to clothing;

(and numerous benefits) refers to the ways in which they derive the benefits of food and drink from them."

Surah: 16 Ayah: 8

﴿ وَٱلْخَيْلَ وَٱلْبِغَالَ وَٱلْحَمِيرَ لِتَرْكَبُوهَا وَزِينَةً ۚ وَيَخْلُقُ مَا لَا تَعْلَمُونَ ۝ ﴾

8. And (He has created) horses, mules and donkeys, for you to ride and as an adornment. And He creates (other) things of which you have no knowledge.

Transliteration

8. Waalkhayla waalbighala waalhameera litarkabooha wazeenatan wayakhluqu ma la taAAlamoona

Tafsir Ibn Kathir

This refers to another category of animals that Allah has created as a blessing for His servants; horses, mules and donkeys, all of which He made for riding and adornment.

This is the main purpose for which these animals were created. It was reported in the Two Sahihs that Jabir bin `Abdullah said: "The Messenger of Allah forbade us to eat the meat of domestic donkeys, but he allowed us to eat the meat of horses." Imam Ahmad and Abu Dawud reported with two chains of narration, each of which meet the conditions of Muslim, that Jabir said: "On the day of Khaybar we slaughtered horses, mules and donkeys. The Messenger of Allah forbade us from eating the mules and donkeys, but he did not forbid us from eating the horses." According to Sahih Muslim, Asma' bint Abi Bakr (may Allah be pleased with them both) said: "At the time of the Messenger of Allah we slaughtered a horse and ate it when we were in Al-Madinah."

Surah: 16 Ayah: 9

﴿ وَعَلَى ٱللَّهِ قَصْدُ ٱلسَّبِيلِ وَمِنْهَا جَآئِرٌ ۚ وَلَوْ شَآءَ لَهَدَىٰكُمْ أَجْمَعِينَ ۝ ﴾

9. And upon Allâh is the responsibility to explain the Straight Path. But there are ways that turn aside (such as Paganism, Judaism and Christianity). And had He willed, He would have guided you all (mankind).

Transliteration

9. WaAAala Allahi qasdu alssabeeli waminha ja-irun walaw shaa lahadakum ajmaAAeena

Tafsir Ibn Kathir

When Allah mentioned the animals which may be used for the purpose of physical journeys, He also referred to the moral, religious routes that people may follow. Often in the Qur'an there is a shift from physical or tangible things to beneficial spiritual and religious matters, as when Allah says,

(And take a provision (with you) for the journey, but the best provision is Taqwa (piety, righteousness).) (2:197) And,

(O Children of Adam! We have granted clothing for you to cover yourselves, as well as for adornment; but the raiment of righteousness, that is better.) (7:26) Since Allah mentioned cattle and other such animals in this Surah, all of which are ridden or can be used in any way necessary, carrying people's necessities for them to distant places and on difficult journeys - then He mentions the ways which people follow to try to reach Him, and explains that the right way is the one that does reach Him. He says:

(And it is up to Allah to show the right way.) This is like the Ayat,

(And verily, this is My straight path, so follow it, and do not follow the (other) paths, for they will separate you away from His path.) (6:153) and,

((Allah) said: "This is the way which will lead straight to Me.") (15:41)

(And it is up to Allah to show the right way.) Mujahid said: "The true way is up to Allah."

(And it is up to Allah to show the right way.) Al-`Awfi said that Ibn `Abbas said: "It is up to Allah to clarify, to explain the guidance and misguidance." This was also reported by `Ali bin Abi Talhah, and was also the opinion of Qatadah and Ad-Dahhak. Hence Allah said:

(But there are ways that stray.) meaning they deviate from the truth. Ibn `Abbas and others said: "These are the different ways," and various opinions and whims, such as Judaism, Christianity and Zoroastrianism. Ibn Mas`ud recited it as (جَائِرٌ وَمِنْكُمْ) "But among you are those who stray. " Then Allah tells us that all of that happens by His will and decree. He says:

(And had He willed, He would have guided you all.) And Allah says:

(If your Lord had willed, then all who are in the earth would have believed.) (10:99)

(And if your Lord had so willed, He could surely, have made humanity one Ummah, but they will not stop disagreeing. Except those for whom your Lord has granted mercy. And it is for this that He did create them; and the Word of your Lord has been fulfilled (i.e. His saying): "Surely, I shall fill Hell with Jinn and men all together.") (11:118-119).

Surah: 16 Ayah: 10 & Ayah: 11

﴿ هُوَ ٱلَّذِىٓ أَنزَلَ مِنَ ٱلسَّمَآءِ مَآءً لَّكُم مِّنْهُ شَرَابٌ وَمِنْهُ شَجَرٌ فِيهِ تُسِيمُونَ

10. He it is Who sends down water (rain) from the sky; from it you drink and from it (grows) the vegetation on which you send your cattle to pasture.

﴿ يُنۢبِتُ لَكُم بِهِ ٱلزَّرْعَ وَٱلزَّيْتُونَ وَٱلنَّخِيلَ وَٱلْأَعْنَٰبَ وَمِن كُلِّ ٱلثَّمَرَٰتِ إِنَّ فِى ذَٰلِكَ لَءَايَةً لِّقَوْمٍ يَتَفَكَّرُونَ ﴿١١﴾ ﴾

11. With it He causes to grow for you the crops, the olives, the date-palms, the grapes, and every kind of fruit. Verily! In this is indeed an evident proof and a manifest sign for people who give thought.

Transliteration

10. Huwa allathee anzala mina alssama-i maan lakum minhu sharabun waminhu shajarun feehi tuseemoona 11. Yunbitu lakum bihi alzzarAAa waalzzaytoona waalnnakheela waal-aAAnaba wamin kulli aththamarati inna fee thalika laayatan liqawmin yatafakkaroona

Tafsir Ibn Kathir

The Blessings of Rain, and explaining how it is one of the Signs

When Allah mentions the blessings of cattle and other animals that He has granted mankind, He then mentions how He has blessed them by sending rain down from the sky above, which has been fulfilling the needs and bringing joy to people and their cattle. Allah says:

(from it you drink) meaning, He made it fresh and pure so that they can drink it, not salty and undrinkable.

(and from it (grows) the vegetation on which you send your cattle to pasture.) meaning, from it He raised plants on which your cattle graze. Ibn `Abbas, `Ikrimah, Ad-Dahhak, Qatadah and Ibn Zayd, all said that this refers to grazing animals including camels.

(With it He causes crops to grow for you, olives, date palms, grapes, and every kind of fruit.) meaning, with this one kind of water, He makes the earth sprout plants with different tastes, colors, scents and shapes. For this reason He says,

(Verily, in this there is indeed an evident proof and a manifest sign for people who give thought.) meaning, this is a sign and a proof that there is no god besides Allah, as He says:

(Is not He (better than your gods) Who created the heavens and the earth, and sends water down for you from the sky, from which We cause wonderful gardens full of beauty and delight to grow You are not able to cause the growth of their trees. Is there any ilah (god) with Allah Nay, but they are a people who make equals (to Him)!) (27:60).

Surah: 16 Ayah: 12 & Ayah: 13

﴿ وَسَخَّرَ لَكُمُ ٱلَّيْلَ وَٱلنَّهَارَ وَٱلشَّمْسَ وَٱلْقَمَرَ ۖ وَٱلنُّجُومُ مُسَخَّرَٰتٌۢ بِأَمْرِهِۦٓ ۗ إِنَّ فِى ذَٰلِكَ لَءَايَٰتٍ لِّقَوْمٍ يَعْقِلُونَ ﴿١٢﴾ ﴾

12. And He has subjected to you the night and the day, and the sun and the moon; and the stars are subjected by His Command. Surely, in this are proofs for people who understand.

﴿ وَمَا ذَرَأَ لَكُمْ فِى ٱلْأَرْضِ مُخْتَلِفًا أَلْوَٰنُهُۥٓ ۗ إِنَّ فِى ذَٰلِكَ لَءَايَةً لِّقَوْمٍ يَذَّكَّرُونَ ﴿١٣﴾ ﴾

13. And whatsoever He has created for you on the earth of varying colors (and qualities from vegetation and fruits (botanical life) and from animal (zoological life)) Verily! In this is a sign for people who remember.

Transliteration

12. Wasakhkhara lakumu allayla waalnnahara waalshshamsa waalqamara waalnnujoomu musakhkharatun bi-amrihi inna fee thalika laayatin liqawmin yaAAqiloona   13. Wama tharaa lakum fee al-ardi mukhtalifan alwanuhu inna fee thalika laayatan liqawmin yaththakkaroona

Tafsir Ibn Kathir

Signs in the Subjection of Night and Day, the Sun and the Moon, and in that which grows on Earth

Allah mentions the mighty signs and immense blessings to be found in His subjection of night and day, which follow one another; the sun and moon, which revolve; the stars, both fixed and moving through the skies, offering light by which people may find their way in the darkness. Each of (these heavenly bodies) travels in its own orbit, which Allah has ordained for it, and travels in the manner prescribed for it, without deviating in any way. All of them are under His subjugation, His control and His decree, as Allah says:

(Indeed, your Lord is Allah, Who created the heavens and the earth in Six Days, and then He rose (Istawa) over the Throne. He brings the night as a cover over the day, seeking it rapidly, and (He created) the sun, the moon, the stars (all) subjected to His command. Surely, His is the creation and commandment. Blessed is Allah, the Lord of all that exists!) (7:54) Thus Allah says;

(Surely, in this are proofs for people who understand.) meaning, they are indications of His immense power and might, for those who think about Allah and understand His signs.

(And whatsoever He has created of varying colors on the earth for you.) When Allah points out the features of the skies, He also points out the wondrous things that He has created on earth, the variety of its animals, minerals, plants and inanimate features, all having different colors and shapes, benefits and qualities.

(Verily, in this is a sign for people who reflect.) meaning (those who remember) the blessings of Allah and give thanks to Him for them.

Surah: 16 Ayah: 14, Ayah: 15, Ayah: 16, Ayah: 17 & Ayah: 18

﴿ وَهُوَ ٱلَّذِى سَخَّرَ ٱلْبَحْرَ لِتَأْكُلُوا۟ مِنْهُ لَحْمًا طَرِيًّا وَتَسْتَخْرِجُوا۟ مِنْهُ حِلْيَةً تَلْبَسُونَهَا وَتَرَى ٱلْفُلْكَ مَوَاخِرَ فِيهِ وَلِتَبْتَغُوا۟ مِن فَضْلِهِۦ وَلَعَلَّكُمْ تَشْكُرُونَ ﴿١٤﴾ ﴾

14. And He it is Who has subjected the sea (to you), that you eat thereof fresh tender meat (i.e. fish), and that you bring forth out of it ornaments to wear. And you see the ships ploughing through it, that you may seek (thus) of His Bounty (by transporting the goods from place to place) and that you may be grateful.

﴿ وَأَلْقَىٰ فِى ٱلْأَرْضِ رَوَاسِىَ أَن تَمِيدَ بِكُمْ وَأَنْهَٰرًا وَسُبُلًا لَّعَلَّكُمْ تَهْتَدُونَ ﴿١٥﴾ ﴾

15. And He has affixed into the earth mountains standing firm, lest it should shake with you, and rivers and roads, that you may guide yourselves.

﴿ وَعَلَٰمَٰتٍ وَبِٱلنَّجْمِ هُمْ يَهْتَدُونَ ﴿١٦﴾ ﴾

16. And landmarks (signposts during the day) and by the stars (during the night), they (mankind) guide themselves.

﴿ أَفَمَن يَخْلُقُ كَمَن لَّا يَخْلُقُ أَفَلَا تَذَكَّرُونَ ﴿١٧﴾ ﴾

17. Is then He, Who creates as one who creates not? Will you not then remember?

﴿ وَإِن تَعُدُّوا۟ نِعْمَةَ ٱللَّهِ لَا تُحْصُوهَآ إِنَّ ٱللَّهَ لَغَفُورٌ رَّحِيمٌ ﴿١٨﴾ ﴾

18. And if you would count the favors of Allâh, never could you be able to count them. Truly! Allâh is Oft-Forgiving, Most Merciful.

Transliteration

14. Wahuwa allathee sakhkhara albahra lita/kuloo minhu lahman tariyyan watastakhrijoo minhu hilyatan talbasoonaha watara alfulka mawakhira feehi walitabtaghoo min fadlihi walaAAallakum tashkuroona   15. Waalqa fee al-ardi rawasiya an tameeda bikum waanharan wasubulan laAAallakum tahtadoona   16.

WaAAalamatin wabialnnajmi hum yahtadoona 17. Afaman yakhluqu kaman la yakhluqu afala tathakkaroona 18. Wa-in taAAuddoo niAAmata Allahi la tuhsooha inna Allaha laghafoorun raheemun

Tafsir Ibn Kathir

Signs in the Oceans, Mountains, Rivers, Roads and Stars

Allah tells us how He has subjected the seas, with their waves lapping the shores, and how He blesses His servants by subjecting the seas for them so that they may travel on them, and by putting fish and whales in them, by making their flesh permissible to eat - whether they are caught alive or dead - at all times, including when people are in a state of Ihram. He has created pearls and precious jewels in the oceans, and made it easy for His servants to recover ornaments that they can wear from the ocean floor. He made the sea such that it carries the ships which plow through it. He is the One Who taught mankind to make ships, which is the inheritance of their forefather Nuh. He was the first one to travel by ship, he was taught how to make them, then people took this knowledge from him and passed it down from generation to generation through the centuries, so that they could travel from country to country and from place to place, bringing goods from here to there and from there to here. Thus Allah says:

(that you may seek from His bounty and that you may perhaps be grateful.) - for His bounty and blessings. Then Allah mentions the earth and how He placed in it mountains standing firm, which make it stable and keep it from shaking in such a manner that the creatures dwelling on it would not be able to live. Hence Allah says,

(And the mountains He has fixed firmly.) (79: 32).

(and rivers and roads) meaning He has made rivers which flow from one place to another, bringing provision for His servants. The rivers arise in one place, and bring provision to people living in another place. They flow through lands and fields and wildernesses, through mountains and hills, until they reach the land whose people they are meant to benefit. They meander across the land, left and right, north and south, east and west - rivers great and small - flowing sometimes and ceasing sometimes, flowing from their sources to the places where the water gathers, flowing rapidly or moving slowly, as decreed by Allah. There is no god besides Him and no Lord except Him. He also made roads or routes along which people travel from one land or city to another, and He even made gaps in the mountains so that there would be routes between them, as He says:

(And We placed broad highways for them to pass through.) (21:31)

(And landmarks) meaning, signs like great mountains and small hills, and so on, things that land and sea travelers use to find their way if they get lost.

(and by the stars (during the night), they (mankind) guide themselves.) meaning, in the darkness of the night. This was the opinion of Ibn `Abbas.

Chapter 16: An-Nahl (The Bee), Verses 001-128 61

Worship is Allah's Right

Then Allah tells us of His greatness, and that worship should be directed to Him alone, not to any of the idols which do not create but are rather themselves created. Thus He says

(Is then He, Who creates, the same as one who does not create Will you not then reflect)(16:17). Then He shows His servants some of the many blessings He granted for them, and the many kinds of things that He has done for them. He says;

(And if you would try to count the favors of Allah, you would never be able to count them. Truly, Allah is Forgiving, Most Merciful.) (16:18) meaning that He pardons and forgives them. If He were to ask you to thank Him for all of His blessings, you would not be able to do so, and if He were to command you to do so, you would be incapable of it. If He punishes you, He is never unjust in His punishment, but He is Forgiving and Most Merciful, He forgives much and rewards for little. Ibn Jarir said: "It means that Allah is Forgiving when you fail to thank Him properly, if you repent and turn to Him in obedience, and strive to do that which pleases Him. He is Merciful to you and does not punish you if you turn to Him and repent."

Surah: 16 Ayah: 19, Ayah: 20 & Ayah: 21

﴿ وَٱللَّهُ يَعْلَمُ مَا تُسِرُّونَ وَمَا تُعْلِنُونَ ﴾

19. And Allâh knows what you conceal and what you reveal.

﴿ وَٱلَّذِينَ يَدْعُونَ مِن دُونِ ٱللَّهِ لَا يَخْلُقُونَ شَيْئًا وَهُمْ يُخْلَقُونَ ﴾

20. Those whom they (Al-Mushrikûn) invoke besides Allâh have not created anything, but are themselves created.

﴿ أَمْوَٰتٌ غَيْرُ أَحْيَآءٍ وَمَا يَشْعُرُونَ أَيَّانَ يُبْعَثُونَ ﴾

21. (They are) dead, not alive; and they know not when they will be raised up.

Transliteration

19. WaAllahu yaAAlamu ma tusirroona wama tuAAlinoona   20. Waallatheena yadAAoona min dooni Allahi la yakhluqoona shay-an wahum yukhlaqoona   21. Amwatun ghayru ahya-in wama yashAAuroona ayyana yubAAathoona

Tafsir Ibn Kathir

Allah tells us that He knows what is hidden in people's hearts as well as what is apparent. He will reward or punish everyone for their deeds on the Day of Resurrection. If their deeds are good then they will be rewarded, and if their deeds are evil, then they will be punished.

The gods of the Idolators are Created, they do not create

Then Allah tells us that the idols which people call on instead of Him cannot create anything, they are themselves created, as Al-Khalil (Ibrahim) said:

("Do you worship that which you (yourselves) carve While Allah has created you and what you make!") (37:-96).

((They are) dead, not alive) means, they are inanimate and lifeless, they do not hear, see, or think.

(and they know not when they will be resurrected.) meaning, they do not know when the Hour will come, so how can anyone hope for any benefit or reward from these idols They should hope for it from the One Who knows all things and is the Creator of all things.

Surah: 16 Ayah: 22 & Ayah: 23

﴿ إِلَـٰهُكُمْ إِلَـٰهٌ وَاحِدٌ ۚ فَالَّذِينَ لَا يُؤْمِنُونَ بِالْآخِرَةِ قُلُوبُهُم مُّنكِرَةٌ وَهُم مُّسْتَكْبِرُونَ ﴾

22. Your Ilâh (God) is One Ilâh (God - Allâh, none has the right to be worshipped but He). But for those who believe not in the Hereafter, their hearts deny (the faith in the Oneness of Allâh), and they are proud.

﴿ لَا جَرَمَ أَنَّ ٱللَّهَ يَعْلَمُ مَا يُسِرُّونَ وَمَا يُعْلِنُونَ ۚ إِنَّهُ لَا يُحِبُّ ٱلْمُسْتَكْبِرِينَ ﴾

23. Certainly, Allâh knows what they conceal and what they reveal. Truly, He likes not the proud.

Transliteration

22. Ilahukum ilahun wahidun faallatheena la yu/minoona bial-akhirati quloobuhum munkiratun wahum mustakbiroona   23. La jarama anna Allaha yaAAlamu ma yusirroona wama yuAAlinoona innahu la yuhibbu almustakbireena

Tafsir Ibn Kathir

None is to be worshipped except Allah

Allah tells us that there is none to be worshipped besides Him, the One, the Unique, the Lone, the Self-Sufficient. He tells us that the hearts of the disbelievers deny that and are astonished by that:

("Has he made the gods (all) into One God! Verily, this is a curious thing!") (38:5).

(And when Allah alone is mentioned, the hearts of those who do not believe in the Hereafter are filled with disgust, and when those besides Him are mentioned, behold, they rejoice!) (39:45).

(and they are proud) meaning they are too proud to worship Allah, and their hearts reject the idea of singling Him out, as Allah says:

(Verily! Those who scorn My worship they will surely enter Hell in humiliation!) (40:60) So here, Allah says;

(Certainly), meaning truly,

(Allah knows what they conceal and what they reveal.) meaning He will requite them for that in full.

(Truly, He does not like the proud.)

Surah: 16 Ayah: 24 & Ayah: 25

﴿ وَإِذَا قِيلَ لَهُم مَّاذَآ أَنزَلَ رَبُّكُمْ قَالُوٓاْ أَسَٰطِيرُ ٱلْأَوَّلِينَ ۝ ﴾

24. And when it is said to them: "What is it that your Lord has sent down (unto Muhammad (peace be upon him))" They say: "Tales of the men of old!"

﴿ لِيَحْمِلُوٓاْ أَوْزَارَهُمْ كَامِلَةً يَوْمَ ٱلْقِيَٰمَةِ وَمِنْ أَوْزَارِ ٱلَّذِينَ يُضِلُّونَهُم بِغَيْرِ عِلْمٍ أَلَا سَآءَ مَا يَزِرُونَ ۝ ﴾

25. They may bear their own burdens in full on the Day of Resurrection, and also of the burdens of those whom they misled without knowledge. Evil indeed is that which they shall bear!

Transliteration

24. Wa-itha qeela lahum matha anzala rabbukum qaloo asateeru al-awwaleena 25. Liyahmiloo awzarahum kamilatan yawma alqiyamati wamin awzari allatheena yudilloonahum bighayri AAilmin ala saa ma yaziroona

Tafsir Ibn Kathir

The Destruction of the Disbelievers and Intensification of their Punishment for rejecting the Revelation

Allah informs us that when it is said to those liars,

("What is it that your Lord has revealed" They say,) not wanting to answer,

("Tales of the men of old!") meaning nothing is revealed to him, what he is reciting to us is just tales of the men of old, taken from the previous Books. As Allah says,

(And they say: "Tales of the ancients, which he has written down, and they are dictated to him morning and afternoon.") (25:5) i.e., they tell lies against the Messenger and say things contradicting one another, but all of it is false, as Allah says,

(Look at the parables they make of you, so they have gone astray, and they are not able to find the right way.)(17:48) Once they have gone beyond the bounds of the truth, whatever they say will be in error. They used to say that he (the Prophet) was a sorcerer, a poet, a soothsayer, or a madman, then they settled on an idea proposed by their leader, an individual known as Al-Walid bin Al-Mughirah Al-Makhzumi, when:

(He thought, and plotted. So let him be cursed, how he plotted! And once more let him be cursed, how he plotted! Then he thought. Then he frowned and he looked in a bad tempered way; then he turned back, and was proud. Then he said: "This is nothing but the magic of old.") (74:18-24) meaning something that had been transmitted and passed down. So they dispersed having agreed on this opinion, may Allah punish them.

(They will bear their own burdens in full on the Day of Resurrection, and also of the burdens of those whom they misled without knowledge.) meaning, `We decreed that they would say that, so they will carry the burden of their own sins and some of the burden of those who followed them and agreed with them,' i.e., they will be held guilty not only for going astray themselves, but also for tempting others and having them follow them. As it says in a Hadith:

«مَنْ دَعَا إِلَى هُدًى كَانَ لَهُ مِنَ الْأَجْرِ مِثْلُ أُجُورِ مَنِ اتَّبَعَهُ، لَا يَنْقُصُ ذَلِكَ مِنْ أُجُورِهِمْ شَيْئًا، وَمَنْ دَعَا إِلَى ضَلَالَةٍ كَانَ عَلَيْهِ مِنَ الْإِثْمِ مِثْلُ آثَامِ مَنِ اتَّبَعَهُ، لَا يَنْقُصُ ذَلِكَ مِنْ آثَامِهِمْ شَيْئًا»

(Whoever invites people to guidance, he will receive a reward like that of those who follow him, without diminishing their reward in the least. And whoever invites people to misguidance, he will bear a burden of sin like that of those who follow him, without diminishing their burden in the least.) Allah says;

(They shall bear their own loads, and other loads besides their own; and they shall be questioned about their false allegations on the Day of Resurrection.) (29:13) Al-`Awfi reported from Ibn `Abbas that it is like the Ayah:

(That they may bear their own burdens in full on the Day of Resurrection, and also of the burdens of those whom they misled without knowledge.) (16:25) Allah says,

(They shall bear their own loads, and other loads besides their own) (29:13). Mujahid said: "They will bear the burden of their own sins, and they will bear the sins of those who obeyed them, but that will not lessen the punishment of those who obeyed them at all."

Surah: 16 Ayah: 26 & Ayah: 27

﴿ قَدْ مَكَرَ ٱلَّذِينَ مِن قَبْلِهِمْ فَأَتَى ٱللَّهُ بُنْيَـٰنَهُم مِّنَ ٱلْقَوَاعِدِ فَخَرَّ عَلَيْهِمُ ٱلسَّقْفُ مِن فَوْقِهِمْ وَأَتَىٰهُمُ ٱلْعَذَابُ مِنْ حَيْثُ لَا يَشْعُرُونَ ۝ ﴾

26. Those before them indeed plotted, but Allâh struck at the foundation of their building, and then the roof fell down upon them, from above them, and the torment overtook them from directions they did not perceive.

﴿ ثُمَّ يَوْمَ ٱلْقِيَـٰمَةِ يُخْزِيهِمْ وَيَقُولُ أَيْنَ شُرَكَآءِىَ ٱلَّذِينَ كُنتُمْ تُشَـٰقُّونَ فِيهِمْ قَالَ ٱلَّذِينَ أُوتُوا۟ ٱلْعِلْمَ إِنَّ ٱلْخِزْىَ ٱلْيَوْمَ وَٱلسُّوٓءَ عَلَى ٱلْكَـٰفِرِينَ ۝ ﴾

27. Then, on the Day of Resurrection, He will disgrace them and will say: "Where are My (so called) partners concerning whom you used to disagree and dispute (with the believers, by defying and disobeying Allâh)?" Those who have been given the knowledge (about the Torment of Allâh for the disbelievers) will say: "Verily! Disgrace and misery this Day are upon the disbelievers.

Transliteration

26. Qad makara allatheena min qablihim faata Allahu bunyanahum mina alqawaAAidi fakharra AAalayhimu alssaqfu min fawqihim waatahumu alAAathabu min haythu la yashAAuroona 27. Thumma yawma alqiyamati yukhzeehim wayaqoolu ayna shuraka-iya allatheena kuntum tushaqqoona feehim qala allatheena ootoo alAAilma inna alkhizya alyawma waalssoo-a AAala alkafireena

Tafsir Ibn Kathir

Discussion about what the previous Peoples did, and what was done to Them

(Those before them indeed plotted,) Al-`Awfi reported that Ibn `Abbas said: "This refers to Namrud (Nimrod), who built the tower." Others said that it refers to Bukhtanassar (Nebuchadnezzar). The correct view is that this is said by way of example, to refute what was done by those who disbelieved in Allah and associated others in worship with Him. As Nuh said,

("And they have hatched a mighty scheme.") (71:22) meaning, they used all sorts of ploys to misguide their people, and tempted them to join them in their Shirk via all possible means. On the Day of Resurrection their followers will say to them:

("Nay, but it was your plotting by night and day, when you ordered us to disbelieve in Allah and set up rivals to Him!") (34:33)

(but Allah struck at the foundation of their building.) meaning, He uprooted it and brought their efforts to naught. This is like the Ayah:

(Every time they kindled the fire of war, Allah extinguished it.) (5:64) and

(But Allah's (torment) reached them from a place where they were not expecting it, and He cast terror into their hearts so that they destroyed their own dwellings with their own hands and the hands of the believers. So then take admonition, O you with eyes (to see).) (59:2) Allah says here:

(but Allah struck at the foundation of their building, and then the roof fell down upon them, from above them, and the torment overtook them from directions they did not perceive. Then, on the Day of Resurrection, He will disgrace them) (16:26-27) meaning, He will expose their scandalous deeds and what they used to hide in their hearts, and He will bring it out in the open. As He says,

(The Day when all the secrets will be (exposed and) examined.) (86:9) They will be displayed and made known, as found in the Two Sahihs, where Ibn `Umar reported that the Messenger of Allah said:

«يُنْصَبُ لِكُلِّ غَادِرٍ لِوَاءٌ يَوْمَ الْقِيَامَةِ عِنْدَ اسْتِهِ بِقَدْرِ غَدْرَتِهِ، فَيُقَالُ: هَذِهِ غَدْرَةُ فُلَانِ ابْنِ فُلَان»

(On the Day of Resurrection a banner will be set up by his backside for every deceitful person, (whose size is) in accordance with the amount of his deceit. It be said, "This is the one who deceived so-and-so, the son of so-and-so.") Thus, what they used to plot in secret will be made public. Allah will humiliate them before all of His creation, and the Lord will say to them, in rebuke and reprimand;

(Where are My (so-called) partners, those over which you caused so much discord) meaning, you fought and made enemies for their sake, so where are they now to help and save you

(Can they help you or (even) help themselves) (26:93)

(Then will (man) have no power, nor any helper.) (86:10) When evidence and proof is established against them, and the Word (of Allah) is justified against them, and they will be unable to give any excuse, realizing that escape is impossible, then

(Those who have been given the knowledge will say) who are the leaders in this world and the Hereafter and who know about the truth in this world and the Hereafter - will say,

(Indeed it is a Day of disgrace and misery for the disbelievers.) meaning, today those who disbelieved in Allah and worshipped others who have no power either to benefit or to harm them are now surrounded by disgrace and punishment.

Surah: 16 Ayah: 28 & Ayah: 29

﴿ ٱلَّذِينَ تَتَوَفَّىٰهُمُ ٱلْمَلَـٰٓئِكَةُ ظَالِمِىٓ أَنفُسِهِمْ ۖ فَأَلْقَوُا۟ ٱلسَّلَمَ مَا كُنَّا نَعْمَلُ مِن سُوٓءٍ ۚ بَلَىٰٓ إِنَّ ٱللَّهَ عَلِيمٌۢ بِمَا كُنتُمْ تَعْمَلُونَ ﴿٢٨﴾ ﴾

28. "Those whose lives the angels take while they are doing wrong to themselves (by disbelief and by associating partners in worship with Allâh and by committing all kinds of crimes and evil deeds)." Then, they will make (false) submission (saying): "We used not to do any evil." (The angels will reply): "Yes! Truly, Allâh is All-Knower of what you used to do.

﴿ فَٱدْخُلُوٓا۟ أَبْوَٰبَ جَهَنَّمَ خَـٰلِدِينَ فِيهَا ۖ فَلَبِئْسَ مَثْوَى ٱلْمُتَكَبِّرِينَ ﴿٢٩﴾ ﴾

29. "So enter the gates of Hell, to abide therein, and indeed, what an evil abode will be for the arrogant."

Transliteration

28. Allatheena tatawaffahumu almala-ikatu thalimee anfusihim faalqawoo alssalama ma kunna naAAmalu min soo-in bala inna Allaha AAaleemun bima kuntum taAAmaloona 29. Faodkhuloo abwaba jahannama khalideena feeha falabi/sa mathwa almutakabbireena

Tafsir Ibn Kathir

The Condition of the Disbeliever during and after Death

Allah informs us of the state of the idolators who are doing wrong to themselves when death approaches and the angels come to seize their evil souls.

(Then, they will (falsely) submit) meaning, they will make it appear as if they used to listen and obey by saying,

(We did not do any evil.) Similarly, on the Day of Resurrection, they will say,

(By Allah, our Lord, we were not idolators.) (6:23)

(On the Day when Allah will resurrect them all together; then they will swear to Him as they swear to you.) (58:18) Allah says, rejecting what they say,

("Yes! Truly, Allah is Most Knowing of what you did. So enter the gates of Hell, to abide therein, and indeed, what an evil abode there is for the arrogant.") (16:28-29), meaning, a miserable position in the abode of humiliation for those who were too arrogant to pay attention to the signs of Allah and follow His Messengers. They will enter Hell from the day they die with their souls, and their bodies will feel the heat and hot winds of their graves. When the Day of Resurrection comes, their souls will be reunited with their bodies, to abide forever in the fire of Hell, and

(It will not be complete enough to kill them nor shall its torment be lightened for them.) (35:36) As Allah says,

(The Fire, they are exposed to it morning and afternoon. And on the Day when the Hour will be established (it will be said to the angels): "Cause Fir'awn's people to enter the severest torment!") (40:46).

Surah: 16 Ayah: 30, Ayah: 31 & Ayah: 32

﴿ ۞ وَقِيلَ لِلَّذِينَ ٱتَّقَوْاْ مَاذَآ أَنزَلَ رَبُّكُمْ ۚ قَالُواْ خَيْرًا ۗ لِّلَّذِينَ أَحْسَنُواْ فِى هَـٰذِهِ ٱلدُّنْيَا حَسَنَةٌ ۚ وَلَدَارُ ٱلْأَخِرَةِ خَيْرٌ ۚ وَلَنِعْمَ دَارُ ٱلْمُتَّقِينَ ۝ ﴾

30. And (when) it is said to those who are the Muttaqûn (pious - see V.2:2) "What is it that your Lord has sent down?" They say: "That which is good." For those who do good in this world, there is good, and the home of the Hereafter will be better. And excellent indeed will be the home (i.e. Paradise) of the Muttaqûn (the pious - see V.2:2).

﴿ جَنَّـٰتُ عَدْنٍ يَدْخُلُونَهَا تَجْرِى مِن تَحْتِهَا ٱلْأَنْهَـٰرُ ۖ لَهُمْ فِيهَا مَا يَشَآءُونَ ۚ كَذَٰلِكَ يَجْزِى ٱللَّهُ ٱلْمُتَّقِينَ ۝ ﴾

31. 'Adn (Eden) Paradise (Gardens of Eternity) which they will enter, under which rivers flow, they will have therein all that they wish. Thus Allâh rewards the Muttaqûn (pious - see V.2:2).

﴿ ٱلَّذِينَ تَتَوَفَّىٰهُمُ ٱلْمَلَـٰٓئِكَةُ طَيِّبِينَ ۙ يَقُولُونَ سَلَـٰمٌ عَلَيْكُمُ ٱدْخُلُواْ ٱلْجَنَّةَ بِمَا كُنتُمْ تَعْمَلُونَ ۝ ﴾

32. Those whose lives the angels take while they are in a pious state (i.e. pure from all evil, and worshipping none but Allâh Alone) saying (to them): Salâmun 'Alaikum (peace be on you) enter you Paradise, because of (the good) which you used to do (in the world)."

Transliteration

30. Waqeela lillatheena ittaqaw matha anzala rabbukum qaloo khayran lillatheena ahsanoo fee hathihi alddunya hasanatun waladaru al-akhirati khayrun walaniAAma daru almuttaqeena 31. Jannatu AAadnin yadkhuloonaha tajree min tahtiha al-anharu lahum feeha ma yashaoona kathalika yajzee Allahu almuttaqeena 32. Allatheena tatawaffahumu almala-ikatu tayyibeena yaqooloona salamun AAalaykumu odkhuloo aljannata bima kuntum taAAmaloona

Tafsir Ibn Kathir

What the Pious say about the Revelation, their Reward and their Condition during and after Death

Here we are told about the blessed, as opposed to the doomed, who, when they are asked,

(What is it that your Lord has revealed) they will reluctantly answer, "He did not reveal anything, these are just the fables of old." But the blessed, on the other hand, will say, "That which is good," meaning - He revealed something good, meaning mercy and blessings for those who followed it and believed in it. Then we are told about Allah's promise to His servants which He revealed to His Messengers. He says:

(For those who do good in this world, there is good) This is like the Ayah,

(Whoever works righteousness - whether male or female - while being a true believer verily, to him We will give a good life, and We shall certainly reward them in proportion to the best of what they used to do.) (16:97), which means that whoever does good in this world, Allah will reward him for his good deeds in this world and in the next. Then we are told that the home of the Hereafter will be better, i.e., better than the life of this world, and that the reward in the Hereafter will be more complete than the reward in this life, as Allah says,

(But those who were given (religious) knowledge said: "Woe to you! The reward of Allah (in the Hereafter) is better) (28:80) and,

(and what is with Allah for the righteous is better.) (3:198) and;

(Although the Hereafter is better and enduring) (87:17). Allah said to His Messenger :

(And indeed the Hereafter is better for you than the present) (93:4). Then Allah describes the abode of the Hereafter, saying,

(And excellent indeed will be the home (i.e. Paradise) of those who have Taqwa.)

(`Adn (Eden) Paradise (Gardens of Eternity)) refers to the home of the Muttaqun, i.e., in the Hereafter they will have Gardens of Eternity in which they will dwell forever.

(under which rivers flow) meaning, between its trees and palaces.

(in it they will have all that they wish) this is like the Ayah:

(in it (there will be) all that souls could desire, and all that eyes could delight in, and in it you will live forever.) (43:71)

(Thus Allah rewards those who have Taqwa.) meaning, this is how Allah rewards everyone who believes in Him, fears Him, and does good deeds. Then Allah tells us about their condition when death approaches them in a good state, i.e., free from Shirk, impurity and all evil. The angels greet them and give them the good news of Paradise, as Allah says:

(Verily, those who say: "Our Lord is Allah (alone)," and then behave righteously, on them the angels will descend (at the time of their death) (saying): "Fear not, nor grieve! But receive the good news of Paradise as you have been promised! We have been your friends in the life of this world and are (so) in the Hereafter. In it you shall have (all) that your souls desire, and in it you shall have (all) that you ask for. An entertainment from (Allah), the Oft-Forgiving, Most Merciful.")(41:30:32) We have already referred to the Hadiths that have been reported on the taking of the soul of the believer and the soul of the disbeliever, when we discussed the Ayah,

(Allah will keep firm those who believe, with the word that stands firm in this world (i.e. they will keep on worshipping Allah Alone and none else), and in the Hereafter. And Allah will cause the wrongdoers to stray, and Allah does as He wills.) (14:27)

Surah: 16 Ayah: 33 & Ayah: 34

﴿ هَلْ يَنظُرُونَ إِلَّا أَن تَأْتِيَهُمُ ٱلْمَلَـٰٓئِكَةُ أَوْ يَأْتِىَ أَمْرُ رَبِّكَ ۚ كَذَٰلِكَ فَعَلَ ٱلَّذِينَ مِن قَبْلِهِمْ ۚ وَمَا ظَلَمَهُمُ ٱللَّهُ وَلَـٰكِن كَانُوٓا۟ أَنفُسَهُمْ يَظْلِمُونَ ۝ ﴾

33. Do they (the disbelievers and polytheists) await but that the angels should come to them (to take away their souls (at death)) or there should come the command (i.e. the torment or the Day of Resurrection) of your Lord? Thus did those before them. And Allâh wronged them not, but they used to wrong themselves.

﴿ فَأَصَابَهُمْ سَيِّـَٔاتُ مَا عَمِلُوا۟ وَحَاقَ بِهِم مَّا كَانُوا۟ بِهِۦ يَسْتَهْزِءُونَ ۝ ﴾

34. Then, the evil results of their deeds overtook them, and that at which they used to mock at surrounded them.

Transliteration

33. Hal yanthuroona illa an ta/tiyahumu almala-ikatu aw ya/tiya amru rabbika kathalika faAAala allatheena min qablihim wama thalamahumu Allahu walakin kanoo anfusahum yathlimoona 34. Faasabahum sayyi-atu ma AAamiloo wahaqa bihim ma kanoo bihi yastahzi-oona

Tafsir Ibn Kathir

The Disbelievers' Refrain from Faith means that They were simply awaiting Punishment

Threatening the idolators for their persistence in falsehood and their conceited delusions about this world, Allah says: Are these people waiting only for the angels to come and take their souls Qatadah said: (Or there comes the command of your Lord) means the Day of Resurrection and the terror that they will go through."

(Thus did those before them.) means, thus did their predecessors and those who were like them among the idolators persist in their Shirk, until they tasted the wrath of Allah and experienced the punishment and torment that they suffered.

(And Allah did not wrong them.) because by sending His Messengers and revealing His Books He gave them enough warning and clearly demonstrated His proofs to them.

(but they were wronging themselves.) meaning, by opposing the Messengers and denying what they brought. For this reason Allah's punishment tormented them. (they were surrounded) meaning, they were overwhelmed by the painful torment.

(by that which they used to mock.) meaning, they used to make fun of the Messengers when they warned them Allah's punishment, and for this it will be said to them on the Day of Resurrection:

(This is the Fire which you used to belie.) (52:14).

Surah: 16 Ayah: 35, Ayah: 36 & Ayah: 37

﴿ وَقَالَ ٱلَّذِينَ أَشْرَكُوا۟ لَوْ شَآءَ ٱللَّهُ مَا عَبَدْنَا مِن دُونِهِۦ مِن شَىْءٍ نَّحْنُ وَلَآ ءَابَآؤُنَا وَلَا حَرَّمْنَا مِن دُونِهِۦ مِن شَىْءٍ ۚ كَذَٰلِكَ فَعَلَ ٱلَّذِينَ مِن قَبْلِهِمْ ۚ فَهَلْ عَلَى ٱلرُّسُلِ إِلَّا ٱلْبَلَٰغُ ٱلْمُبِينُ ﴿٣٥﴾

35. And those who joined others in worship with Allâh said: "If Allâh had so willed, neither we nor our fathers would have worshipped aught but Him, nor would we have forbidden anything without (Command from) Him." So did those before them. Then! Are the Messengers charged with anything but to convey clearly the Message?

﴿ وَلَقَدْ بَعَثْنَا فِى كُلِّ أُمَّةٍ رَّسُولًا أَنِ ٱعْبُدُوا۟ ٱللَّهَ وَٱجْتَنِبُوا۟ ٱلطَّٰغُوتَ ۖ فَمِنْهُم مَّنْ هَدَى ٱللَّهُ وَمِنْهُم مَّنْ حَقَّتْ عَلَيْهِ ٱلضَّلَٰلَةُ ۚ فَسِيرُوا۟ فِى ٱلْأَرْضِ فَٱنظُرُوا۟ كَيْفَ كَانَ عَٰقِبَةُ ٱلْمُكَذِّبِينَ ﴿٣٦﴾

36. And verily, We have sent among every Ummah (community, nation) a Messenger (proclaiming): "Worship Allâh (Alone), and avoid (or keep away from) Tâghût (all false deities, etc. i.e. do not worship Tâghût besides Allâh)." Then of them were some whom Allâh guided and of them were some upon whom the straying was justified. So travel through the land and see what was the end of those who denied (the truth).

﴿ إِن تَحْرِصْ عَلَىٰ هُدَىٰهُمْ فَإِنَّ ٱللَّهَ لَا يَهْدِى مَن يُضِلُّ ۖ وَمَا لَهُم مِّن نَّٰصِرِينَ ﴿٣٧﴾

37. If you (O Muhammad (peace be upon him)) covet for their guidance, then verily Allâh guides not those whom He makes to go astray (or none can guide him whom Allâh sends astray). And they will have no helpers.

Transliteration

35. Waqala allatheena ashrakoo law shaa Allahu ma AAabadna min doonihi min shay-in nahnu wala abaona wala harramna min doonihi min shay-in kathalika faAAala allatheena min qablihim fahal AAala alrrusuli illa albalaghu almubeenu 36. Walaqad baAAathna fee kulli ommatin rasoolan ani oAAbudoo Allaha waijtaniboo alttaghoota faminhum man hada Allahu waminhum man haqqat AAalayhi alddalalatu faseeroo fee al-ardi faonthuroo kayfa kana AAaqibatu almukaththibeena 37. In tahris AAala hudahum fa-inna Allaha la yahdee man yudillu wama lahum min nasireena

Tafsir Ibn Kathir

The Idolators Argument that their Shirk was Divinely decreed, and the Refutation of this Claim

Allah tells us about the idolators delusion over their Shirk, and the excuse they claimed for it based on the idea that it is ordained by divine decree. He says:

((They say:) "If Allah had so willed, neither we nor our fathers would have worshipped any but Him, nor would we have forbidden anything without (a command from) Him.") They had superstitious customs dealing with certain animals, e.g. the Bahirah the Sa'ibah and the Wasilah and other things that they had invented and innovated by themselves, with no revealed authority. The essence of what they said was: "If Allah hated what we did, He would have stopped it by punishing us, and He would not have enabled us to do it." Rejecting their confusing ideas, Allah says:

(Are the Messengers charged with anything but to clearly convey the Message) meaning, the matter is not as you claim. It is not the case that Allah did not rebuke your behavior; rather, He did rebuke you, and in the strongest possible terms, and He emphatically forbade you from such behavior. To every nation - that is, to every generation, to every community of people - He sent a Messenger. All of the Messengers called their people to worship Allah (Alone) as well as forbidding them from worshipping anything or anybody except Him.

(Worship Allah (Alone), and shun the Taghut (all false deities).) Allah continued sending Messengers to mankind with this Message, from the first incidence of Shirk that appeared among the Children of Adam, in the people to whom Nuh was sent - the first Messenger sent by Allah to the people of this earth - until He sent the final Messenger, Muhammad , whose call was addressed to both men and Jinn, in the east and in the west. All of the Messengers brought the same Message, as Allah says:

(And We did not send any Messenger before you (O Muhammad) but We revealed to him (saying): None has the right to be worshipped but I (Allah), so worship Me (alone and none else).") (21:25)

(And ask (O Muhammad) those Messengers of Ours whom We sent before you: "Did We ever appointed to be worshipped besides the Most Gracious (Allah)") (43:45) And in this Ayah, Allah says:

(And We have indeed sent a Messenger to every Ummah (community, nation) (saying): "Worship Allah (alone), and shun the Taghut (all false deities).") So how could any of the idolators say,

(If Allah had so willed, we would not have worshipped any but Him,) The legislative will of Allah is clear and cannot be taken as an excuse by them, because He had forbidden them to do that upon the tongue of His Messengers, but by His universal will (i.e., by which He allows things to occur even though they do not please Him) He allowed them to do that as it was decreed for them. So there is no argument in that for them. Allah created Hell and its people both the Shayatin (devils) and disbelievers, but He does not like His servants to disbelieve. And this point constitutes the strongest proof and the most unquestionable wisdom. Then Allah informs us that He rebuked them with punishment in this world, after the Messengers issued their warning, thus He says:

(Then among them were some whom Allah guided, and among them were some who deserved to be left to stray. So travel through the land and see the end of those who denied (the truth).) This means: ask about what happened to those who went against the Messengers and rejected the truth, see how:

(Allah destroyed them completely, and a similar (end awaits) the disbelievers.) (47:10) and,

(And indeed those before them belied (the Messengers of Allah), so then how terrible was My denial (punishment)) (67:18) Then Allah told His Messenger that his eagerness to guide them will be of no benefit to them if Allah wills that they should be misguided, as He says:

(And for whoever Allah wills to try with error, you can do nothing for him against Allah) (5:41). Nuh said to his people:

("And my advice will not profit you, even if I wish to give you good counsel, if Allah's will is to keep you astray.")(11:34). In this Ayah, Allah says:

((Even) if you desire that they be guided, then verily, Allah does not guide those whom He allowed to stray,) As Allah says:

(Whomsoever Allah allows to stray, then there is no guide for him; and He lets them wander blindly in their transgressions.) (7:186)

(Truly! Those deserving the Word (wrath) of your Lord will not believe, even if every sign should come to them - until they see the painful torment) (10:96-97).

(then verily, Allah) meaning, this is the way in which Allah does things. If He wills a thing, then it happens, and if He does not will a thing, then it does not happen. For this reason Allah says:

(Allah does not guide those whom He allowed to stray,) meaning the one whom He has caused to go astray, so who can guide him apart from Allah. No one.

(And they will have no helpers.) means, they will have no one to save them from the punishment of Allah,

(Surely, His is the creation and commandment. Blessed is Allah, the Lord of all that exists!) (7:54).

Surah: 16 Ayah: 38, Ayah: 39 & Ayah: 40

﴿ وَأَقْسَمُواْ بِٱللَّهِ جَهْدَ أَيْمَـٰنِهِمْ لَا يَبْعَثُ ٱللَّهُ مَن يَمُوتُ بَلَىٰ وَعْدًا عَلَيْهِ حَقًّا وَلَـٰكِنَّ أَكْثَرَ ٱلنَّاسِ لَا يَعْلَمُونَ ﴾

38. And they swear by Allâh their strongest oaths, that Allâh will not raise up him who dies. Yes, (He will raise them up), - a promise (binding) upon Him in truth, but most of mankind know not.

﴿ لِيُبَيِّنَ لَهُمُ ٱلَّذِى يَخْتَلِفُونَ فِيهِ وَلِيَعْلَمَ ٱلَّذِينَ كَفَرُوٓاْ أَنَّهُمْ كَانُواْ كَـٰذِبِينَ ﴾

39. In order that He may make manifest to them the truth of that wherein they differ, and that those who disbelieved (in Resurrection, and in the Oneness of Allâh) may know that they were liars.

﴿ إِنَّمَا قَوْلُنَا لِشَىْءٍ إِذَآ أَرَدْنَـٰهُ أَن نَّقُولَ لَهُ كُن فَيَكُونُ ﴾

40. Verily! Our Word unto a thing when We intend it, is only that We say unto it: "Be!" - and it is.

Transliteration

38. Waaqsamoo biAllahi jahda aymanihim la yabAAathu Allahu man yamootu bala waAAdan AAalayhi haqqan walakinna akthara alnnasi la yaAAlamoona   39. Liyubayyina lahumu allathee yakhtalifoona feehi waliyaAAlama allatheena kafaroo annahum kanoo kathibeena   40. Innama qawluna lishay-in itha aradnahu an naqoola lahu kun fayakoonu

Tafsir Ibn Kathir

The Resurrection after Death is true, there is Wisdom behind it, and it is easy for Allah

Allah tells us that the idolators swore by Allah their strongest oaths, meaning that they made oaths swore fervently that Allah would not resurrect the one who died. They considered that to be improbable, and did not believe the Messengers when they told them about that, swearing that it could not happen. Allah said, refuting them:

(Yes), meaning it will indeed happen,

(a promise (binding) upon Him in truth,) - meaning it is inevitable, (but most of mankind know not.) means, because of their ignorance they oppose the Messengers and fall into disbelief. Then Allah mentions His wisdom and the reason why He will resurrect mankind physically on the Day of Calling (between the people of Fire and of Paradise). He says,

(In order that He may make clear to them) means, to mankind,

(what they differed over,) means, every dispute.

(that He may requite those who do evil with that which they have done (i. e. punish them in Hell), and reward those who do good, with what is best (i.e. Paradise).) (53:31)

(and so that those who disbelieved may know that they were liars.) meaning that they lied in their oaths and their swearing that Allah would not resurrect those who die. Thus they will be pushed down by force to the Fire with horrible force on the Day of Resurrection, and the guards of Hell will say to them:

(This is the Fire which you used to belie. Is this magic or do you not see. Taste its heat, and whether you are tolerant of it or intolerant of it - it is all the same. You are only being requited for what you have done.) (52:14-16). Then Allah tells us about His ability to do whatever He wills, and that nothing is impossible for Him on earth or in heaven. When He wants a thing, all He has to do is say to it "Be!" and it is. The Resurrection is one such thing, when He wants it to happen, all He will have to do is issue the command once, and it will happen as He wills, as He says:

(And Our commandment is but one as the twinkling of an eye) (54:50) and,

(The creation of you all and the resurrection of you all are only as (the creation and resurrection of) a single person.) (31:28) And in this Ayah, Allah says:

(Verily, Our Word to a thing when We intend it, is only that We say to it: "Be!" - and it is.) meaning, We issue the command once, and then it happens. Allah does not need to repeat or confirm whatever He commands, because there is nothing that can stop Him or oppose Him. He is the One, the Compelling, the Almighty, whose power, might and dominion have subjected all things. None has the right to be worshipped except Him, and there is no Lord other than Him.

Surah: 16 Ayah: 41 & Ayah: 42

﴿ وَٱلَّذِينَ هَاجَرُواْ فِى ٱللَّهِ مِنۢ بَعْدِ مَا ظُلِمُواْ لَنُبَوِّئَنَّهُمْ فِى ٱلدُّنْيَا حَسَنَةً وَلَأَجْرُ ٱلْأَخِرَةِ أَكْبَرُ لَوْ كَانُواْ يَعْلَمُونَ ۝ ﴾

41. And as for those who emigrated for the Cause of Allâh, after they had been wronged, We will certainly give them goodly residence in this world, but indeed the reward of the Hereafter will be greater; if they but knew!

$$\text{﴿ ٱلَّذِينَ صَبَرُوا۟ وَعَلَىٰ رَبِّهِمْ يَتَوَكَّلُونَ ۝ ﴾}$$

42. (They are) those who remained patient (in this world for Allâh's sake), and put their trust in their Lord (Allâh Alone).

Transliteration

41. Waallatheena hajaroo fee Allahi min baAAdi ma thulimoo lanubawwi-annahum fee alddunya hasanatan walaajru al-akhirati akbaru law kanoo yaAAlamoona 42. Allatheena sabaroo waAAala rabbihim yatawakkaloona

Tafsir Ibn Kathir

The Reward of the Muhajirin

Allah tells us about the reward of those who migrated for His sake, seeking His pleasure, those who left their homeland behind, brothers and friends, hoping for the reward of Allah. This may have been revealed concerning those who migrated to Ethiopia, those whose persecution at the hands of their own people in Makkah was so extreme that they left them and went to Ethiopia so that they would be able to worship their Lord. Among the most prominent of these migrants were `Uthman bin `Affan and his wife Ruqayyah, the daughter of the Messenger of Allah , Ja`far bin Abi Talib, the cousin of the Messenger , and Abu Salamah bin `Abdul-Asad, among a group of almost eighty sincere and faithful men and women, may Allah be pleased with them. Allah promised them a great reward in this world and the next. Allah said:

(We will certainly give them good residence in this world,) Ibn `Abbas, Ash-Sha`bi and Qatadah said: (this means) "Al-Madinah." It was also said that it meant "good provision". This was the opinion of Mujahid. There is no contradiction between these two opinions, for they left their homes and wealth, but Allah compensated them with something better in this world. Whoever gives up something for the sake of Allah, Allah compensates him with something that is better for him than that, and this is what happened. He gave them power throughout the land and caused them to rule over the people, so they became governors and rulers, and each of them became a leader of the pious. Allah tells us that His reward for the Muhajirin in the Hereafter is greater than that which He gave them in this world, as He says:

(but indeed the reward of the Hereafter will be greater) meaning, greater than that which We have given you in this world.

(if they but knew!) means, if those who stayed behind and did not migrate with them only knew what Allah prepared for those who obeyed Him and followed His Messenger . Then Allah describes them as:

(those who remained patient, and put their trust in their Lord.) (16:42), meaning, they bore their people's persecution with patience, putting their trust in Allah Who made their end good in this world and the Hereafter.

Chapter 16: An-Nahl (The Bee), Verses 001-128

Surah: 16 Ayah: 43 & Ayah: 44

﴿ وَمَآ أَرْسَلْنَا مِن قَبْلِكَ إِلَّا رِجَالًا نُّوحِىٓ إِلَيْهِمْ ۚ فَسْـَٔلُوٓاْ أَهْلَ ٱلذِّكْرِ إِن كُنتُمْ لَا تَعْلَمُونَ ﴾

43. And We sent not (as Our Messengers) before you (O Muhammad (peace be upon him)) any but men, whom We inspired, (to preach and invite mankind to believe in the Oneness of Allâh). So ask (you, O pagans of Makkah) of those who know the Scripture (learned men of the Taurât (Torah) and the Injeel (Gospel)) if you know not.

﴿ بِٱلْبَيِّنَـٰتِ وَٱلزُّبُرِ ۗ وَأَنزَلْنَآ إِلَيْكَ ٱلذِّكْرَ لِتُبَيِّنَ لِلنَّاسِ مَا نُزِّلَ إِلَيْهِمْ وَلَعَلَّهُمْ يَتَفَكَّرُونَ ﴾

44. With clear signs and Books (We sent the Messengers). And We have also sent down unto you (O Muhammad (peace be upon him)) the Dhikr (reminder and the advice (i.e. the Qur'ân)) that you may explain clearly to men what is sent down to them, and that they may give thought.

Transliteration

43. Wama arsalna min qablika illa rijalan noohee ilayhim fais-aloo ahla aththikri in kuntum la taAAlamoona   44. Bialbayyinati waalzzuburi waanzalna ilayka aththikra litubayyina lilnnasi ma nuzzila ilayhim walaAAallahum yatafakkaroona

Tafsir Ibn Kathir

Only Human Messengers have been Sent

Ad-Dahhak said, reporting from Ibn `Abbas: "When Allah sent Muhammad as a Messenger, the Arabs, or some of them, denied him and said, `Allah is too great to send a human being as a Messenger.' Then Allah revealed:

(Is it a wonder to people that We have sent Our Inspiration to a man from among themselves (saying): "Warn mankind...") and He said,

(And We sent not (as Our Messengers) before you (O Muhammad) any but men, whom We sent Revelation. So ask Ahl Adh-Dhikr, if you know not.). meaning, (ask) the people of the previous Books, were the Messengers that were sent to them humans or angels If they were angels, then you have the right to find this strange, but if they were human, then you have no grounds to deny that Muhammad is a Messenger. Allah says:

(And We sent not before you (as Messengers) any but men to whom We revealed, from among the people of townships.) (12:109) and not from among the people of heaven as you say." It was reported by Mujahid from Ibn `Abbas that what is meant by Ahl Adh-Dhikr is the People of the Book. This is as Allah says:

(Say: "Glorified be my Lord! Am I anything but a man, sent as a Messenger" And nothing prevented men from believing when the guidance came to them, except that they said: "Has Allah sent a man as (His) Messenger") (17:93-94)

(And We never sent before you (O Muhammad) any of the Messengers but verily, they ate food and walked in the markets.) (25:20)

(And We did not create them (the Messengers, with) bodies that did not eat food, nor were they immortals.)(21:8)

(Say (O Muhammad): "I am not a new thing among the Messengers. ") (46:9),

(Say (O Muhammad): "I am only a man like you. It has been revealed to me.") (18:110) Then Allah informs those who doubt that a Messenger can be a human to ask those who have knowledge of the previous Scriptures about the Prophets who came before: were their Prophets humans or angels Then Allah mentions that He has sent them,

(with clear signs), meaning proof and evidence, and

(and Books (Zubur)), meaning Scriptures. Ibn `Abbas, Mujahid, Ad-Dahhak and others said: Zubur is the plural of Zabur, and the Arabs say, Zaburtul-Kitab meaning, "I wrote the book." Allah says:

(And everything they have done is noted in (their) Records (of deeds) (Zubur)) (54:52)

(And indeed We have written in Az-Zabur after the Dhikr that My righteous servant shall inherit the land (i.e. the land of Paradise).) (21:105) Then Allah says:

(And We have also revealed the Dhikr to you), meaning the Qur'an,

(so that you may clearly explain to men what was revealed to them,) meaning, sent down from their Lord, because you know the meaning of what Allah has revealed to you, and because of your understanding and adherence to it, and because We know that you are the best of creation and the leader of the Children of Adam. So that you may explain in detail what has been mentioned in brief, and explain what is not clear.

(so that perhaps they may reflect.) meaning, they should examine themselves and be guided by it, so that they may attain the victory of salvation in this world and the next.

Surah: 16 Ayah: 45, Ayah: 46 & Ayah: 47

﴿ أَفَأَمِنَ ٱلَّذِينَ مَكَرُواْ ٱلسَّيِّـَٔاتِ أَن يَخْسِفَ ٱللَّهُ بِهِمُ ٱلْأَرْضَ أَوْ يَأْتِيَهُمُ ٱلْعَذَابُ مِنْ حَيْثُ لَا يَشْعُرُونَ ﴿٤٥﴾ ﴾

45. Do then those who devise evil plots feel secure that Allâh will not sink them into the earth, or that the torment will not seize them from directions they perceive not?

﴿ أَوَيَأْخُذَهُمْ فِي تَقَلُّبِهِمْ فَمَا هُم بِمُعْجِزِينَ ۝ ﴾

46. Or that He may catch them in the midst of their going to and fro (in their jobs), so that there be no escape for them (from Allâh's punishment)?

﴿ أَوَيَأْخُذَهُمْ عَلَىٰ تَخَوُّفٍ فَإِنَّ رَبَّكُمْ لَرَءُوفٌ رَّحِيمٌ ۝ ﴾

47. Or that He may catch them with gradual wasting (of their wealth and health). Truly! Your Lord is indeed full of Kindness, Most Merciful?

Transliteration

45. Afaamina allatheena makaroo alssayyi-ati an yakhsifa Allahu bihimu al-arda aw ya/tiyahumu alAAathabu min haythu la yashAAuroona   46. Aw ya/khuthahum fee taqallubihim fama hum bimuAAjizeena   47. Aw ya/khuthahum AAala takhawwufin fa-inna rabbakum laraoofun raheemun

Tafsir Ibn Kathir

How the Guilty can feel Secure

Allah informs us about His patience, and how He delays the punishment for the sinners who do evil things and call others to do likewise, plotting to call others to do evil - even though He is able to make the earth swallow them or to bring His wrath upon them.

(from where they do not perceive it), meaning in such a way that they do not know where it comes from. As Allah says:

(Do you feel secure that He Who is over the heaven (Allah), will not cause you to sink into the earth, when it quakes Or do you feel secure that He Who is over the heaven (Allah), will not send a storm of stones upon you Then you shall know how My warning really is.) (67:16-17).

(Or that He may punish them in the midst of their going to and fro) meaning, when they are busy with their daily business, travel, and other distracting activities. Qatadah and As-Suddi said:

(Their going to and fro) means their journeys." As Allah says:

(Did the people of the towns feel secure against the coming of Our punishment by night while they were asleep Or, did the people of the towns feel secure against the coming of Our punishment in the forenoon while they were playing) (7:97-98)

(so that there be no escape for them (from Allah's punishment)) meaning, it is not impossible for Allah, no matter what their situation.

(Or that He may punish them where they fear it most) meaning, or Allah will take from them what they most fear, which is even more frightening, because when the thing you most fear to happen does happen, this is even worse. Hence Al-`Awfi reported that Ibn `Abbas said that,

(Or that He may punish them where they fear it most) means that Allah is saying: If I wish, I can take him after the death of his companion and after he has become frightened of that.' This was also reported from Mujahid, Ad-Dahhak, Qatadah and others. Then Allah says:

(Indeed your Lord is full of kindness, Most Merciful.) meaning, because He does not hasten to punish, as was reported in the Two Sahihs:

«لَا أَحَدَ أَصْبَرُ عَلَى أَذًى سَمِعَهُ مِنَ اللهِ، إِنَّهُمْ يَجْعَلُونَ لَهُ وَلَدًا وَهُوَ يَرْزُقُهُمْ وَيُعَافِيهِم»

(No one is more patient in the case of hearing offensive speech than Allah, for they attribute to Him a son, while He (alone) is giving them provision and good health.) And it is also recorded in Two Sahihs,

«إِنَّ اللهَ لَيُمْلِي لِلظَّالِمِ حَتَّى إِذَا أَخَذَهُ لَمْ يُفْلِتْه»

(Allah will let the wrongdoer continue until, when He begins to punish him, He will never let him go.) Then the Messenger of Allah recited:

(وَكَذَلِكَ مِّن قَرْيَةٍ أَمْلَيْتُ لَهَا وَهِيَ ظَـلِمَةٌ ثُمَّ أَخَذْتُهَا وَإِلَيَّ الْمَصِيرُ)

(Such is the punishment of your Lord when He seizes the (population of) towns while they are doing wrong. Indeed, His punishment is painful, (and) severe) (11:102) And Allah says:

(And many a township did I give respite while it was given to wrongdoing. Then I punished it. And to Me is the (final) return (of all).) (22:48)

Surah: 16 Ayah: 48, Ayah: 49 & Ayah: 50

﴿أَوَلَمْ يَرَوْاْ إِلَى مَا خَلَقَ اللَّهُ مِن شَىْءٍ يَتَفَيَّؤُاْ ظِلَـلُهُ عَنِ الْيَمِينِ وَالشَّمَآئِلِ سُجَّدًا لِّلَّهِ وَهُمْ دَاخِرُونَ ۝﴾

48. Have they not observed things that Allâh has created: (how) their shadows incline to the right and to the left, making prostration unto Allâh, and they are lowly?

Chapter 16: An-Nahl (The Bee), Verses 001-128

﴿ وَلِلَّهِ يَسْجُدُ مَا فِى ٱلسَّمَـٰوَٰتِ وَمَا فِى ٱلْأَرْضِ مِن دَآبَّةٍ وَٱلْمَلَـٰٓئِكَةُ وَهُمْ لَا يَسْتَكْبِرُونَ ﴿٤٩﴾ ﴾

49. And to Allâh prostate all that is in the heavens and all that is in the earth, of the moving (living) creatures and the angels, and they are not proud (i.e. they worship their Lord (Allâh) with humility).

﴿ يَخَافُونَ رَبَّهُم مِّن فَوْقِهِمْ وَيَفْعَلُونَ مَا يُؤْمَرُونَ ﴿٥٠﴾ ﴾

50. They fear their Lord above them, and they do what they are commanded.

Transliteration

48. Awa lam yaraw ila ma khalaqa Allahu min shay-in yatafayyao thilaluhu AAani alyameeni waalshshama-ili sujjadan lillahi wahum dakhiroona 49. Walillahi yasjudu ma fee alssamawati wama fee al-ardi min dabbatin waalmala-ikatu wahum la yastakbiroona 50. Yakhafoona rabbahum min fawqihim wayafAAaloona ma yu/maroona

Tafsir Ibn Kathir

Everything prostrates to Allah

Allah informs us about His might, majesty and pride, meaning that all things submit themselves to Him and every created being - animate and inanimate, as well as the responsible - humans and Jinns, and the angels - all humble themselves before Him. He tells us that everything that has a shadow leaning to the right and the left, i.e., in the morning and the evening, is by its shadow, prostrating to Allah. Mujahid said, "When the sun passes its zenith, everything prostrates to Allah, may He be glorified." This was also said by Qatadah, Ad-Dahhak and others.

(while they are humble) means, they are in a state of humility. Mujahid also said: "The prostration of every thing is its shadow", and he mentioned the mountains and said that their prostrations are their shadows. Abu Ghalib Ash-Shaybani said: "The waves of the sea are its prayers". It is as if reason is attributed to these inanimate objects when they are described as prostrating, so Allah says:

(And to Allah prostrate all that are in the heavens and all that are in the earth, of the moving creatures) As Allah says:

(And to Allah (alone) all who are in the heavens and the earth fall in prostration, willingly or unwillingly, and so do their shadows in the mornings and in the afternoons.) (13:15)

(and the angels, and they are not proud.) means, they prostrate to Allah and are not too proud to worship Him.

(They fear their Lord above them) means, they prostrate out of fear of their Lord, may He be glorified.

(and they do what they are commanded.) meaning they continually obey Allah, doing what He tells them to do and avoiding that which He forbids.

Surah: 16 Ayah: 51, Ayah: 52, Ayah: 53, Ayah: 54 & Ayah: 55

﴿ ۞ وَقَالَ ٱللَّهُ لَا تَتَّخِذُوٓاْ إِلَـٰهَيۡنِ ٱثۡنَيۡنِۖ إِنَّمَا هُوَ إِلَـٰهٞ وَٰحِدٞۖ فَإِيَّـٰیَ فَٱرۡهَبُونِ ۝ ﴾

51. And Allâh said (O mankind!): "Take not ilâhain (two gods in worship). Verily, He (Allâh) is (the) only One Ilâh (God). Then, fear Me (Allâh (glorified and exalted be He) much (and Me Alone), i.e. be away from all kinds of sins and evil deeds that Allâh has forbidden and do all that Allâh has ordained and worship none but Allâh).

﴿ وَلَهُۥ مَا فِی ٱلسَّمَـٰوَٰتِ وَٱلۡأَرۡضِ وَلَهُ ٱلدِّينُ وَاصِبًاۚ أَفَغَيۡرَ ٱللَّهِ تَتَّقُونَ ۝ ﴾

52. To Him belongs all that is in the heavens and (all that is in) the earth and Ad-Dîn Wâsiba is His ((i.e. perpetual sincere obedience to Allâh is obligatory). None has the right to be worshipped but Allâh)) Will you then fear any other than Allâh?

﴿ وَمَا بِكُم مِّن نِّعۡمَةٖ فَمِنَ ٱللَّهِۖ ثُمَّ إِذَا مَسَّكُمُ ٱلضُّرُّ فَإِلَيۡهِ تَجۡـَٔرُونَ ۝ ﴾

53. And whatever of blessings and good things you have, it is from Allâh. Then, when harm touches you, unto Him you cry aloud for help.

﴿ ثُمَّ إِذَا كَشَفَ ٱلضُّرَّ عَنكُمۡ إِذَا فَرِيقٞ مِّنكُم بِرَبِّهِمۡ يُشۡرِكُونَ ۝ ﴾

54. Then, when He has removed the harm from you, behold! some of you associate others in worship with their Lord (Allâh).

﴿ لِيَكۡفُرُواْ بِمَآ ءَاتَيۡنَـٰهُمۡۚ فَتَمَتَّعُواْ فَسَوۡفَ تَعۡلَمُونَ ۝ ﴾

55. So (as a result of that) they deny (with ungratefulness) that (Allâh's Favors) which We have bestowed on them! Then enjoy yourselves (your short stay), but you will come to know (with regrets).

Transliteration

51. Waqala Allahu la tattakhithoo ilahayni ithnayni innama huwa ilahun wahidun fa-iyyaya fairhabooni   52. Walahu ma fee alssamawati waal-ardi walahu alddeenu wasiban afaghayra Allahi tattaqoona   53. Wama bikum min niAAmatin famina Allahi thumma itha massakumu alddurru fa-ilayhi taj-aroona   54. Thumma itha kashafa alddurra AAankum itha fareequn minkum birabbihim yushrikoona 55. Liyakfuroo bima ataynahum fatamattaAAoo fasawfa taAAlamoona

Tafsir Ibn Kathir

Allah Alone is Deserving of Worship

Allah tells us that there is no god but He, and that no one else should be worshipped except Him, alone, without partners, for He is the Sovereign, Creator, and Lord of all things.

(His is the religion Wasiba) Ibn `Abbas, Mujahid, `Ikrimah, Maymun bin Mahran, As-Suddi, Qatadah and others said that this means forever. It was also reported that Ibn `Abbas said, "It means obligatory." Mujahid said: "It means purely for Him," i.e., worship is due to Him Alone, from whoever is in the heavens and on earth. As Allah says:

(Do they seek other than the religion of Allah, while to Him submitted all creatures in the heavens and the earth, willingly or unwillingly. And to Him shall they all be returned.) (3:83) This is in accordance with the opinion of Ibn `Abbas and `Ikrimah, which is that this Ayah is merely stating the case. According to the opinion of Mujahid, it is by way of instruction, i.e., it is saying: You had better fear associating partners in worship with Me, and be sincere in your obedience to Me. As Allah says:

(Surely, the pure religion (sincere devotion) is for Allah only.) (39:3) Then Allah tells us that He is the One Who has the power to benefit and harm, and that the provisions, blessings, good health and help, His servants enjoy are from His bounty and graciousness towards them.

(Then, when harm touches you, to Him you cry aloud for help.) meaning because you know that none has the power to remove that harm except for Him, so when you are harmed, you turn to ask Him for help and beg Him for aid. As Allah says:

(And when harm touches you at sea, those that you call upon vanish, except for Him. But when He brings you safe to land, you turn away. And man is ever ungrateful.)(17:67) Here, Allah tells us:

(Then, when He has removed the harm from you, behold! some of you associate others in worship with their Lord (Allah). So they are ungrateful for that which We have given them!) (16:54-55) It was said that the Lam here (translated as "So") is an indicator of sequence, or that it serves an explanatory function, meaning, `We decreed that they would conceal the truth and deny the blessings that Allah has bestowed upon them. He is the One Who bestows blessings and the One Who removes distress.' Then Allah threatens them, saying:

(Then enjoy yourselves) meaning, do what you like and enjoy what you have for a little while.

(but you will soon come to know.) meaning the consequences of that.

Surah: 16 Ayah: 56, Ayah: 57, Ayah: 58, Ayah: 59 & Ayah: 60

﴿ وَيَجْعَلُونَ لِمَا لَا يَعْلَمُونَ نَصِيبًا مِّمَّا رَزَقْنَاهُمْ ۗ تَاللَّهِ لَتُسْأَلُنَّ عَمَّا كُنتُمْ تَفْتَرُونَ ۝ ﴾

56. And they assign a portion of that which We have provided them unto what they know not (false deities). By Allâh, you shall certainly be questioned about (all) that you used to fabricate.

﴿ وَيَجْعَلُونَ لِلَّهِ الْبَنَاتِ سُبْحَانَهُ ۙ وَلَهُم مَّا يَشْتَهُونَ ۝ ﴾

57. And they assign daughters unto Allâh! - Glorified (and Exalted) be He above all that they associate with Him! And unto themselves what they desire;

﴿ وَإِذَا بُشِّرَ أَحَدُهُم بِالْأُنثَىٰ ظَلَّ وَجْهُهُ مُسْوَدًّا وَهُوَ كَظِيمٌ ۝ ﴾

58. And when the news of (the birth of) a female (child) is brought to any of them, his face becomes dark, and he is filled with inward grief!

﴿ يَتَوَارَىٰ مِنَ الْقَوْمِ مِن سُوءِ مَا بُشِّرَ بِهِ ۚ أَيُمْسِكُهُ عَلَىٰ هُونٍ أَمْ يَدُسُّهُ فِي التُّرَابِ ۗ أَلَا سَاءَ مَا يَحْكُمُونَ ۝ ﴾

59. He hides himself from the people because of the evil of that whereof he has been informed. Shall he keep her with dishonor or bury her in the earth? Certainly, evil is their decision.

﴿ لِلَّذِينَ لَا يُؤْمِنُونَ بِالْآخِرَةِ مَثَلُ السَّوْءِ ۖ وَلِلَّهِ الْمَثَلُ الْأَعْلَىٰ ۚ وَهُوَ الْعَزِيزُ الْحَكِيمُ ۝ ﴾

60. For those who believe not in the Hereafter is an evil description, and for Allâh is the highest description. And He is the All-Mighty, the All-Wise.

Transliteration

56. WayajAAaloona lima la yaAAlamoona naseeban mimma razaqnahum taAllahi latusalunna AAamma kuntum taftaroona 57. WayajAAaloona lillahi albanati subhanahu walahum ma yashtahoona 58. Wa-itha bushshira ahaduhum bialontha thalla wajhuhu muswaddan wahuwa katheemun 59. Yatawara mina alqawmi min soo-i ma bushshira bihi ayumsikuhu AAala hoonin am yadussuhu fee altturabi ala saa ma yahkumoona 60. Lillatheena la yu/minoona bial-akhirati mathalu alssaw-i walillahi almathalu al-aAAla wahuwa alAAazeezu alhakeemu

Chapter 16: An-Nahl (The Bee), Verses 001-128

Tafsir Ibn Kathir

Among the Behavior of the Idolators was vowing to Things that Allah had provided for Them to their gods

Allah tells us about some of the heinous deeds of those who used to perform baseless worship of other gods besides Him, such as idols and statues, with no grounds for doing so. They gave their idols a share of that which Allah had provided for them,

(They say: "This is for Allah," according to their claim, "and this is for our partners." But the share of their "partners" is not directed to Allah, while the share of Allah is directed to their "partners"! How evil is that with which they judge) (6:136) That is they assigned a share for their idols as well as Allah, but they gave preference to their gods over Him, so Allah swore by His Almighty Self to question them about these lies and fabrications. He will most certainly call them to account for it and give them the unrelenting punishment in the fire of Hell. So He says,

(By Allah, you shall certainly be questioned about (all) that you used to fabricate.) Then Allah tells us how they used to regard the angels, who are servants of the Most Merciful, as being female, and that they considered them to be Allah's daughters, and they worshipped them with Him. In all of the above, they made very serious errors. They attributed offspring to Him when He has no offspring, then they assigned Him the kind of offspring they regarded as inferior, namely daughters, which they did not even want for themselves, as He said:

(Are the males for you and the females for Him That is indeed an unfair division!) (53:21-22) And Allah says here:

(And they assign daughters unto Allah! Glorified (and Exalted) is He.) meaning, above their claims and fabrications.

(But no! It is from their falsehood that they say: "Allah has begotten." They are certainly liars! Has He (then) chosen daughters rather than sons What is the matter with you How do you decide) (37:151-154)

(And for themselves, what they desire;) meaning they choose the males for themselves, rejecting the daughters that they assign to Allah. Exalted be Allah far above what they say!

The Idolators' Abhorrence for Daughters

(And when the news of (the birth of) a female (child) is brought to any of them, his face becomes dark) meaning with distress and grief.

(and he is filled with inner grief!) meaning he is silent because of the intensity of the grief he feels.

(He hides himself from the people) meaning he does not want anyone to see him.

(because of the evil of that whereof he has been informed. Shall he keep her with dishonor or bury her in the earth) meaning should he keep her, humiliating her, not letting her inherit from him and not taking care of her, preferring his male children over her

(or bury her in the earth) meaning bury her alive, as they used to do during the days of ignorance. How could they dislike something so intensely, yet attribute it to Allah

(Certainly, evil is their decision.) meaning how evil are the words they say, the way they want to share things out and the things they attribute to Him. As Allah says:

(And if one of them is informed of the news of (the birth of a girl) that which he sets forth as a parable to the Most Gracious (Allah), his face becomes dark, and he is filled with grief!) (43:17). Here, Allah says:

(For those who do not believe in the Hereafter there is an evil description,) meaning, only imperfection is to be attributed to

(and for Allah is the highest description) meaning He is absolutely perfect in all ways and this absolute perfection is His Alone.

(And He is the All-Mighty, the All-Wise.)

Surah: 16 Ayah: 61 & Ayah: 62

﴿ وَلَوْ يُؤَاخِذُ اللَّهُ النَّاسَ بِظُلْمِهِم مَّا تَرَكَ عَلَيْهَا مِن دَآبَّةٍ وَلَكِن يُؤَخِّرُهُمْ إِلَىٰ أَجَلٍ مُّسَمًّى فَإِذَا جَآءَ أَجَلُهُمْ لَا يَسْتَـْخِرُونَ سَاعَةً وَلَا يَسْتَقْدِمُونَ ﴾

61. And if Allâh were to seize mankind for their wrong-doing, He would not leave on it (the earth) a single moving (living) creature, but He postpones them for an appointed term and when their term comes, neither can they delay nor can they advance it an hour (or a moment).

﴿ وَيَجْعَلُونَ لِلَّهِ مَا يَكْرَهُونَ وَتَصِفُ أَلْسِنَتُهُمُ الْكَذِبَ أَنَّ لَهُمُ الْحُسْنَىٰ لَا جَرَمَ أَنَّ لَهُمُ النَّارَ وَأَنَّهُم مُّفْرَطُونَ ﴾

62. They assign to Allâh that which they dislike (for themselves), and their tongues assert the falsehood that the better things will be theirs. No doubt for them is the Fire, and they will be the first to be hastened on into it, and left there neglected. (Tafsir Al-Qurtubî)

Transliteration

61. Walaw yu-akhithu Allahu alnnasa bithulmihim ma taraka AAalayha min dabbatin walakin yuakhkhiruhum ila ajalin musamman fa-itha jaa ajaluhum la yasta/khiroona saAAatan wala yastaqdimoona 62. WayajAAaloona lillahi ma yakrahoona watasifu alsinatuhumu alkathiba anna lahumu alhusna la jarama anna lahumu alnnara waannahum mufratoona

Tafsir Ibn Kathir

Allah does not immediately punish for Disobedience

Allah tells us about His patience with His creatures, even though they do wrong. If He were to punish them for what they have done, there would be no living creature left on the face of the earth, i.e., He would have destroyed every animal on earth after destroying the sons of Adam. But the Lord - magnificent is His glory - is forbearing and He covers people's faults. He waits until the appointed time, i.e., He does not rush to punish them. If He did, then there would be no one left. Ibn Jarir reported that Abu Salamah said: "Abu Hurayrah heard a man saying, `The wrongdoer harms no one but himself.' He turned to him and said, `That is not true, by Allah! Even the buzzard dies in its nest because of the sins of the wrongdoer.'"

They attribute to Allah what They Themselves dislike

(They assign to Allah that which they dislike (for themselves),) meaning, daughters, and partners, who are merely His servants, yet none of them would like to have someone sharing in his wealth.

(and their tongues assert the lie that the better things will be theirs.) This is a denunciation of their claims that better things will be theirs in this world, and in the Hereafter. Allah tells us about what some of them said, as in the Ayat:

(And if We give man a taste of mercy from Us, and then take it from him, verily! He is hopelessly, ungrateful. But if We let him taste of goodness after harm has touched him, he is sure to say: "Ills have departed from me." Surely, he is cheerful, and boastful (ungrateful to Allah).) (11:9-10)

(And if We give him a taste of mercy from Us, after some adversity has touched him, he is sure to say: "This is due to me; I do not think that the Hour will occur. But if I am brought back to my Lord, then , with Him, there will surely be the best for me." Then, We will certainly show the disbelievers what they have done, and We shall make them taste severe torment.) (41:50)

(Have you seen the one who disbelieved in Our Ayat and said: "I shall certainly be given wealth and children (if I came back to life).") (19:77) Allah tells us about one of the two men:

(He went into his garden while wronging himself. He said: "I do not think that this will ever perish. And I do not think that the Hour will ever come, and if indeed I am brought back to my Lord, (on the Day of Resurrection), then surely, I shall find better than this when I return to Him.") (18:35-36) These people combined bad deeds with the false hopes of being rewarded with good for those bad deeds, which is impossible. Thus Allah refuted their false hopes, when He said:

(No doubt), meaning, truly it is inevitable that

(for them is the Fire), meaning, on the Day of Resurrection.

(and they will be forsaken). Mujahid, Sa`id bin Jubayr, Qatadah and others said: "This means they will be forgotten and neglected there." This is like the Ayah:

(So today We forget them just as they forgot meeting on this day of theirs.) (7:51). It was also reported from Qatadah that,

(they will be forsaken) means 'they are hastened into the Fire.' There is no contradiction between the two, because they will be hastened into the Fire on the Day of Resurrection, then they will be forgotten there, i.e., left to dwell there for eternity.

Surah: 16 Ayah: 63, Ayah: 64 & Ayah: 65

﴿ تَٱللَّهِ لَقَدْ أَرْسَلْنَآ إِلَىٰٓ أُمَمٍ مِّن قَبْلِكَ فَزَيَّنَ لَهُمُ ٱلشَّيْطَـٰنُ أَعْمَـٰلَهُمْ فَهُوَ وَلِيُّهُمُ ٱلْيَوْمَ وَهُمْ عَذَابٌ أَلِيمٌ ۝ ﴾

63. By Allâh, We indeed sent (Messengers) to the nations before you (O Muhammad (peace be upon him)) but Shaitân (Satan) made their deeds fair-seeming to them. So he (Satan) is their Wali (helper) today (i.e. in this world), and theirs will be a painful torment.

﴿ وَمَآ أَنزَلْنَا عَلَيْكَ ٱلْكِتَـٰبَ إِلَّا لِتُبَيِّنَ لَهُمُ ٱلَّذِى ٱخْتَلَفُوا۟ فِيهِ وَهُدًى وَرَحْمَةً لِّقَوْمٍ يُؤْمِنُونَ ۝ ﴾

64. And We have not sent down the Book (the Qur'an) to you (O Muhammad (peace be upon him)) except that you may explain clearly unto them those things in which they differ, and (as) a guidance and a mercy for a folk who believe.

﴿ وَٱللَّهُ أَنزَلَ مِنَ ٱلسَّمَآءِ مَآءً فَأَحْيَا بِهِ ٱلْأَرْضَ بَعْدَ مَوْتِهَآ إِنَّ فِى ذَٰلِكَ لَـَٔايَةً لِّقَوْمٍ يَسْمَعُونَ ۝ ﴾

65. And Allâh sends down water (rain) from the sky, then He revives the earth therewith after its death. Verily, in this is a sign (clear proof) for people who listen (obey Allâh).

Transliteration

63. TaAllahi laqad arsalna ila omamin min qablika fazayyana lahumu alshshaytanu aAAmalahum fahuwa waliyyuhumu alyawma walahum AAathabun aleemun 64. Wama anzalna AAalayka alkitaba illa litubayyina lahumu allathee ikhtalafoo feehi wahudan warahmatan liqawmin yu/minoona 65. WaAllahu anzala mina alssama-i maan faahya bihi al-arda baAAda mawtiha inna fee thalika laayatan liqawmin yasmaAAoona

Chapter 16: An-Nahl (The Bee), Verses 001-128

Tafsir Ibn Kathir

Finding Consolation in the Reminder of Those Who came before

Allah says, `He sent Messengers to the nations of the past, and they were rejected. You, O Muhammad, have an example in your brothers among the Messengers, so do not be distressed by your people's rejection. As for the idolators' rejection of the Messengers, the reason for this is that the Shaytan made their deeds attractive to them.'

(So today he (Shaytan) is their helper,) meaning they will be suffering punishment while Shaytan is their only helper, and he cannot save them, so they have no one to answer their calls for help, and theirs is a painful punishment.

The Reason why the Qur'an was revealed

Then Allah says to His Messenger that He has revealed the Book to him to explain the truth to mankind in matters which they dispute over. So the Qur'an is a decisive arbitrator for every issue that they argue about.

(and (as) a guidance) meaning, for their hearts.

(and a mercy) meaning, for the one who adheres to it.

(for a people who believe.) Just as Allah causes the Qur'an to bring life to hearts that were dead from disbelief, so He brings the earth to life after it has died, by sending down water from the sky.

(Surely that is a sign for people who listen.) meaning those who understand the words and their meanings.

Surah: 16 Ayah: 66 & Ayah: 67

﴿ وَإِنَّ لَكُمْ فِى ٱلْأَنْعَٰمِ لَعِبْرَةً ۖ نُّسْقِيكُم مِّمَّا فِى بُطُونِهِۦ مِنۢ بَيْنِ فَرْثٍ وَدَمٍ لَّبَنًا خَالِصًا سَآئِغًا لِّلشَّٰرِبِينَ ۝ ﴾

66. And verily! In the cattle, there is a lesson for you. We give you to drink of that which is in their bellies, from between excretions and blood, pure milk; palatable to the drinkers.

﴿ وَمِن ثَمَرَٰتِ ٱلنَّخِيلِ وَٱلْأَعْنَٰبِ تَتَّخِذُونَ مِنْهُ سَكَرًا وَرِزْقًا حَسَنًا ۗ إِنَّ فِى ذَٰلِكَ لَءَايَةً لِّقَوْمٍ يَعْقِلُونَ ۝ ﴾

67. And from the fruits of date-palms and grapes, you derive strong drink and a goodly provision. Verily, therein is indeed a sign for people who have wisdom.

Transliteration

66. Wa-inna lakum fee al-anAAami laAAibratan nusqeekum mimma fee butoonihi min bayni farthin wadamin labanan khalisan sa-ighan lilshsharibeena 67. Wamin thamarati alnnakheeli waal-aAAnabi tattakhithoona minhu sakaran warizqan hasanan inna fee thalika laayatan liqawmin yaAAqiloona

Tafsir Ibn Kathir

Lessons and Blessings in Cattle and the Fruit of the Date-palm and Grapevine

(there is for you) - O mankind -

(in the cattle) - meaning camels, cows and sheep,

(a lesson) meaning a sign and an evidence of the wisdom, power, mercy and kindness of the Creator.

(We have made a drink for you out of what is in its belly) meaning its singular forms refers to one cattle, or it could refer to the whole species. For cattle are the creatures which provide a drink from what is in their bellies and in another Ayah it is `in their bellies.' Either way is plausible. He said,

(from between excretions and blood, pure milk;) meaning it is free of blood, and is pure in its whiteness, taste and sweetness. It is between excrement and blood in the belly of the animal, but each of them goes its own way after the food has been fully digested in its stomach. The blood goes to the veins, the milk goes to the udder, the urine goes to the bladder and the feces goes to the anus. None of them gets mixed with another after separating, and none of them is affected by the other.

(pure milk; palatable to the drinkers.) meaning nothing to cause one to choke on it. When Allah mentions milk and how He has made it a palatable drink for mankind, He follows this with a reference to the drinks that people make from the fruits of the date palm and grapevine, and what they used to do with intoxicating Nabidh (drink made from dates) before it was forbidden. Thus He reminds them of His blessings, and says:

(And from the fruits of date palms and grapes, you derive strong drink) This indicates that it was permissible to drink it before it was forbidden. It also indicates that strong drink (i.e., intoxicating drink) derived from dates is the same as strong drink derived from grapes. Also forbidden are strong drinks derived from wheat, barley, corn and honey, as is explained in detail in the Sunnah.

(strong drink and a goodly provision.) Ibn `Abbas said: "Strong drink is the product of these two fruits that is forbidden, and the good provision is what is permitted of them." According to another report: "Strong drink is its unlawful, and the goodly provision is its lawful," referring to the fruits when they are dried, like dates and raisins, or products derived from them such as molasses, vinegar and wine (of grapes, dates) which are permissible to drink before they become strong (becomes alcoholic), as was stated in the Sunnah.

(There is indeed a sign in this for those of reason.) It is appropriate to mention reason here, because it is the noblest feature of man. Hence Allah forbade this Ummah from drinking intoxicants, in order to protect their ability to reason. Allah says:

(And We placed gardens of date palms and grapes in it, and We caused springs of water to gush forth in it. So that they may eat of its fruit - while their hands did not make it. Will they not then give thanks Glory be to Him Who created all the pairs of that which the earth produces, as well as their own (human) kind (male and female), and of that which they know not.) (36:34-36)

Surah: 16 Ayah: 68 & Ayah: 69

﴿ وَأَوْحَىٰ رَبُّكَ إِلَى ٱلنَّحْلِ أَنِ ٱتَّخِذِى مِنَ ٱلْجِبَالِ بُيُوتًا وَمِنَ ٱلشَّجَرِ وَمِمَّا يَعْرِشُونَ ۝ ﴾

68. And your Lord inspired the bee, saying: "Take you habitations in the mountains and in the trees and in what they erect.

﴿ ثُمَّ كُلِى مِن كُلِّ ٱلثَّمَرَٰتِ فَٱسْلُكِى سُبُلَ رَبِّكِ ذُلُلاً ۚ يَخْرُجُ مِنْ بُطُونِهَا شَرَابٌ مُّخْتَلِفٌ أَلْوَٰنُهُ فِيهِ شِفَآءٌ لِّلنَّاسِ ۗ إِنَّ فِى ذَٰلِكَ لَآيَةً لِّقَوْمٍ يَتَفَكَّرُونَ ۝ ﴾

69. "Then, eat of all fruits, and follow the ways of your Lord made easy (for you)." There comes forth from their bellies, a drink of varying color wherein is healing for men. Verily, in this is indeed a sign for people who think.

Transliteration

68. Waawha rabbuka ila alnnahli ani ittakhithee mina aljibali buyootan wamina alshshajari wamimma yaAArishoona 69. Thumma kulee min kulli alththamarati faoslukee subula rabbiki thululan yakhruju min butooniha sharabun mukhtalifun alwanuhu feehi shifaon lilnnasi inna fee thalika laayatan liqawmin yatafakkaroona

Tafsir Ibn Kathir

In the Bee and its Honey there is Blessing and a Lesson

What is meant by inspiration here is guidance. The bee is guided to make its home in the mountains, in trees and in structures erected by man. The bee's home is a solid structure, with its hexagonal shapes and interlocking forms there is no looseness in its combs. Then Allah decrees that the bee will have permission to eat from all fruits and to follow the ways which Allah has made easy for it, wherever it wants to go in the vast spaces of the wilderness, valleys and high mountains. Then each bee comes back to its hive without swerving to the right or left, it comes straight back to its home where its offspring and honey are. It makes wax from its wings, and regurgitates honey from its mouth, and lays eggs from its rear, then the next morning it goes out to the fields again.

(and follow the routes of your Lord made easy (for you)) Qatadah and `Abdur-Rahman bin Zayd bin Aslam said: "This means, in an obedient way", understanding it to be a description of the route of migration. Ibn Zayd said that this is like the Ayah:

(And We have subdued them for them so that some they may ride and some they may eat.) (36:72) He said: "Do you not see that they move the bees' home from one land to another, and the bees follow them" The first opinion is clearly the more likely, as it describes the routes that the bees follow, i.e., `follow these routes as they are easy for you.' This was stated by Mujahid. Ibn Jarir said that both opinions are correct.

(There comes forth from their bellies, a drink of varying colors, wherein is healing for men.) (meaning, honey, that is) white, yellow, red, or of other good colors, depending on the different things that the bees eat.

(in which there is a cure for men.) meaning there is a cure in honey for diseases that people suffer from. Some of those who spoke about the study of Prophetic medicine said that if (Allah) had said, `in which there is the cure for men', then it would be the remedy for all diseases, but He said, `in which there is a cure for men', meaning that it is the right treatment for every "cold" disease, because it is "hot", and a disease should be treated with its opposite. Al-Bukhari and Muslim recorded in their Sahihs from Qatadah from Abu Al-Mutawakkil `Ali bin Dawud An-Naji from Abu Sa`id Al-Khudri that a man came to the Messenger of Allah and said, "My brother is suffering from diarrhea". He said,

«اسْقِهِ عَسَلًا»

(Give him honey to drink.) The man went and gave him honey, then he came back and said, "O Messenger of Allah! I gave him honey to drink, and he only got worse." The Prophet said,

«اذْهَبْ فَاسْقِهِ عَسَلًا»

(Go and give him honey to drink.) So he went and gave him honey, then he came back and said, "O Messenger of Allah! it only made him worse." The Prophet said,

«صَدَقَ اللهُ وَكَذَبَ بَطْنُ أَخِيكَ، اذْهَبْ فَاسْقِهِ عَسَلًا»

(Allah speaks the truth and your brother's stomach is lying. Go and give him honey to drink.) So he went and gave him honey, and he recovered." It is reported in the Two Sahihs from `A'ishah, may Allah be pleased with her, that the Messenger of Allah used to like sweet things and honey. This is the wording of Al-Bukhari, who also reported in his Sahih from Ibn `Abbas that the Messenger of Allah said:

»الشِّفَاءُ فِي ثَلَاثَةٍ: فِي شَرْطَةِ مِحْجَمٍ، أَوْ شَرْبَةِ عَسَلٍ، أَوْ كَيَّةٍ بِنَارٍ، وَأَنْهَى أُمَّتِي عَنِ الْكَيِّ«

(Healing is to be found in three things: the cut made by the cupper, or drinking honey, or in branding with fire (cauterizing), but I have forbidden my Ummah to use branding.)

(There is indeed a sign in that for people who reflect.) meaning in the fact that Allah inspires this weak little creature to travel through the vast fields and feed from every kind of fruit, then gather it for wax and honey, which are some of the best things, in this is a sign for people who think about the might and power of the bee's Creator Who causes all of this to happen. From this they learn that He is the Initiator, the All-Powerful, the All-Wise, the All-Knowing, the Most Generous, the Most Merciful.

Surah: 16 Ayah: 70

﴿ وَٱللَّهُ خَلَقَكُمْ ثُمَّ يَتَوَفَّىٰكُمْ ۚ وَمِنكُم مَّن يُرَدُّ إِلَىٰٓ أَرْذَلِ ٱلْعُمُرِ لِكَىْ لَا يَعْلَمَ بَعْدَ عِلْمٍ شَيْـًٔا ۚ إِنَّ ٱللَّهَ عَلِيمٌ قَدِيرٌ ﴾

70. And Allâh has created you and then He will cause you to die; and of you there are some who are sent back to senility, so that they know nothing after having known (much). Truly! Allâh is All-Knowing, All-Powerful.

Transliteration

70. WaAllahu khalaqakum thumma yatawaffakum waminkum man yuraddu ila arthali alAAumuri likay la yaAAlama baAAda AAilmin shay-an inna Allaha AAaleemun qadeerun

Tafsir Ibn Kathir

In Man there is a Lesson

Allah tells us that He is controlling the affairs of His servants. He is the One Who created them out of nothing, then He will cause them to die. But there are some of them that He allows to grow old, which is a physical weakness, as Allah says:

(Allah is He Who created you in (a state of) weakness, then gave you strength after weakness, then after strength gave (you) weakness) (30:54)

(so that they know nothing after having known.) meaning, after he knew things, he will reach a stage where he knows nothing because of weakness of mind due to old age and senility. Thus Al-Bukhari, when commenting on this Ayah, reported a narration from Anas bin Malik that the Messenger of Allah used to pray:

«أَعُوذُ بِكَ مِنَ الْبُخْلِ وَالْكَسَلِ وَالْهَرَمِ، وَأَرْذَلِ الْعُمُرِ وَعَذَابِ الْقَبْرِ، وَفِتْنَةِ الدَّجَّالِ وَفِتْنَةِ الْمَحْيَا وَالْمَمَاتِ»

(I seek refuge with You from miserliness, laziness, old age, senility, the punishment of the grave, the Fitnah of the Dajjal and the trials of life and death.) Zuhayr bin Abi Sulma said, in his famous Mu`allaqah: "I became exhausted from the responsibilities of life. Whoever lives for eighty years, no wonder he is tired. I saw death hitting people like a crazed camel, and whoever it hit dies, but whoever is not hit lives until he grows old."

Surah: 16 Ayah: 71

﴿ وَٱللَّهُ فَضَّلَ بَعْضَكُمْ عَلَىٰ بَعْضٍ فِى ٱلرِّزْقِ فَمَا ٱلَّذِينَ فُضِّلُوا۟ بِرَآدِّى رِزْقِهِمْ عَلَىٰ مَا مَلَكَتْ أَيْمَٰنُهُمْ فَهُمْ فِيهِ سَوَآءٌ أَفَبِنِعْمَةِ ٱللَّهِ يَجْحَدُونَ ﴾

71. And Allâh has preferred some of you above others in wealth and properties. Then, those who are preferred will by no means hand over their wealth and properties to those (slaves) whom their right hands possess, so that they may be equal with them in respect thereof. Do they then deny the Favor of Allâh?

Transliteration

71. WaAllahu faddala baAAdakum AAala baAAdin fee alrrizqi fama allatheena fuddiloo biraddee rizqihim AAala ma malakat aymanuhum fahum feehi sawaon afabiniAAmati Allahi yajhadoona

Tafsir Ibn Kathir

There is a Sign and a Blessing in Matters of People's Livelihood

Allah explains to the idolators the ignorance and disbelief involved in their claim that Allah has partners while also admitting that these partners are His servants. In their Talbiyah for Hajj, they used to say, "Here I am, there are no partners for You except Your own partner, You own him and everything he owns." Allah says, denouncing them: `You would not accept for your servant to have an equal share in your wealth, so how is it that Allah would accept His servant to be His equal in divinity and glory As Allah says elsewhere:

(He sets forth a parable for you from yourselves: Do you have partners among those whom your right hands possess (i.e. your servant) to share as equals in the wealth We have granted you, those whom you fear as you fear each other) (30:28) Al-`Awfi reported that Ibn `Abbas mentioned this Ayah, saying, "Allah is saying - `If they did

Chapter 16: An-Nahl (The Bee), Verses 001-128

not want their servant to have a share with them in their wealth and wives, how can My servant have a share with Me in My power' Thus Allah says:

(Do they then deny the favor of Allah)" According to another report, Ibn `Abbas said: "How can they accept for Me that which they do not accept for themselves"

(Do they then deny the favor of Allah) meaning, they assign to Allah a share of the tilth and cattle which He has created. They denied His blessings and associated others in worship with Him. Al-Hasan Al-Basri said: "Umar bin Al-Khattab wrote this letter to Abu Musa Al-Ash`ari: `Be content with your provision in this world, for the Most Merciful has honored some of His servants over others in terms of provision as a test of both. The one who has been given plenty is being tested to see if he will give thanks to Allah and fulfill the duties which are his by virtue of his wealth...'" It was reported by Ibn Abi Hatim.

Surah: 16 Ayah: 72

﴿ وَٱللَّهُ جَعَلَ لَكُم مِّنْ أَنفُسِكُمْ أَزْوَٰجًا وَجَعَلَ لَكُم مِّنْ أَزْوَٰجِكُم بَنِينَ وَحَفَدَةً وَرَزَقَكُم مِّنَ ٱلطَّيِّبَٰتِ ۚ أَفَبِٱلْبَٰطِلِ يُؤْمِنُونَ وَبِنِعْمَتِ ٱللَّهِ هُمْ يَكْفُرُونَ ۝ ﴾

72. And Allâh has made for you Azwaj (mates or wives) of your own kind, and has made for you, from your wives, sons and grandsons, and has bestowed on you good provision. Do they then believe in false deities and deny the Favor of Allâh (by not worshipping Allâh Alone).

Transliteration

72. WaAllahu jaAAala lakum min anfusikum azwajan wajaAAala lakum min azwajikum baneena wahafadatan warazaqakum mina alttayyibati afabialbatili yu/minoona wabiniAAmati Allahi hum yakfuroona

Tafsir Ibn Kathir

Among His Blessings and Signs are Mates, Children and Grandchildren

Allah mentions the blessing He has bestowed upon His servant by giving them mates from among themselves, mates of their own kind. If He had given them mates of another kind, there would be no harmony, love and mercy between them. But out of His mercy He has made the Children of Adam male and female, and has made the females wives or mates for the males. Then Allah mentions that from these wives He creates children and grandchildren, one's children's children. This was the opinion of Ibn `Abbas, `Ikrimah, Al-Hasan, Ad-Dahhak and Ibn Zayd. Shu`bah said, narrating from Abu Bishr from Sa`id bin Jubayr from Ibn `Abbas: "Children and grandchildren, who are one's children and one's children's children." It was also said that this means servants and helpers, or it means sons-in-law or in-laws. I say: if we understand

(grandsons) to refer back to wives, then it must mean children, children's children, and sons-in-law, because they are the husbands of one's daughter or the children of one's wife.

(and has granted you good provisions.) meaning your food and drink. Then Allah denounces those who associate others in worship with the One Who bestows blessings on them:

(Do they then believe in false deities), meaning idols and rivals to Allah

(and deny the favor of Allah) meaning, by concealing the blessings that Allah has given them and attributing them to others. According to a Sahih Hadith, the Prophet said:

«إِنَّ اللهَ يَقُولُ لِلْعَبْدِ يَوْمَ الْقِيَامَةِ مُمْتَنًّا عَلَيْهِ: أَلَمْ أُزَوِّجْكَ؟ أَلَمْ أُكْرِمْكَ؟ أَلَمْ أُسَخِّرْ لَكَ الْخَيْلَ وَالْإِبِلَ، وَأَذَرْكَ تَرْأَسُ وَتَرْبَعُ؟»

(Allah will say to His servant on the Day of Resurrection, reminding him of His blessings: "Did I not give you a wife Did I not honor you Did I not subject horses and camels to your use, and cause you to occupy a position of leadership and honor")

Surah: 16 Ayah: 73 & Ayah: 74

﴿ وَيَعْبُدُونَ مِن دُونِ ٱللَّهِ مَا لَا يَمْلِكُ لَهُمْ رِزْقًا مِّنَ ٱلسَّمَـٰوَٰتِ وَٱلْأَرْضِ شَيْـًٔا وَلَا يَسْتَطِيعُونَ ﴿٧٣﴾ ﴾

73. And they worship others besides Allâh - such as do not and cannot own any provision for them from the heavens or the earth.

﴿ فَلَا تَضْرِبُوا۟ لِلَّهِ ٱلْأَمْثَالَ إِنَّ ٱللَّهَ يَعْلَمُ وَأَنتُمْ لَا تَعْلَمُونَ ﴿٧٤﴾ ﴾

74. So put not forward similitudes for Allâh (as there is nothing similar to Him, nor He resembles anything). Truly! Allâh knows and you know not.

Transliteration

73. WayaAAbudoona min dooni Allahi ma la yamliku lahum rizqan mina alssamawati waal-ardi shayan wala yastateeAAoona   74. Fala tadriboo lillahi al-amthala inna Allaha yaAAlamu waantum la taAAlamoona

Tafsir Ibn Kathir

Denouncing the Worship of anything besides Allah

Allah tells us about the Mushrikin who worship others besides Him, even though He alone is the bountiful Provider, the Creator and Sustainer, without partners or associates, but they still worship idols and make rivals for Him. He says:

(such as do not have power to grant them any provision from the heavens or the earth) meaning, nobody can cause rain to fall, or make plants and trees grow. They cannot do these things for them-selves, even if they wanted to. Thus Allah says:

(So do not give examples on behalf of Allah.) meaning, do not set up rivals to Him or describe anything as being like Him.

(Truly, Allah knows and you know not.) meaning, He knows and bears witness that there is no god but Him, but you are ignorant and associate others in worship with Him.

Surah: 16 Ayah: 75

﴿ ۞ ضَرَبَ ٱللَّهُ مَثَلًا عَبْدًا مَّمْلُوكًا لَّا يَقْدِرُ عَلَىٰ شَىْءٍ وَمَن رَّزَقْنَٰهُ مِنَّا رِزْقًا حَسَنًا فَهُوَ يُنفِقُ مِنْهُ سِرًّا وَجَهْرًا ۖ هَلْ يَسْتَوُۥنَ ۚ ٱلْحَمْدُ لِلَّهِ ۚ بَلْ أَكْثَرُهُمْ لَا يَعْلَمُونَ

75. Allâh puts forward the example (of two men - a believer and a disbeliever); a slave (disbeliever) under the possession of another, he has no power of any sort, and (the other), a man (believer) on whom We have bestowed a good provision from Us, and he spends thereof secretly and openly. Can they be equal? (By no means). All the praises and thanks are to Allâh. Nay! (But) most of them know not.

Transliteration

75. Daraba Allahu mathalan AAabdan mamlookan la yaqdiru AAala shay-in waman razaqnahu minna rizqan hasanan fahuwa yunfiqu minhu sirran wajahran hal yastawoona alhamdu lillahi bal aktharuhum la yaAAlamoona

Tafsir Ibn Kathir

The Example of the Believer and the Disbeliever, or the Idol and the True God

Al-`Awfi reported that Ibn `Abbas said: "This is the example which Allah gives of the disbeliever and the believer." This was also the view of Qatadah and Ibn Jarir. The servant who has no power over anything is like the disbeliever, and the one who is given good provisions and spends of them secretly and openly is like the believer. Ibn Abi Najih reported that Mujahid said: "This is an example given of the idol and the True God - can they be the same" Once the difference between them is so clear and so obvious, no one can be unaware of it except the one who is foolish. Allah says: (All the praises and thanks are to Allah. Nay! (But) most of them know not.)

Surah: 16 Ayah: 76

﴿ وَضَرَبَ ٱللَّهُ مَثَلًا رَّجُلَيْنِ أَحَدُهُمَآ أَبْكَمُ لَا يَقْدِرُ عَلَىٰ شَىْءٍ وَهُوَ كَلٌّ عَلَىٰ مَوْلَىٰهُ أَيْنَمَا يُوَجِّههُّ لَا يَأْتِ بِخَيْرٍ هَلْ يَسْتَوِى هُوَ وَمَن يَأْمُرُ بِٱلْعَدْلِ وَهُوَ عَلَىٰ صِرَٰطٍ مُّسْتَقِيمٍ ۝ ﴾

76. And Allâh puts forward (another) example of two men, one of them dumb, who has no power over anything (disbeliever), and he is a burden on his master, whichever way he directs him, he brings no good. Is such a man equal to one (believer in the Islâmic Monotheism) who commands justice, and is himself on the Straight Path?

Transliteration

76. Wadaraba Allahu mathalan rajulayni ahaduhuma abkamu la yaqdiru AAala shay-in wahuwa kallun AAala mawlahu aynama yuwajjihhu la ya/ti bikhayrin hal yastawee huwa waman ya/muru bialAAadli wahuwa AAala siratin mustaqeemin

Tafsir Ibn Kathir

Another Example

Mujahid said, "This also refers to idols and the True God, may He be exalted." Meaning that the idol is dumb and cannot speak or say anything, good or otherwise. It cannot do anything at all, no words, no action, it is dependent and is a burden on its master.

(whichever way he directs him,) meaning, wherever he sends him

(he brings no good.) meaning, he does not succeed in what he wants.

(Is such a man equal) meaning, a man who has these attributes

(to one who commands justice) meaning fairness, one whose words are true and whose deeds are righteous.

(and is himself on the straight path) Al-`Awfi reported that Ibn `Abbas said: "This is also an example of the disbeliever and the believer", as in the previous Ayah.

Surah: 16 Ayah: 77, Ayah: 78 & Ayah: 79

﴿ وَلِلَّهِ غَيْبُ ٱلسَّمَٰوَٰتِ وَٱلْأَرْضِ وَمَآ أَمْرُ ٱلسَّاعَةِ إِلَّا كَلَمْحِ ٱلْبَصَرِ أَوْ هُوَ أَقْرَبُ إِنَّ ٱللَّهَ عَلَىٰ كُلِّ شَىْءٍ قَدِيرٌ ۝ ﴾

77. And to Allâh belongs the Unseen of the heavens and the earth. And the matter of the Hour is not but as a twinkling of the eye, or even nearer. Truly! Allâh is Able to do all things.

Chapter 16: An-Nahl (The Bee), Verses 001-128

﴿ وَٱللَّهُ أَخْرَجَكُم مِّنۢ بُطُونِ أُمَّهَـٰتِكُمْ لَا تَعْلَمُونَ شَيْـًٔا وَجَعَلَ لَكُمُ ٱلسَّمْعَ وَٱلْأَبْصَـٰرَ وَٱلْأَفْـِٔدَةَ لَعَلَّكُمْ تَشْكُرُونَ ۝ ﴾

78. And Allâh has brought you out from the wombs of your mothers while you know nothing. And He gave you hearing, sight, and hearts that you might give thanks (to Allâh).

﴿ أَلَمْ يَرَوْا۟ إِلَى ٱلطَّيْرِ مُسَخَّرَٰتٍ فِى جَوِّ ٱلسَّمَآءِ مَا يُمْسِكُهُنَّ إِلَّا ٱللَّهُ إِنَّ فِى ذَٰلِكَ لَـَٔايَـٰتٍ لِّقَوْمٍ يُؤْمِنُونَ ۝ ﴾

79. Do they not see the birds held (flying) in the midst of the sky? None holds them but Allâh (none gave them the ability to fly but Allâh). Verily, in this are clear Ayât (proofs and signs) for people who believe (in the Oneness of Allâh).

Transliteration

77. Walillahi ghaybu alssamawati waal-ardi wama amru alssaAAati illa kalamhi albasari aw huwa aqrabu inna Allaha AAala kulli shay-in qadeerun 78. WaAllahu akhrajakum min butooni ommahatikum la taAAlamoona shay-an wajaAAala lakumu alssamAAa waal-absara waal-af-idata laAAallakum tashkuroona 79. Alam yaraw ila alttayri musakhkharatin fee jawwi alssama-i ma yumsikuhunna illa Allahu inna fee thalika laayatin liqawmin yu/minoona

Tafsir Ibn Kathir

The Unseen belongs to Allah and only He has Knowledge of the Hour

Allah tells us of the perfection of His knowledge and ability to do all things, by telling us that He alone knows the Unseen of the heavens and the earth. No one knows anything about such things except for what Allah informs about as He wills. His complete power, which no one can oppose or resist, means that when He wants a thing, He only has to say to it "Be!" and it is, as Allah says:

(And Our commandment is but one as the twinkling of an eye.) (54:50) meaning, whatever He wills happens in blinking. Thus Allah says here:

(And the matter of the Hour is not but as a twinkling of the eye, or even nearer. Truly, Allah is Able to do all things.) iElsewhere, Allah says:

(The processes of creating you all and resurrecting you all are but like that of (the creation and resurrection of) a single person.) (31:28)

Among the Favors Allah has granted People are Hearing, Sight and the Heart

Then Allah mentions His blessings to His servants in that He brought them from their mothers' wombs not knowing a thing, then He gives them hearing to recognize voices, sight to see visible things and hearts - meaning reason - whose seat, according to the correct view, is the heart, although it was also said that its seat is the brain. With his reason, a person can distinguish between what is harmful and what is beneficial. These abilities and senses develop gradually in man. The more he grows, the more his hearing, vision and reason increase, until they reach their peak. Allah has created these faculties in man to enable him to worship his Lord, so he uses all these organs, abilities and strengths to obey his Master. Al-Bukhari reported in his Sahih from Abu Hurayrah that the Messenger of Allah said:

«يَقُولُ تَعَالَى: مَنْ عَادَى لِي وَلِيًّا فَقَدْ بَارَزَنِي بِالْحَرْبِ، وَمَا تَقَرَّبَ إِلَيَّ عَبْدِي بِشَيْءٍ أَفْضَلَ مِنْ أَدَاءِ مَا افْتَرَضْتُ عَلَيْهِ، وَلَا يَزَالُ عَبْدِي يَتَقَرَّبُ إِلَيَّ بِالنَّوَافِلِ حَتَّى أُحِبَّهُ، فَإِذَا أَحْبَبْتُهُ كُنْتُ سَمْعَهُ الَّذِي يَسْمَعُ بِهِ، وَبَصَرَهُ الَّذِي يُبْصِرُ بِهِ، وَيَدَهُ الَّتِي يَبْطِشُ بِهَا، وَرِجْلَهُ الَّتِي يَمْشِي بِهَا، وَلَئِنْ سَأَلَنِي لَأُعْطِيَنَّهُ، وَلَئِنْ دَعَانِي لَأُجِيبَنَّهُ، وَلَئِنِ اسْتَعَاذَ بِي لَأُعِيذَنَّهُ، وَمَا تَرَدَّدْتُ فِي شَيْءٍ أَنَا فَاعِلُهُ تَرَدُّدِي فِي قَبْضِ نَفْسِ عَبْدِي الْمُؤْمِنِ يَكْرَهُ الْمَوْتَ وَأَكْرَهُ مَسَاءَتَهُ وَلَا بُدَّ لَهُ مِنْهُ»

(Allah says: "Whoever takes My friend as an enemy, has declared war on Me. My servant does not draw near to Me with anything better than his doing that which I have enjoined upon him, and My servant keeps drawing near to Me by doing Nawafil (supererogatory) deeds until I love him. And when I love him, I am his hearing with which he hears, his vision with which he sees, his hand with which he strikes and his foot with which he walks. Were he to ask Me for anything, I would give it to him, if he were to call on Me, I would respond, if he were to seek Me for refuge I would surely grant him it. I do not hesitate to do anything as I hesitate to take the soul of My believing servant, because he hates death and I hate to upset him, but it is inevitable.") The meaning of the Hadith is that when a person is sincere in his obedience towards Allah, all his deeds are done for the sake of Allah, so he only hears for the sake of Allah, he only sees for the sake of Allah - meaning he only listens to or looks at what has been allowed by Allah. He does not strike or walk except in obedience to Allah, seeking Allah's help in all of these things. Thus in some versions of the Hadith, narrated outside the Sahih, after the phrase "his foot with which he walks", there is added:

«فَبِي يَسْمَعُ، وَبِي يُبْصِرُ، وَبِي يَبْطِشُ، وَبِي يَمْشِي»

(So through Me he hears, through Me he sees, through Me he strikes and through Me he walks.) Thus Allah says:

(And He gave you hearing, sight, and hearts that you might give thanks.) Elsewhere, He says:

(Say it is He Who has created you, and endowed you with hearing and seeing, and hearts. Little thanks you give. Say: "It is He Who has created you on the earth, and to Him shall you be gathered (in the Hereafter).") (67:23-24)

In the Subjection of the Birds in the Sky there is a Sign

Then Allah tells His servants to look at the birds held (flying) in the sky, between heaven and earth, and how He has caused them to fly with their wings in the sky. They are held up only by Him, it is He Who gave them the strength to do that, subjecting the air to carry them and support them. As Allah says in Surat Al-Mulk:

(Do they not see the birds above them, spreading their wings out and folding them in None holds them up except the Most Gracious (Allah). Verily, He is the All-Seer of everything.) (67:19) And here Allah says:

(Verily, in this are clear signs for people who believe.)

Surah: 16 Ayah: 80, Ayah: 81, Ayah: 82 & Ayah: 83

﴿ وَٱللَّهُ جَعَلَ لَكُم مِّنۢ بُيُوتِكُمْ سَكَنًا وَجَعَلَ لَكُم مِّن جُلُودِ ٱلْأَنْعَٰمِ بُيُوتًا تَسْتَخِفُّونَهَا يَوْمَ ظَعْنِكُمْ وَيَوْمَ إِقَامَتِكُمْ ۙ وَمِنْ أَصْوَافِهَا وَأَوْبَارِهَا وَأَشْعَارِهَآ أَثَٰثًا وَمَتَٰعًا إِلَىٰ حِينٍ ﴾

80. And Allâh has made for you in your homes an abode, and made for you out of the hides of the cattle (tents for) dwelling, which you find so light (and handy) when you travel and when you stay (in your travels); and of their wool, fur, and hair (sheep wool, camel fur, and goat hair), furnishings and articles of convenience (e.g. carpets, blankets), comfort for a while.

﴿ وَٱللَّهُ جَعَلَ لَكُم مِّمَّا خَلَقَ ظِلَٰلًا وَجَعَلَ لَكُم مِّنَ ٱلْجِبَالِ أَكْنَٰنًا وَجَعَلَ لَكُمْ سَرَٰبِيلَ تَقِيكُمُ ٱلْحَرَّ وَسَرَٰبِيلَ تَقِيكُم بَأْسَكُمْ ۚ كَذَٰلِكَ يُتِمُّ نِعْمَتَهُۥ عَلَيْكُمْ لَعَلَّكُمْ تُسْلِمُونَ ﴾

81. And Allâh has made for you out of that which He has created shades, and has made for you places of refuge in the mountains, and has made for you garments to protect you from the heat (and cold), and coats of mail to protect you from your (mutual) violence. Thus does He perfect His Favor unto you, that you may submit yourselves to His Will (in Islâm).

﴿ فَإِن تَوَلَّوْا۟ فَإِنَّمَا عَلَيْكَ ٱلْبَلَٰغُ ٱلْمُبِينُ ﴾

82. Then, if they turn away, your duty (O Muhammad (peace be upon him)) is only to convey (the Message) in a clear way.

﴿يَعْرِفُونَ نِعْمَتَ ٱللَّهِ ثُمَّ يُنكِرُونَهَا وَأَكْثَرُهُمُ ٱلْكَـٰفِرُونَ ۝﴾

83. They recognize the Grace of Allâh, yet they deny it (by worshipping others besides Allâh) and most of them are disbelievers (deny the Prophethood of Muhammad (peace be upon him))

Transliteration

80. WaAllahu jaAAala lakum min buyootikum sakanan wajaAAala lakum min juloodi al-anAAami buyootan tastakhiffoonaha yawma thaAAnikum wayawma iqamatikum wamin aswafiha waawbariha waashAAariha athathan wamataAAan ila heenin 81. WaAllahu jaAAala lakum mimma khalaqa thilalan wajaAAala lakum mina aljibali aknanan wajaAAala lakum sarabeela taqeekumu alharra wasarabeela taqeekum ba/sakum kathalika yutimmu niAAmatahu AAalaykum laAAallakum tuslimoona 82. Fa-in tawallaw fa-innama AAalayka albalaghu almubeenu 83. YaAArifoona niAAmata Allahi thumma yunkiroonaha waaktharuhumu alkafiroona

Tafsir Ibn Kathir

Homes, Furnishings and Clothing are also Blessings from Allah

Allah mentions His great blessings for His servant in that He has given them homes to dwell in and protect themselves with, in which they find all kinds of benefits. He has also given them homes from the hides of cattle, i.e., leather, which are light and easy to carry on journeys and can be erected wherever they stop, whether they are traveling or are settled. Thus Allah says:

(which you find so light when you travel and when you camp;)

(out of their wool, fur and hair) refers to sheep, camels and goats respectively.

(furnishings) meaning what you take from them, i.e., wealth. It was also said that it means articles of convenience, or clothing. The correct view is more general in meaning than this; it means that you make carpets, clothing and other things from their wool, hair etc., which you use as wealth and for trade. Ibn `Abbas said: `Al-Athath means articles of convenience and comfort." This was also the view of Mujahid, `Ikrimah, Sa`id bin Jubayr, Al-Hasan, `Atiyah Al-`Awfi, `Ata' Al-Khurasani, Ad-Dahhak and Qatadah. The phrase,

(for a while) means, until the appointed time.

Shade, Places of Refuge in the Mountains, Garments and Coats of Mail are also Blessings from Allah

(And Allah has made shade for you out of that which He has created,) Qatadah said: "This means trees."

Chapter 16: An-Nahl (The Bee), Verses 001-128

(and He has made places of refuge in the mountains for you,) meaning fortresses and strongholds.

(and He has made garments for you to protect you from the heat,) meaning clothing of cotton, linen and wool.

(and coats of mail to protect you from your violence.) such as shields made of layers of sheet iron, coats of mail and so on.

(Thus does He perfect His favor for you,) meaning, thus He gives you what you need to go about your business, so that this will help you to worship and obey Him.

(that you may submit yourselves to His will). This is interpreted by the majority to mean submitting to Allah or becoming Muslim.

All the Messenger has to do is convey the Message

(Then, if they turn away,) meaning, after this declaration and reminder, do not worry about them.

(your duty (O Muhammad) is only to convey (the Message) in a clear way), and you have delivered the Message to them.

(They recognize the grace of Allah, yet they deny it) meaning they know that Allah is the One Who grants these blessings to them, and that He is Bountiful towards them, but they still deny this by worshipping others besides Him and thinking that their help and provisions come from others besides Him.

(and most of them are disbelievers.)

Surah: 16 Ayah: 84, Ayah: 85, Ayah: 86, Ayah: 87 & Ayah: 88

﴿ وَيَوْمَ نَبْعَثُ مِن كُلِّ أُمَّةٍ شَهِيدًا ثُمَّ لَا يُؤْذَنُ لِلَّذِينَ كَفَرُواْ وَلَا هُمْ يُسْتَعْتَبُونَ ۝ ﴾

84. And (remember) the Day when We shall raise up from each nation a witness (their Messenger), then, those who have disbelieved will not be given leave (to put forward excuses), nor will they be allowed (to return to the world) to repent and ask for Allâh's Forgiveness (of their sins).

﴿ وَإِذَا رَءَا ٱلَّذِينَ ظَلَمُواْ ٱلْعَذَابَ فَلَا يُخَفَّفُ عَنْهُمْ وَلَا هُمْ يُنظَرُونَ ۝ ﴾

85. And when those who did wrong (the disbelievers) will see the torment, then it will not be lightened unto them, nor will they be given respite.

$$\left\{ \text{وَإِذَا رَءَا ٱلَّذِينَ أَشْرَكُوا۟ شُرَكَآءَهُمْ قَالُوا۟ رَبَّنَا هَٰٓؤُلَآءِ شُرَكَآؤُنَا ٱلَّذِينَ كُنَّا نَدْعُوا۟ مِن دُونِكَ ۖ فَأَلْقَوْا۟ إِلَيْهِمُ ٱلْقَوْلَ إِنَّكُمْ لَكَٰذِبُونَ ۝ } \right\}$$

86. And when those who associated partners with Allâh see their (Allâh's so-called) partners, they will say: "Our Lord! These are our partners whom we used to invoke besides you." But they will throw back their word at them (and say): "Surely! You indeed are liars!"

$$\left\{ \text{وَأَلْقَوْا۟ إِلَى ٱللَّهِ يَوْمَئِذٍ ٱلسَّلَمَ ۖ وَضَلَّ عَنْهُم مَّا كَانُوا۟ يَفْتَرُونَ ۝ } \right\}$$

87. And they will offer (their full) submission to Allâh (Alone) on that Day, and their invented false deities (all that they used to invoke besides Allâh, e.g. idols, saints, priests, monks, angels, jinn, Jibrîl (Gabriel), Messengers) will vanish from them.

$$\left\{ \text{ٱلَّذِينَ كَفَرُوا۟ وَصَدُّوا۟ عَن سَبِيلِ ٱللَّهِ زِدْنَٰهُمْ عَذَابًا فَوْقَ ٱلْعَذَابِ بِمَا كَانُوا۟ يُفْسِدُونَ ۝ } \right\}$$

88. Those who disbelieved and hinder (men) from the Path of Allâh, for them We will add torment over the torment because they used to spread corruption (by disobeying Allâh themselves, as well as ordering others (mankind) to do so).

Transliteration

84. Wayawma nabAAathu min kulli ommatin shaheedan thumma la yu/thanu lillatheena kafaroo wala hum yustaAAtaboona 85. Wa-itha raa allatheena thalamoo alAAathaba fala yukhaffafu AAanhum wala hum yuntharoona 86. Wa-itha raa allatheena ashrakoo shurakaahum qaloo rabbana haola-i shurakaona allatheena kunna nadAAoo min doonika faalqaw ilayhimu alqawla innakum lakathiboona 87. Waalqaw ila Allahi yawma-ithin alssalama wadalla AAanhum ma kanoo yaftaroona 88. Allatheena kafaroo wasaddoo AAan sabeeli Allahi zidnahum AAathaban fawqa alAAathabi bima kanoo yufsidoona

Tafsir Ibn Kathir

The Plight of the Idolators on the Day of Judgement

Allah tells us about the predicament of the idolators on the Day when they will be resurrected in the realm of the Hereafter. He will raise a witness from every nation - that is - their Prophet, to testify about their response to the Message he conveyed from Allah.

(then, those who disbelieved will not be given leave.) meaning, they will not be allowed to offer any excuse, as Allah says:

(That will be a Day when they do not speak. And they will not be permitted to present any excuse) (77:35-36). Hence, Allah says:

(nor will they be allowed (to return to the world) to repent and ask for Allah's forgiveness. And once those who did wrong see) meaning those who associated others in worship with Allah,

(the torment, it will not decrease for them,) meaning it will not be reduced for them even for a moment.

(nor will they be given respite.) meaning, it will not be delayed for them, rather they will be taken quickly from the place of gathering, with no calling to account. Then Hell will be brought forth, pulled by seventy thousand ropes, each of which is held by seventy thousand angels, and a neck will stretch forth from Hell towards the people, and it will expel a gust of hot air. No one will be left but will fall to his knees. Then it (the neck that is stretched forth) will say, "I have been entrusted to deal with every stubborn, arrogant one who joined another god with Allah," and so and so, mentioning different types of people, as was reported in the Hadith. Then it will come down upon them and pick them up from where they are standing as a bird picks up a seed. Allah says:

(When it (Hell) sees them from a far place, they will hear its raging and its roaring. And when they are thrown into a narrow part of it, chained together, they will cry for destruction. Today, do not scream for one destruction, but scream repeatedly for destruction.) (25:12-14)

(And the guilty shall see the Fire and apprehend that they are about to fall into it. And they will find no way to avoid it.) (18:53)

(If only those who disbelieved knew (about the time) when they will not be able to protect their faces nor their backs from the Fire, and they have no help. Nay, it (the Fire) will come upon them all of a sudden and will perplex them, and they will have no power to avert it nor will they have any respite.) (21:39-40)

The gods of the Idolators will disown Them at the Time when They need them most

Then Allah tells us that their gods will disown them when they need them most. He says:

(And when those who associated partners with Allah see their partners) meaning, those whom they used to worship in this world.'

(they will say: "Our Lord! These are our partners whom we used to call upon besides you." But they will throw their statements back at them (saying): "You are indeed liars!") i.e., those gods will say to them, `you are lying. We never commanded you to worship us.' Allah says:

(And who is more astray than one who calls upon others besides Allah, such as will not answer him till the Day of Resurrection, and who are (even) unaware of their invocations to them And when the people are gathered (on the Day of Resurrection), they (false deities) will become their enemies and will deny their worship,) (46:5-6)

(And they have taken gods besides Allah, that they might give them honor, power and glory. Nay, but they will deny their worship, and become their adversaries (on the Day of Resurrection).) (19:81-82) Al-Khalil (Ibrahim) said:

(but on the Day of Resurrection, you will disown each other) (29:25) And Allah says:

(And it will be said (to them): "Call upon your partners") (28:64) And there are many other similar Ayat.

Everything will surrender to Allah on the Day of Resurrection

(And they will offer (their full) submission to Allah on that Day,) Qatadah and `Ikrimah said: "They will humble themselves and surrender on that Day," i.e., they will all surrender to Allah, there will not be anyone who does not hear and obey. As Allah says:

(How clearly will they see and hear, the Day when they will appear before Us!) (19:38) meaning, they will see and hear better than they have ever seen and heard before. And Allah says:

(And if you only could see when the guilty hang their heads before their Lord (saying): "Our Lord! We have now seen and heard.") (32:12)

(And (all) faces shall be humbled before the Ever Living, the Sustainer.) (20:111) meaning, they will humble and submit themselves.

(And they will offer (their full) submission to Allah on that Day, and what they falsely invented will wander away from them.) The things that they used to worship which were all based on fabrications and lies, will all disappear, and they will have no helper or supporter, and no one to turn to.

Those among the Idolators who corrupted Others will receive a Greater Punishment

Then Allah tells us:

(Those who disbelieved and tried to obstruct the path of Allah, for them We will add torment) meaning one punishment for their disbelief and another punishment for turning others away from following the truth, as Allah says:

(And they prevent others from him and they themselves keep away from him) (6:26) meaning they forbade others to follow him and they themselves shunned him, but:

(they destroyed only themselves, while they do not realize it.) This is evidence that there will be varying levels of punishment for the disbelievers, just as there will be varying degrees of Paradise for the believers, as Allah says:

(For each one there is double (torment), but you know not.) (7:38)

Surah: 16 Ayah: 89

﴿ وَيَوْمَ نَبْعَثُ فِى كُلِّ أُمَّةٍ شَهِيدًا عَلَيْهِم مِّنْ أَنفُسِهِمْ وَجِئْنَا بِكَ شَهِيدًا عَلَىٰ هَـٰؤُلَاءِ وَنَزَّلْنَا عَلَيْكَ ٱلْكِتَـٰبَ تِبْيَـٰنًا لِّكُلِّ شَىْءٍ وَهُدًى وَرَحْمَةً وَبُشْرَىٰ لِلْمُسْلِمِينَ ﴾ ۝

89. And (remember) the Day when We shall raise up from every nation a witness against them from amongst themselves. And We shall bring you (O Muhammad (peace be upon him)) as a witness against these. And We have sent down to you the Book (the Qur'an) as an exposition of everything, a guidance, a mercy, and glad tidings for those who have submitted themselves (to Allâh as Muslims).

Transliteration

89. Wayawma nabAAathu fee kulli ommatin shaheedan AAalayhim min anfusihim waji/na bika shaheedan AAala haola-i wanazzalna AAalayka alkitaba tibyanan likulli shay-in wahudan warahmatan wabushra lilmuslimeena

Tafsir Ibn Kathir

Every Prophet will bear Witness against his Nation on the Day of Resurrection

Allah addressed His servant and Messenger Muhammad, saying:

(And on the Day when We resurrect a witness from each nation from among themselves, and We bring you (O Muhammad) as a witness against these.), meaning, your Ummah. The Ayah means: remember that Day and its terrors, and the great honor and high position that Allah has bestowed upon you. This Ayah is like the Ayah with which `Abdullah bin Mas`ud ended when he recited to the Messenger of Allah from the beginning of Surat An-Nisa'. When he reached the Ayah:

(How (will it be) then, when We bring from each nation a witness and We bring you (O Muhammad) as a witness against these) (4:41) the Messenger of Allah said to him:

«حَسْبُكَ»

(Enough.) Ibn Mas`ud said: "I turned to him and saw his eyes streaming with tears."

The Qur'an explains Everything

(And We revealed the Book (the Qur'an) to you as an explanation of everything,) Ibn Mas`ud said: "(Allah) made it clear that in this Qur'an there is complete knowledge about everything." The Qur'an contains all kinds of beneficial knowledge, such as reports of what happened in the past, information about what is yet to come, what is lawful and unlawful, and what people need to know about their worldly affairs, their religion, their livelihood in this world, and their destiny in the Hereafter.

(a guidance) means, for their hearts.

(a mercy, and good news for the Muslims.) Al-Awza`i said:

(And We have revealed the Book (the Qur'an) as an explanation of everything,) meaning, with the Sunnah. This is the reason why the phrase,

(And We have revealed the Book to you) is mentioned immediately after the phrase,

(And We shall bring you (O Muhammad) as a witness against these.) the meaning - and Allah knows best - is that the One Who obligated you to convey the Book which He revealed to you, will also ask you about that on the Day of Resurrection.

(Then We shall indeed question those (people) to whom it (the Book) was sent and We shall indeed question the Messengers.) (7:6)

(So by your Lord We question them all about what they did.) (15:92-92)

(On the Day when Allah gathers the Messengers together and says to them: "What was the response you received (to your Message)" They will say: "We have no knowledge, indeed only You are the Knower of all that is hidden.") (5:109) And Allah says:

(Verily, He Who obligated the Qur'an upon you (O Muhammad) will surely bring you back to the return.) (28:85) meaning, the One Who gave you the obligation of conveying the Qur'an will bring you back to Him, and your return will be on the Day of Resurrection, and He will question you about you commission of the duty He gave you. This is one of the opinions, and it presents a good understanding of it.

Surah: 16 Ayah: 90

﴿ ۞ إِنَّ ٱللَّهَ يَأْمُرُ بِٱلْعَدْلِ وَٱلْإِحْسَـٰنِ وَإِيتَآئِ ذِى ٱلْقُرْبَىٰ وَيَنْهَىٰ عَنِ ٱلْفَحْشَآءِ وَٱلْمُنكَرِ وَٱلْبَغْىِ يَعِظُكُمْ لَعَلَّكُمْ تَذَكَّرُونَ ۞ ﴾

90. Verily, Allâh enjoins Al-'dl (i.e. justice and worshipping none but Allâh Alone - Islâmic Monotheism) and Al-Ihsân (i.e. to be patient in performing your duties to Allâh, totally for Allâh's sake and in accordance with the Sunnah (legal ways) of the Prophet (peace be upon him in a perfect manner), and giving (help) to kith and kin (i.e. all that Allâh has ordered you to give them e.g., wealth, visiting, looking after them, or any other kind of help), and forbids Al-Fahshâ' (i.e. all evil deeds, e.g. illegal sexual acts, disobedience of parents, polytheism, to tell lies, to give false witness, to kill a life without right), and Al-Munkar (i.e. all that is prohibited by Islâmic law: polytheism of every kind, disbelief and every kind of evil deeds), and Al-Baghy (i.e. all kinds of oppression), He admonishes you, that you may take heed.

Transliteration

90. Inna Allaha ya/muru bialAAadli waal-ihsani wa-eeta-i thee alqurba wayanha AAani alfahsha-i waalmunkari waalbaghyi yaAAithukum laAAallakum tathakkaroona

Tafsir Ibn Kathir

The Command to be Fair and Kind

Allah tells us that He commands His servant to be just, i.e., fair and moderate, and that He encourages kindness and good treatment. As He says:

(And if you punish them, then punish them with the like of that with which you were afflicted. But if you have patience with them, then it is better for those who are patient.) (16:126)

(The recompense for an offense is an offense the like thereof; but whoever forgives and makes reconciliation, his reward is with Allah.) (42:40)

(and wounds equal for equal. But if anyone remits the retaliation by way of charity, it shall count as atonement for him.) (5:45) And there are other Ayat which support the institution of justice in Islam, as well as encouraging a fair and generous attitude.

The Command to maintain the Ties of Kinship and the prohibition of Immoral Sins, Evil and Tyranny

(and giving (help) to relatives,) meaning that Allah is commanding us to uphold the ties of kinship, as He says:

(And give the relative his due and to the poor and to the wayfarer. But do not spend wastefully in the manner of a spendthrift.) (17:26)

(and He forbids immoral sins, and evil) Fahsha' refers to all things that are forbidden, and Munkar refers to those forbidden deeds that are committed openly by the one who does them. Hence Allah says elsewhere:

(Say (O Muhammad): "(But) the things that my Lord has indeed forbidden are the indecencies, whether committed openly or secretly) (7:33) Baghy refers to aggression towards people. In a Hadith, the Prophet said:

«مَا مِنْ ذَنْبٍ أَجْدَرَ أَنْ يُعَجِّلَ اللهُ عُقُوبَتَهُ فِي الدُّنْيَا مَعَ مَا يَدَّخِرُ لِصَاحِبِهِ فِي الْآخِرَةِ مِنَ الْبَغْيِ وَقَطِيعَةِ الرَّحِمِ»

(There is no sin more deserving of having its punishment hastened in this world, as well as what is reserved in the Hereafter for the one who does it, than tyrannical aggression and cutting the ties of kinship.)

(He admonishes you,) meaning, He commands what He commands you of good and He forbids what He forbids you of evil;

(so that perhaps you may take heed) Ash-Sha`bi reported that Shatiyr bin Shakl said: "I heard Ibn Mas`ud say: `The most comprehensive Ayah in the Qur'an is in Surat An-Nahl:

(Verily, Allah enjoins justice and kindness...)'" It was reported by Ibn Jarir.

The Eyewitness Account of `Uthman

Concerning the revelation of this Ayah, Imam Ahmad reported a Hasan Hadith from `Abdullah bin `Abbas who said: "While the Messenger of Allah was sitting in the courtyard of his house, `Uthman bin Maz`un passed by and smiled at the Messenger of Allah. The Messenger of Allah said to him,

«أَلَا تَجْلِسُ؟»

(Won't you sit down) He said, `Certainly.' So the Messenger of Allah sat facing him, and while they were talking, the Messenger of Allah began looking up at the sky, looking at it for a while, then he brought his gaze down until he was looking at the ground to his right. Then the Messenger of Allah turned slightly away from his companion `Uthman to where he was looking. Then he began to tilt his head as if trying to understand something, and Ibn Maz`un was looking on. When the matter was finished and he had understood what had been said to him, the Messenger of Allah stared at the sky again as he had the first time, looking at whatever he could see until it disappeared. Then he turned back to face `Uthman again. `Uthman said, `O Muhammad, I have never seen you do anything like you did today while I was sitting with you.' The Messenger of Allah said:

«وَمَا رَأَيْتَنِي فَعَلْتُ؟»

(What did you see me do) `Uthman said: `I saw you staring at the sky, then you lowered your gaze until you were looking to your right, then you turned to him and left me. Then you tilted your head as if you were trying to understand something that was being said to you.' The Messenger of Allah said,

«وَفَطِنْتَ لِذَلِكَ؟»

(Did you notice that) `Uthman said, `Yes'. The Messenger of Allah said:

«أَتَانِي رَسُولُ اللهِ آنِفًا وَأَنْتَ جَالِسٌ»

Chapter 16: An-Nahl (The Bee), Verses 001-128

(A messenger from Allah came to me just now, when you were sitting here.) `Uthman said, `A messenger from Allah' The Messenger of Allah said,

《نَعَم》

(Yes.) `Uthman said, `And what did he say to you' The Messenger of Allah said:

(إِنَّ اللَّهَ يَأْمُرُ بِالْعَدْلِ وَالْإِحْسَانِ)

(Verily, Allah orders justice and kindness...) `Uthman said: `That was when faith was established in my heart and I began to love Muhammad ." It is a Hasan Hadith having a good connected chain of narrators in which their hearing it from each other is clear.

Surah: 16 Ayah: 91 & Ayah: 92

﴿ وَأَوْفُوا بِعَهْدِ اللَّهِ إِذَا عَاهَدتُّمْ وَلَا تَنقُضُوا الْأَيْمَانَ بَعْدَ تَوْكِيدِهَا وَقَدْ جَعَلْتُمُ اللَّهَ عَلَيْكُمْ كَفِيلًا إِنَّ اللَّهَ يَعْلَمُ مَا تَفْعَلُونَ ۝ ﴾

91. And fulfill the Covenant of Allâh (Bai'ah: pledge for Islâm) when you have covenanted, and break not the oaths after you have confirmed them - and indeed you have appointed Allâh your surety. Verily! Allâh knows what you do.

﴿ وَلَا تَكُونُوا كَالَّتِي نَقَضَتْ غَزْلَهَا مِنْ بَعْدِ قُوَّةٍ أَنكَاثًا تَتَّخِذُونَ أَيْمَانَكُمْ دَخَلًا بَيْنَكُمْ أَن تَكُونَ أُمَّةٌ هِيَ أَرْبَىٰ مِنْ أُمَّةٍ إِنَّمَا يَبْلُوكُمُ اللَّهُ بِهِ ۚ وَلَيُبَيِّنَنَّ لَكُمْ يَوْمَ الْقِيَامَةِ مَا كُنتُمْ فِيهِ تَخْتَلِفُونَ ۝ ﴾

92. And be not like her who undoes the thread which she has spun after it has become strong, by taking your oaths a means of deception among yourselves, lest a nation may be more numerous than another nation. Allâh only tests you by this (i.e. who obeys Allâh and fulfills Allâh's Covenant and who disobeys Allâh and breaks Allâh's Covenant). And on the Day of Resurrection, He will certainly make clear to you that wherein you used to differ (i.e. a believer confesses and believes in the Oneness of Allâh and in the Prophethood of Prophet Muhammad (peace be upon him) which the disbeliever denies and that is their difference amongst them in the life of this world).

Transliteration

91. Waawfoo biAAahdi Allahi itha AAahadtum wala tanqudoo al-aymana baAAda tawkeediha waqad jaAAaltumu Allaha AAalaykum kafeelan inna Allaha yaAAlamu ma tafAAaloona 92. Wala takoonoo kaallatee naqadat ghazlaha min baAAdi quwwatin ankathan tattakhithoona aymanakum dakhalan baynakum an takoona ommatun hiya

arba min ommatin innama yablookumu Allahu bihi walayubayyinanna lakum yawma alqiyamati ma kuntum feehi takhtalifoona

Tafsir Ibn Kathir

The Command to fulfill the Covenant

This is one of the commands of Allah, to fulfill covenants, keep promises and to fulfill oaths after confirming them. Thus Allah says: (and do not break the oaths after you have confirmed them) There is no conflict between this and the Ayat:

(And do not use Allah as an excuse in your oaths) (2:224)

(That is the expiation for oaths when you have sworn. And protect your oaths.) (5:89) meaning, do not forgo your oaths without offering the penance. There is also no conflict between this Ayah (16:91) and the Hadith reported in the Two Sahihs according to which the Prophet said:

«إِنِّي وَاللهِ إِنْ شَاءَ اللهُ لَا أَحْلِفُ عَلَى يَمِينٍ فَأَرَى غَيْرَهَا خَيْرًا مِنْهَا إِلَّا أَتَيْتُ الَّذِي هُوَ خَيْرٌ وَتَحَلَّلْتُهَا وَفِي رِوَايَةٍ وَكَفَّرْتُ عَنْ يَمِينِي»

(By Allah, if Allah wills, I will not swear an oath and then realize that something else is better, but I do that which is better and find a way to free myself from the oath. According to another report he said: "and I offer penance for my oath. ") There is no contradiction at all between all of these texts and the Ayah under discussion here, which is:

(and do not break the oaths after you have confirmed them) because these are the kinds of oaths that have to do with covenants and promises, not the kind that have to do with urging oneself to do something or preventing him from doing something. Therefore Mujahid said concerning this Ayah:

(and do not break the oaths after you have confirmed them) "The oath here refers to oaths made during Jahiliyyah." This supports the Hadith recorded by Imam Ahmad from Jubayr bin Mut`im, who said that the Messenger of Allah said:

«لَا حِلْفَ فِي الْإِسْلَامِ، وَأَيُّمَا حِلْفٍ كَانَ فِي الْجَاهِلِيَّةِ فَإِنَّهُ لَا يَزِيدُهُ الْإِسْلَامُ إِلَّا شِدَّةً»

(There is no oath in Islam, and any oath made during the Jahiliyyah is only reinforced by Islam.) This was also reported by Muslim. The meaning is that Islam does not need oaths as they were used by the people of the Jahiliyyah; adherence to Islam is sufficient to do away with any need for what they used to customarily give oaths for. In the Two Sahihs it was reported that Anas said: "The Messenger of Allah () swore the treaty of allegiance between the Muhajirin (emigrants) and the Ansar (helpers) in our house. " This means that he established brotherhood between them, and they used to inherit from one another, until Allah abrogated that. And Allah knows best.

(Verily, Allah knows what you do.) This is a warning and a threat to those who break their oaths after confirming them. (And do not be like the one who undoes the thread which she has spun, after it has become strong,) `Abdullah bin Kathir and As-Suddi said: "This was a foolish woman in Makkah. Everytime she spun thread and made it strong, she would undo it again." Mujahid, Qatadah and Ibn Zayd said: "This is like the one who breaks a covenant after confirming it." This view is more correct and more apparent, whether or not there was a woman in Makkah who undid her thread after spinning it. The word Ankathan could be referring back to the word translated as "undoes", reinforcing the meaning, or it could be the predicate of the verb "to be", meaning, do not be Ankathan, the plural of Nakth (breach, violation), from the word Nakith (perfidious). Hence after this, Allah says:

(by taking your oaths as a means of deception among yourselves) meaning for the purposes of cheating and tricking one another.

(when one group is more numerous than another group.) meaning, you swear an oath with some people if they are more in number than you, so that they can trust you, but when you are able to betray them you do so. Allah forbids that, by showing a case where treachery might be expected or excused, but He forbids it. If treachery is forbidden in such a case, then in cases where one is in a position of strength it is forbidden more emphatically. Mujahid said: "They used to enter into alliances and covenants, then find other parties who were more powerful and more numerous, so they would cancel the alliance with the first group and make an alliance with the second who were more powerful and more numerous. This is what they were forbidden to do." Ad-Dahhak, Qatadah and Ibn Zayd said something similar.

(Allah only tests you by this) Sa`id bin Jubayr said: "This means (you are tested) by the large numbers." This was reported by Ibn Abi Hatim. Ibn Jarir said: "It means (you are being tested) by His command to you to adhere to your covenants."

(And on the Day of Resurrection, He will certainly clarify that which you differed over.) Everyone will be rewarded or punished in accordance with his deeds, good or evil.

Surah: 16 Ayah: 93, Ayah: 94, Ayah: 95 & Ayah: 96

﴿ وَلَوْ شَآءَ ٱللَّهُ لَجَعَلَكُمْ أُمَّةً وَٰحِدَةً وَلَٰكِن يُضِلُّ مَن يَشَآءُ وَيَهْدِى مَن يَشَآءُ وَلَتُسْـَٔلُنَّ عَمَّا كُنتُمْ تَعْمَلُونَ ۝ ﴾

93. And had Allâh willed, He could have made you (all) one nation, but He sends astray whom He wills and guides whom He wills. But you shall certainly be called to account for what you used to do.

﴿ وَلَا تَتَّخِذُوٓاْ أَيْمَـٰنَكُمْ دَخَلَۢا بَيْنَكُمْ فَتَزِلَّ قَدَمٌۢ بَعْدَ ثُبُوتِهَا وَتَذُوقُواْ ٱلسُّوٓءَ بِمَا صَدَدتُّمْ عَن سَبِيلِ ٱللَّهِ وَلَكُمْ عَذَابٌ عَظِيمٌ ۞ ﴾

94. And make not your oaths, a means of deception among yourselves, lest a foot may slip after being firmly planted, and you may have to taste the evil (punishment in this world) of having hindered (men) from the Path of Allâh (i.e. Belief in the Oneness of Allâh and His Messenger, Muhammad (peace be upon him)) and yours will be a great torment (i.e. the Fire of Hell in the Hereafter).

﴿ وَلَا تَشْتَرُواْ بِعَهْدِ ٱللَّهِ ثَمَنًا قَلِيلًا إِنَّمَا عِندَ ٱللَّهِ هُوَ خَيْرٌ لَّكُمْ إِن كُنتُمْ تَعْلَمُونَ ۞ ﴾

95. And purchase not a small gain at the cost of Allâh's Covenant. Verily! What is with Allâh is better for you if you did but know.

﴿ مَا عِندَكُمْ يَنفَدُ وَمَا عِندَ ٱللَّهِ بَاقٍ وَلَنَجْزِيَنَّ ٱلَّذِينَ صَبَرُوٓاْ أَجْرَهُم بِأَحْسَنِ مَا كَانُواْ يَعْمَلُونَ ۞ ﴾

96. Whatever is with you, will be exhausted, and whatever is with Allâh (of good deeds) will remain. And those who are patient, We will certainly pay them a reward in proportion to the best of what they used to do.

Transliteration

93. Walaw shaa Allahu lajaAAalakum ommatan wahidatan walakin yudillu man yashao wayahdee man yashao walatus-alunna AAamma kuntum taAAmaloona   94. Wala tattakhithoo aymanakum dakhalan baynakum fatazilla qadamun baAAda thubootiha watathooqoo alssoo-a bima sadadtum AAan sabeeli Allahi walakum AAathabun AAatheemun   95. Wala tashtaroo biAAahdi Allahi thamanan qaleelan innama AAinda Allahi huwa khayrun lakum in kuntum taAAlamoona   96. Ma AAindakum yanfadu wama AAinda Allahi baqin walanajziyanna allatheena sabaroo ajrahum bi-ahsani ma kanoo yaAAmaloona

Tafsir Ibn Kathir

If Allah had willed, He would have made all of Humanity one Nation

Allah says:

(And had Allah willed, He would have made you) meaning - O mankind,

((all) one nation,) This is like the Ayah:

(And had your Lord willed, all of those on earth would have believed together.) (10:99), meaning, He could have created harmony among them, and there would not be any differences, conflicts or hatred between them.

(And if your Lord had so willed, He would surely, have made mankind one Ummah (nation or community), but they will not cease to disagree. Except him on whom your Lord has bestowed His mercy, and for that did He create them.) (11:118-119) Similarly, Allah says here:

(but He allows whom He wills to stray and He guides whom He wills.) Then on the Day of Resurrection, He will ask them all about their deeds, and will reward or punish them even equal to a scalish thread in the long slit of a date stone or the size of a speck on the back of a date stone, or even a thin membrane of the date stone.

The Prohibition on taking an Oath for Purposes of Treachery

Then Allah warns His servant against taking oaths as means of deception, i.e., using them for treacherous purposes, lest a foot should slip after being firmly planted. This is an analogy describing one who was on the right path but then deviated and slipped from the path of guidance because of an unfulfilled oath that involved hindering people from the path of Allah. This is because if a disbeliever were to find that after having agreed to a covenant, then the believer betrayed him, then the believer will have hindered him from entering Islam. Thus Allah says:

(and you taste the evil of having hindered from the path of Allah, and you will suffer a terrible punishment.)

Do not break Oaths for the sake of Worldly Gain

Then Allah says:

(And do not use an oath by Allah for the purchase of little value.) meaning, do not neglect an oath sworn in the Name of Allah for the sake of this world and its attractions, for they are few, and even if the son of Adam were to gain this world and all that is in it, that which is with Allah is better for him, i.e., the reward of Allah is better for the one who puts his hope in Him, believes in Him, seeks Him and fulfills his oaths in the hope of that which Allah has promised. This is why Allah says:

(if you only knew. Whatever you have will be exhausted,) meaning, it will come to an end and will vanish, because it is only there for a certain, limited time.

(and what is with Allah will remain.) meaning, His reward for you in Paradise will remain, without interruption or end, because it is eternal and will never change nor disappear.

(And to those who are patient, We will certainly grant them their rewards in proportion to the best of what they used to do.) Here the Lord swears, with the Lam of affirmation, that He will reward the patient for the best of their deeds, i.e., He will forgive them for their bad deeds.

Surah: 16 Ayah: 97

$$ ﴿ مَنْ عَمِلَ صَـٰلِحًا مِّن ذَكَرٍ أَوْ أُنثَىٰ وَهُوَ مُؤْمِنٌ فَلَنُحْيِيَنَّهُ حَيَوٰةً طَيِّبَةً وَلَنَجْزِيَنَّهُمْ أَجْرَهُم بِأَحْسَنِ مَا كَانُوا۟ يَعْمَلُونَ ۝ ﴾ $$

97. Whoever works righteousness - whether male or female - while he (or she) is a true believer (of Islâmic Monotheism) verily, to him We will give a good life (in this world with respect, contentment and lawful provision), and We shall pay them certainly a reward in proportion to the best of what they used to do (i.e. Paradise in the Hereafter).

Transliteration

97. Man AAamila salihan min thakarin aw ontha wahuwa mu/minun falanuhyiyannahu hayatan tayyibatan walanajziyannahum ajrahum bi-ahsani ma kanoo yaAAmaloona

Tafsir Ibn Kathir

Righteous Deeds and their Reward

This is a promise from Allah to those Children of Adam, male or female, who do righteous deeds - deeds in accordance with the Book of Allah and the Sunnah of His Prophet, with a heart that believes in Allah and His Messenger, while believing that these deeds are commanded and enjoined by Allah. Allah promises that He will give them a good life in this world and that He will reward them according to the best of their deeds in the Hereafter. The good life includes feeling tranquillity in all aspects of life. It has been reported that Ibn `Abbas and a group (of scholars) interpreted it to mean good, lawful provisions. It was reported that `Ali bin Abi Talib interpreted as contentment. This was also the opinion of Ibn `Abbas, `Ikrimah and Wahb bin Munabbih. `Ali bin Abi Talhah recorded from Ibn `Abbas that it meant happiness. Al-Hasan, Mujahid and Qatadah said: "None gets (this) good life (mentioned) except in Paradise." Ad-Dahhak said: "It means lawful provisions and worship in this life". Ad-Dahhak also said: "It means working to obey Allah and finding joy in that." The correct view is that a good life includes all of these things. as found in the Hadith recorded by Imam Ahmad from `Abdullah bin `Amr that the Messenger of Allah said:

$$ «قَدْ أَفْلَحَ مَنْ أَسْلَمَ، وَرُزِقَ كَفَافًا، وَقَنَّعَهُ اللهُ بِمَا آتَاهُ» $$

(He who submits (becomes a Muslim) has succeeded, is given sufficient provisions, and is content with Allah for what he is given.) It was also recorded by Muslim.

Surah: 16 Ayah: 98, Ayah: 99 & Ayah: 100

$$ ﴿ فَإِذَا قَرَأْتَ ٱلْقُرْءَانَ فَٱسْتَعِذْ بِٱللَّهِ مِنَ ٱلشَّيْطَـٰنِ ٱلرَّجِيمِ ۝ ﴾ $$

98. So when you want to recite the Qur'ân, seek refuge with Allâh from Shaitân (Satan), the outcast (the cursed one).

Chapter 16: An-Nahl (The Bee), Verses 001-128

﴿ إِنَّهُۥ لَيْسَ لَهُۥ سُلْطَـٰنٌ عَلَى ٱلَّذِينَ ءَامَنُوا۟ وَعَلَىٰ رَبِّهِمْ يَتَوَكَّلُونَ ۝ ﴾

99. Verily! He has no power over those who believe and put their trust only in their Lord (Allâh).

﴿ إِنَّمَا سُلْطَـٰنُهُۥ عَلَى ٱلَّذِينَ يَتَوَلَّوْنَهُۥ وَٱلَّذِينَ هُم بِهِۦ مُشْرِكُونَ ۝ ﴾

100. His power is only over those who obey and follow him (Satan), and those who join partners with Him (Allâh i.e. those who are Mushrikûn i.e. polytheists. See Verse 6:121).

Transliteration

98. Fa-itha qara/ta alqur-ana faistaAAith biAllahi mina alshshaytani alrrajeemi 99. Innahu laysa lahu sultanun AAala allatheena amanoo waAAala rabbihim yatawakkaloona 100. Innama sultanuhu AAala allatheena yatawallawnahu waallatheena hum bihi mushrikoona

Tafsir Ibn Kathir

The Command to seek Refuge with Allah before reciting the Qur'an

This is a command from Allah to His servants upon the tongue of His Prophet , telling them that when they want to read Qur'an, they should seek refuge with Allah from the cursed Shaytan. The Hadiths mentioned about seeking refuge with Allah (Isti`adhah), were quoted in our discussion at the beginning of this Tafsir, praise be to Allah. The reason for seeking refuge with Allah before reading is that the reader should not get confused or mixed up, and that the Shaytan would not confuse him or stop him from thinking about and pondering over the meaning of what he reads. Hence the majority of scholars said that refuge should be sought with Allah before starting to read.

(Verily, he has no power over those who believe and put their trust only in their Lord.) Ath-Thawri said: "He has no power to make them commit a sin they will not repent from." Others said: it means that he has no argument for them. Others said it is like the Ayah: (Except Your chosen servants amongst them.) (15:40) (His power is only over those who obey and follow him (Shaytan),) Mujahid said: "Those who obey him." Others said, "Those who take him as their protector instead of Allah."

(and those who join partners with Him.) means, those who associate others in worship with Allah.

Surah: 16 Ayah: 101 & Ayah: 102

﴿ وَإِذَا بَدَّلْنَآ ءَايَةً مَّكَانَ ءَايَةٍ وَٱللَّهُ أَعْلَمُ بِمَا يُنَزِّلُ قَالُوٓا۟ إِنَّمَآ أَنتَ مُفْتَرٍۭ بَلْ أَكْثَرُهُمْ لَا يَعْلَمُونَ ۝ ﴾

101. And when We change a Verse (of the Qur'ân,) in place of another - and Allâh knows best what He sends down - they (the disbelievers) say: "You (O

Muhammad (peace be upon him)) are but a Muftari! (forger, liar)." Nay, but most of them know not.

﴿ قُلْ نَزَّلَهُۥ رُوحُ ٱلْقُدُسِ مِن رَّبِّكَ بِٱلْحَقِّ لِيُثَبِّتَ ٱلَّذِينَ ءَامَنُوا۟ وَهُدًى وَبُشْرَىٰ لِلْمُسْلِمِينَ ﴾

102. Say (O Muhammad (peace be upon him)) Ruh-ul-Qudus (Jibrîl (Gabriel)) has brought it (the Qur'ân) down from your Lord with truth, that it may make firm and strengthen (the Faith of) those who believe, and as a guidance and glad tidings to those who have submitted (to Allâh as Muslims).

Transliteration

101. Wa-itha baddalna ayatan makana ayatin waAllahu aAAlamu bima yunazzilu qaloo innama anta muftarin bal aktharuhum la yaAAlamoona 102. Qul nazzalahu roohu alqudusi min rabbika bialhaqqi liyuthabbita allatheena amanoo wahudan wabushra lilmuslimeena

Tafsir Ibn Kathir

The Idolators' Accusation that the Prophet was a Liar since some Ayat were abrogated, and the Refutation of their Claim

Allah tells us of the weak minds of the idolators, and their lack of faith and conviction. He explains that it is impossible for them to have faith when He has decreed that they are doomed. When they saw that some rulings had been changed by being abrogated, they said to the Messenger of Allah :

(You are but a forger) meaning one who tells lies. But Allah is the Lord Who does whatever He wills, and rules as He wants.

(And when We change a verse (of the Qur'an) in place of another) Mujahid said: this means, "We remove one and put another in its place." Qatadah said: this is like the Ayah:

(Whatever verse We change (abrogate) or omit (the abrogated)...)" (2:106). Allah said, in response to them: (Say: "Ruh-ul-Qudus has brought it...") meaning, Jibril,

(from your Lord with truth,) meaning, with truthfulness and justice

(for the conviction of those who believe,) so that they will believe what was revealed earlier and what was revealed later, and humble themselves towards Allah.

(and as a guide and good news for the Muslims.) meaning He has made it a guide and good news to the Muslims who believe in Allah and His Messengers.

Surah: 16 Ayah: 103

$$ \text{﴿ وَلَقَدْ نَعْلَمُ أَنَّهُمْ يَقُولُونَ إِنَّمَا يُعَلِّمُهُ بَشَرٌ لِّسَانُ ٱلَّذِى يُلْحِدُونَ إِلَيْهِ أَعْجَمِىٌّ وَهَـٰذَا لِسَانٌ عَرَبِىٌّ مُّبِينٌ ﴾} $$

103. And indeed We know that they (polytheists and pagans) say: "It is only a human being who teaches him (Muhammad (peace be upon him))" The tongue of the man they refer to is foreign, while this (the Qur'ân) is a clear Arabic tongue.

Transliteration

103. Walaqad naAAlamu annahum yaqooloona innama yuAAallimuhu basharun lisanu allathee yulhidoona ilayhi aAAjamiyyun wahatha lisanun AAarabiyyun mubeenun

Tafsir Ibn Kathir

The Idolators' Claim that the Qur'an was taught by a Human, and the Refutation of their Claim

Allah tells us about the idolators' lies, allegations, and slander when they claimed that this Qur'an which Muhammad had recited for them, was actually taught to him by a human. They referred to a foreign (i.e., non-Arab) man who lived among them as the servant of some of the clans of Quraysh and who used to sell goods by As-Safa. Maybe the Messenger of Allah used to sit with him sometimes and talk to him a little, but he was a foreigner who did not know much Arabic, only enough simple phrases to answer questions when he had to. So in refutation of their claims of fabrication, Allah said:

(The tongue of the man they refer to is foreign, while this (the Qur'an) is a (in) clear Arabic tongue.) meaning, how could it be that this Qur'an with its eloquent style and perfect meanings, which is more perfect than any Book revealed to any previously sent Prophet, have been learnt from a foreigner who hardly speaks the language No one with the slightest amount of common sense would say such a thing.

Surah: 16 Ayah: 104 & Ayah: 105

$$ \text{﴿ إِنَّ ٱلَّذِينَ لَا يُؤْمِنُونَ بِـَٔايَـٰتِ ٱللَّهِ لَا يَهْدِيهِمُ ٱللَّهُ وَلَهُمْ عَذَابٌ أَلِيمٌ ﴾} $$

104. Verily! Those who believe not in the Ayât (proofs, evidences, verses, lessons, signs, revelations, etc.) of Allâh, Allâh will not guide them and theirs will be a painful torment.

$$ \text{﴿ إِنَّمَا يَفْتَرِى ٱلْكَذِبَ ٱلَّذِينَ لَا يُؤْمِنُونَ بِـَٔايَـٰتِ ٱللَّهِ وَأُوْلَـٰئِكَ هُمُ ٱلْكَـٰذِبُونَ ﴾} $$

105. It is only those who believe not in the Ayât (proofs, evidences, verses, lessons, signs, revelations, etc.) of Allâh, who fabricate falsehood, and it is they who are liars.

Transliteration

104. Inna allatheena la yu/minoona bi-ayati Allahi la yahdeehimu Allahu walahum AAathabun aleemun 105. Innama yaftaree alkathiba allatheena la yu/minoona bi-ayati Allahi waola-ika humu alkathiboona

Tafsir Ibn Kathir

(Verily, those who do not believe in Allah's Ayat,) Allah will not guide them, and theirs will be a painful punishment, meaning, the disbelievers and heretics who are known to the people as liars. The Messenger Muhammad , on the other hand, was the most honest and righteous of people, the most perfect in knowledge, deeds, faith and conviction. He was known among his people for his truthfulness and no one among them had any doubts about that - to such an extent that they always addressed him as Al-Amin (the Trustworthy) Muhammad. Thus when Heraclius, the king of the Romans, asked Abu Sufyan about the attributes of the Messenger of Allah , one of the things he said to him was, "Did you ever accuse him of lying before he made his claim" Abu Sufyan said, "No". Heraclius said, "He would refrain from lying about people and then go and fabricate lies about Allah"

Surah: 16 Ayah: 106, Ayah: 107, Ayah: 108 & Ayah: 109

﴿ مَن كَفَرَ بِٱللَّهِ مِنۢ بَعْدِ إِيمَٰنِهِۦٓ إِلَّا مَنْ أُكْرِهَ وَقَلْبُهُۥ مُطْمَئِنٌّۢ بِٱلْإِيمَٰنِ وَلَٰكِن مَّن شَرَحَ بِٱلْكُفْرِ صَدْرًا فَعَلَيْهِمْ غَضَبٌ مِّنَ ٱللَّهِ وَلَهُمْ عَذَابٌ عَظِيمٌ ﴾

106. Whoever disbelieved in Allâh after his belief, except him who is forced thereto and whose heart is at rest with Faith; but such as open their breasts to disbelief, on them is wrath from Allâh, and theirs will be a great torment.

﴿ ذَٰلِكَ بِأَنَّهُمُ ٱسْتَحَبُّوا۟ ٱلْحَيَوٰةَ ٱلدُّنْيَا عَلَى ٱلْءَاخِرَةِ وَأَنَّ ٱللَّهَ لَا يَهْدِى ٱلْقَوْمَ ٱلْكَٰفِرِينَ ﴾

107. That is because they loved and preferred the life of this world over that of the Hereafter. And Allâh guides not the people who disbelieve.

﴿ أُو۟لَٰٓئِكَ ٱلَّذِينَ طَبَعَ ٱللَّهُ عَلَىٰ قُلُوبِهِمْ وَسَمْعِهِمْ وَأَبْصَٰرِهِمْ وَأُو۟لَٰٓئِكَ هُمُ ٱلْغَٰفِلُونَ ﴾

108. They are those upon whose hearts, hearing (ears) and sight (eyes) Allâh has set a seal. And they are the heedless!

$$\lambda \text{ جَرَمَ أَنَّهُمْ فِى ٱلْأَخِرَةِ هُمُ ٱلْخَـٰسِرُونَ}$$ ﴿١٠٩﴾

109. No doubt, in the Hereafter, they will be the losers.

Transliteration

106. Man kafara biAllahi min baAAdi eemanihi illa man okriha waqalbuhu mutma-innun bial-eemani walakin man sharaha bialkufri sadran faAAalayhim ghadabun mina Allahi walahum AAathabun AAatheemun 107. Thalika bi-annahumu istahaboo alhayata alddunya AAala al-akhirati waanna Allaha la yahdee alqawma alkafireena 108. Ola-ika allatheena tabaAAa Allahu AAala quloobihim wasamAAihim waabsarihim waola-ika humu alghafiloona 109. La jarama annahum fee al-akhirati humu alkhasiroona

Tafsir Ibn Kathir

Allah's Wrath against the Apostate, except for the One Who is forced into Disbelief

Allah tells us that He is angry with them who willingly disbelieve in Him after clearly believing in Him, who open their hearts to disbelief finding peace in that, because they understood the faith yet they still turned away from it. They will suffer severe punishment in the Hereafter, because they preferred this life to the Hereafter, and they left the faith for the sake of this world and Allah did not guide their hearts and help them to stand firm in the true religion. He put a seal on their hearts so that they would not be able to understand what is beneficial for them, and He sealed their ears and eyes so that they would not benefit from them. Their faculties did not help them at all, so they are unaware of what is going to happen to them.

(No doubt) means, it is inevitable, and no wonder that those who are like this -

(in the Hereafter, they will be the losers.) meaning, they will lose themselves and their families on the Day of Resurrection.

(except one who was forced while his heart is at peace with the faith) This is an exception in the case of one who utters statements of disbelief and verbally agrees with the Mushrikin because he is forced to do so by the beatings and abuse to which he is subjected, but his heart refuses to accept what he is saying, and he is, in reality, at peace with his faith in Allah and His Messenger . The scholars agreed that if a person is forced into disbelief, it is permissible for him to either go along with them in the interests of self-preservation, or to refuse, as Bilal did when they were inflicting all sorts of torture on him, even placing a huge rock on his chest in the intense heat and telling him to admit others as partners with Allah. He refused, saying, "Alone, Alone." And he said, "By Allah, if I knew any word more annoying to you than this, I would say it." May Allah be pleased with him. Similarly, when the Liar Musaylimah asked Habib bin Zayd Al-Ansari, "Do you bear witness that Muhammad is the Messenger of Allah" He said, "Yes." Then Musaylimah asked, "Do you bear witness that I am the messenger of Allah" Habib said, "I do not hear you." Musaylimah kept cutting him, piece by piece, but he remained steadfast insisting on his words. It is better and preferable for the Muslim to remain steadfast in his religion, even if that leads to him being killed, as was mentioned by Al-Hafiz Ibn `Asakir in his biography of `Abdullah bin Hudhafah Al-Sahmi, one of the Companions. He said that he was taken prisoner by the Romans, who brought him to their king. The king said, "Become a Christian, and I will give you a share of my kingdom and my daughter in marriage." `Abdullah said: "If you were to give me all that you possess and all that Arabs possess to make me give up the religion of Muhammad even for an instant, I would not do it." The king said, "Then I will kill you." `Abdullah said, "It is up to you." The king gave orders that he should be crucified, and commanded his archers to shoot near his hands and feet while ordering him to become a Christian, but he still refused. Then the king gave orders that he should be brought down, and that a big vessel made of copper be brought and heated up. Then, while `Abdullah was watching, one of the Muslim prisoners was brought out and thrown into it, until all that was left of him was scorched bones. The king ordered him to become a Christian, but he still refused. Then he ordered that `Abdullah be thrown into the vessel, and he was brought back to the pulley to be thrown in. `Abdullah wept, and the king hoped that he would respond to him, so he called him, but `Abdullah said, "I only weep because I have only one soul with which to be thrown into this vessel at this moment for the sake of Allah; I wish that I had as many souls as there are hairs on my body with which I could undergo this torture for the sake of Allah." According to some reports, the king imprisoned him and deprived him of food and drink for several days, then he sent him wine and pork, and he did not come near them. Then the king called him and asked him, "What stopped you from eating" `Abdullah said, "It is permissible for me (under these circumstances), but I did not want to give you the opportunity to gloat." The king said to him, "Kiss my head and I will let you go." `Abdullah said, "And will you release all the Muslim prisoners with me" The king said, "Yes." So `Abdullah kissed his head and he released him and all the other Muslim prisoners he was holding. When he came back, `Umar bin Al-Khattab said, "Every Muslim should kiss the head of `Abdullah bin Hudhafah, and I will be the first to do so." And he stood up and kissed his head. May Allah be pleased with them both.

Surah: 16 Ayah: 110 & Ayah: 111

﴿ ثُمَّ إِنَّ رَبَّكَ لِلَّذِينَ هَاجَرُواْ مِنۢ بَعْدِ مَا فُتِنُواْ ثُمَّ جَٰهَدُواْ وَصَبَرُوٓاْ إِنَّ رَبَّكَ مِنۢ بَعْدِهَا لَغَفُورٌ رَّحِيمٌ ۝ ﴾

110. Then, verily! Your Lord - for those who emigrated after they had been put to trials and thereafter strove hard and fought (for the Cause of Allâh) and were patient, verily, your Lord afterward is, Oft-Forgiving, Most Merciful.

﴿ ۞ يَوْمَ تَأْتِى كُلُّ نَفْسٍ تُجَٰدِلُ عَن نَّفْسِهَا وَتُوَفَّىٰ كُلُّ نَفْسٍ مَّا عَمِلَتْ وَهُمْ لَا يُظْلَمُونَ ۝ ﴾

111. (Remember) the Day when every person will come up pleading for himself, and every one will be paid in full for what he did (good or evil, belief or disbelief in the life of this world) and they will not be dealt with unjustly.

Transliteration

110. Thumma inna rabbaka lillatheena hajaroo min baAAdi ma futinoo thumma jahadoo wasabaroo inna rabbaka min baAAdiha laghafoorun raheemun 111. Yawma ta/tee kullu nafsin tujadilu AAan nafsiha watuwaffa kullu nafsin ma AAamilat wahum la yuthlamoona

Tafsir Ibn Kathir

The One who is forced to renounce Islam will be forgiven if He does Righteous Deeds afterwards

This refers to another group of people who were oppressed in Makkah and whose position with their own people was weak, so they went along with them when they were tried by them. Then they managed to escape by emigrating, leaving their homeland, families and wealth behind, seeking the pleasure and forgiveness of Allah. They joined the believers and fought with them against the disbelievers, bearing hardship with patience. Allah tells them that after this, meaning after their giving in when put to the test, He will forgive them and show mercy to them when they are resurrected.

((Remember) the Day when every person will come pleading) meaning making a case in his own defence.

(for himself.) means, no one else will plead on his behalf; not his father, not his son, nor his brother, nor his wife.

(and every one will be paid in full for what he did,) meaning whatever he did, good or evil.

(and they will not be dealt with unjustly.) meaning there will be no decrease in the reward for good, and no increase in the punishment for evil. They will not be dealt with unjustly in the slightest way.

Surah: 16 Ayah: 112 & Ayah: 113

﴿ وَضَرَبَ ٱللَّهُ مَثَلًا قَرْيَةً كَانَتْ ءَامِنَةً مُّطْمَئِنَّةً يَأْتِيهَا رِزْقُهَا رَغَدًا مِّن كُلِّ مَكَانٍ فَكَفَرَتْ بِأَنْعُمِ ٱللَّهِ فَأَذَاقَهَا ٱللَّهُ لِبَاسَ ٱلْجُوعِ وَٱلْخَوْفِ بِمَا كَانُوا۟ يَصْنَعُونَ ۝

112. And Allâh puts forward the example of a township (Makkah), that dwelt secure and well content: its provision coming to it in abundance from every place, but it (its people) denied the Favors of Allâh (with ungratefulness). So Allâh made it

taste the extreme of hunger (famine) and fear, because of that (evil, i.e. denying Prophet Muhammad (peace be upon him)) which they (its people) used to do.

﴿ وَلَقَدْ جَآءَهُمْ رَسُولٌ مِّنْهُمْ فَكَذَّبُوهُ فَأَخَذَهُمُ ٱلْعَذَابُ وَهُمْ ظَٰلِمُونَ ۝ ﴾

113. And verily, there had come unto them a Messenger (Muhammad (peace be upon him)) from among themselves, but they denied him, so the torment overtook them while they were Zâlimûn (polytheists and wrong-doers).

Transliteration

112. Wadaraba Allahu mathalan qaryatan kanat aminatan mutma-innatan ya/teeha rizquha raghadan min kulli makanin fakafarat bi-anAAumi Allahi faathaqaha Allahu libasa aljooAAi waalkhawfi bima kanoo yasnaAAoona 113. Walaqad jaahum rasoolun minhum fakaththaboohu faakhathahumu alAAathabu wahum thalimoona

Tafsir Ibn Kathir

The Example of Makkah

This example refers to the people of Makkah, which had been secure, peaceful and stable, a secure sanctuary while men were being snatched away from everywhere outside of it. Whoever entered Makkah, he was safe, and he had no need to fear, as Allah said:

(And they say: "If we follow the guidance with you, we would be snatched away from our land." Have We not established a secure sanctuary (Makkah) for them, to which are brought fruits of all kinds, a provision from Ourselves.) (28:57) Similarly, Allah says here:

(its provision coming to it in abundance) meaning, with ease and in plenty,

(from every place, but it (its people) denied the favors of Allah.) meaning, they denied the blessings of Allah towards them, the greatest of which was Muhammad being sent to them, as Allah said:

(Have you not seen those who have changed the favors of Allah into disbelief, and caused their people to dwell in the abode of destruction; Hell, in which they will burn, - and what an evil place to settle in!) (14:28-29). Hence Allah replaced their former blessings with the opposite, and said:

(So Allah made it taste extreme hunger (famine) and fear,) meaning, He inflicted it and made them taste of hunger after fruits of all kinds and provision in abundance from every place had been brought to it. This was when they defied the Messenger of Allah and insisted on opposing him, so he supplicated against them, asking Allah to send them seven years like the seven years of Yusuf (i.e., seven years of famine), and they were stricken with a year in which everything that they had was destroyed, and they ate `Alhaz', which is the hair of the camel mixed with its blood when it is slaughtered.

(and fear). This refers to the fact that their sense of security was replaced with fear of the Messenger of Allah and his Companions after they had migrated to Al-Madinah. They feared the power and the attack of his armies, and they started to lose and face the destruction of everything that belonged to them, until Allah made it possible for His Messenger to conquer Makkah. This happened because of their evil deeds, their wrongdoing and their rejection of the Messenger that Allah sent to them from among themselves. He reminded them of this blessing in the Ayah:

(Indeed, Allah blessed the believers when He sent Messenger from among themselves to them.) (3:164) and,

(So have Taqwa of Allah! O men of understanding who have believed, Allah has indeed revealed to you a reminder (this Qur'an). (And has also sent to you) a Messenger.) (65:10-11) and:

(Similarly (as a blessing), We have sent a Messenger to you from among you, reciting Our Ayat to you, and purifying you, and teaching you the Book (the Qur'an) and the Hikmah (i.e. Sunnah).) Until

(and do not be ungrateful.) (2:151-152) Allah changed the situation of the disbelievers and made it the opposite of what it had been, so they lived in fear after being secure, they were hungry after having plenty of provisions. After the believers lived in fear, Allah granted them security, giving them ample provisions after they lived in poverty, making them rulers, governors and leaders of mankind. This is what we say about the example that was given of the people of Makkah. It was also the opinion of Al-`Awfi and Ibn `Abbas, Mujahid, Qatadah, `Abdur-Rahman bin Zayd bin Aslam, and Malik narrated it from Az-Zuhri as well. May Allah have mercy on them all.

Surah: 16 Ayah: 114, Ayah: 115, Ayah: 116 & Ayah: 117

﴿ فَكُلُواْ مِمَّا رَزَقَكُمُ ٱللَّهُ حَلَٰلًا طَيِّبًا وَٱشْكُرُواْ نِعْمَتَ ٱللَّهِ إِن كُنتُمْ إِيَّاهُ تَعْبُدُونَ ﴾

114. So eat of the lawful and good food which Allâh has provided for you. And be grateful for the Favor of Allâh, if it is He Whom you worship.

﴿ إِنَّمَا حَرَّمَ عَلَيْكُمُ ٱلْمَيْتَةَ وَٱلدَّمَ وَلَحْمَ ٱلْخِنزِيرِ وَمَآ أُهِلَّ لِغَيْرِ ٱللَّهِ بِهِۦ فَمَنِ ٱضْطُرَّ غَيْرَ بَاغٍ وَلَا عَادٍ فَإِنَّ ٱللَّهَ غَفُورٌ رَّحِيمٌ ﴾

115. He has forbidden you only Al-Maitah (meat of a dead animal), blood, the flesh of swine, and any animal which is slaughtered as a sacrifice for others than Allâh (or has been slaughtered for idols or on which Allâh's Name has not been mentioned while slaughtering). But if one is forced by necessity, without willful disobedience, and not transgressing, - then, Allâh is Oft-Forgiving, Most Merciful.

﴿ وَلَا تَقُولُوا لِمَا تَصِفُ أَلْسِنَتُكُمُ ٱلْكَذِبَ هَٰذَا حَلَٰلٌ وَهَٰذَا حَرَامٌ لِتَفْتَرُوا عَلَى ٱللَّهِ ٱلْكَذِبَ إِنَّ ٱلَّذِينَ يَفْتَرُونَ عَلَى ٱللَّهِ ٱلْكَذِبَ لَا يُفْلِحُونَ ۝ ﴾

116. And say not concerning that which your tongues put forth falsely: "This is lawful and this is forbidden," so as to invent lies against Allâh. Verily, those who invent lies against Allâh will never prosper.

﴿ مَتَٰعٌ قَلِيلٌ وَلَهُمْ عَذَابٌ أَلِيمٌ ۝ ﴾

117. A passing brief enjoyment (will be theirs), but they will have a painful torment.

Transliteration

114. Fakuloo mimma razaqakumu Allahu halalan tayyiban waoshkuroo niAAmata Allahi in kuntum iyyahu taAAbudoona 115. Innama harrama AAalaykumu almaytata waalddama walahma alkhinzeeri wama ohilla lighayri Allahi bihi famani idturra ghayra baghin wala AAadin fa-inna Allaha ghafoorun raheemun 116. Wala taqooloo lima tasifu alsinatukumu alkathiba hatha halalun wahatha haramun litaftaroo AAala Allahi alkathiba inna allatheena yaftaroona AAala Allahi alkathiba la yuflihoona 117. MataAAun qaleelun walahum AAathabun aleemun

Tafsir Ibn Kathir

The Command to eat Lawful Provisions and to be Thankful, and an Explanation of what is Unlawful

Allah orders His believing servants to eat the good and lawful things that He has provided, and to give thanks to Him for that, for He is the Giver and Originator of all favors, Who alone deserves to be worshipped, having no partners or associate. Then Allah mentions what He has forbidden things which harm them in both religious and worldly affairs, i.,e., dead meat, blood and the flesh of pigs.

(and any animal which is slaughtered as a sacrifice for other than Allah.) meaning, it was slaughtered with the mention of a name other than that of Allah. Nevertheless,

(But if one is forced by necessity.) meaning, if one needs to do it, without deliberately disobeying or transgressing, then,

(Allah is Pardoning, Most Merciful.) We have already discussed a similar Ayah in Surat Al-Baqarah, and there is no need to repeat it here. And to Allah be praise. Then Allah forbids us to follow the ways of the idolators who declare things to be permitted or forbidden based upon their own whims and whatever names they agree on, such as the Bahirah (a she-camel whose milk was spared for the idols and nobody was allowed to milk it), the Sa'ibah (a she-camel let loose for free pasture for their false gods, idols, etc., and nothing was allowed to be carried on it), the Wasilah (a she-camel set free for idols because it has given birth to a she-camel at its first delivery and then again gives birth to a she-camel at its second delivery) and the Ham (a stallion camel freed from work for the sake of their idols, after it had finished a number of acts of copulation assigned for it), and so on. All of these were laws and customs that were invented during jahiliyyah. Then Allah says:

(And do not describe what your tongues have lied about, saying: "This is lawful and this is forbidden," to invent lies against Allah.) This includes everyone who comes up with an innovation (Bid`ah) for which he has no evidence from the Shari`ah, or whoever declares something lawful that Allah has forbidden, or whoever declares something unlawful that Allah has permitted, only because it suits his opinions or whim to do so.

(describe what...) meaning, do not speak lies because of what your tongues put forth. Then Allah warns against that by saying:

(Verily, those who invent lies against Allah, will never succeed.) meaning, either in this world or the Hereafter. As for this world, it is transient pleasure, and in the Hereafter, theirs will be a severe punishment, as Allah says:

(We let them enjoy for a little while, then in the end We will drive them into an unrelenting punishment.) (31:24) and

(Verily, those who invent a lie against Allah, will never be successful. (A brief) enjoyment in this world! and then to Us will be their return, then We shall make them taste the severest torment because they disbelieved.) (10:69-70)

Surah: 16 Ayah: 118 & Ayah: 119

﴿ وَعَلَى ٱلَّذِينَ هَادُواْ حَرَّمْنَا مَا قَصَصْنَا عَلَيْكَ مِن قَبْلُ ۖ وَمَا ظَلَمْنَٰهُمْ وَلَٰكِن كَانُوٓاْ أَنفُسَهُمْ يَظْلِمُونَ ۝ ﴾

118. And unto those who are Jews, We have forbidden such things as We have mentioned to you (O Muhammad (peace be upon him)) before (see Verse 6:146). And We wronged them not, but they used to wrong themselves.

﴿ ثُمَّ إِنَّ رَبَّكَ لِلَّذِينَ عَمِلُواْ ٱلسُّوٓءَ بِجَهَٰلَةٍ ثُمَّ تَابُواْ مِنۢ بَعْدِ ذَٰلِكَ وَأَصْلَحُوٓاْ إِنَّ رَبَّكَ مِنۢ بَعْدِهَا لَغَفُورٌ رَّحِيمٌ ۝ ﴾

119. Then, verily! Your Lord - for those who do evil (commit sins and are disobedient to Allâh) in ignorance and afterward repent and do righteous deeds, verily, your Lord thereafter, (to such) is Oft-Forgiving, Most Merciful.

Transliteration

118. WaAAala allatheena hadoo harramna ma qasasna AAalayka min qablu wama thalamnahum walakin kanoo anfusahum yathlimoona   119. Thumma inna rabbaka lillatheena AAamiloo alssoo-a bijahalatin thumma taboo min baAAdi thalika waaslahoo inna rabbaka min baAAdiha laghafoorun raheemun

Tafsir Ibn Kathir

Some Good Things were Forbidden for the Jews

After mentioning that He has forbidden us to eat dead meat, blood, the flesh of swine, and any animal which is slaughtered as a sacrifice for others than Allah, and after making allowances for cases of necessity - which is part of making things easy for this Ummah, because Allah desires ease for us, not hardship - Allah then mentions what He forbade for the Jews in their laws before they were abrogated, and the restrictions, limitations and difficulties involved therein. He tells us:

(And for those who are Jews, We have forbidden such things as We have mentioned to you before.) meaning in Surat Al-An`am, where Allah says:

(And unto those who are Jews, We forbade every (animal) with undivided hoof, and We forbade them the fat of the ox and the sheep except what adheres to their backs) Until,

(We are indeed truthful) (6:146) Hence Allah says here:

(And We did not wrong them,) meaning, in the restrictions that We imposed upon them.

(but they wronged themselves.) meaning, they deserved that. This is like the Ayah:

(Because of the wrong committed of those who were Jews, We prohibited certain good foods which had been lawful for them - and (also) for their hindering many from Allah's way.) (4:160) Then Allah tells us, honoring and remin- ding believers who have sinned of His blessings, that who- ever among them repents, He will accept his repentance, as He says:

(Then, your Lord for those who did evil out of ignorance) Some of the Salaf said that this means that everyone who disobeys Allah is ignorant.

(and afterward repent and do righteous deeds) meaning, they give up the sins they used to commit and turn to doing acts of obedience to Allah.

(verily, after that, your Lord is...) means, after that mistake

(...Pardoning, Most Merciful.)

Surah: 16 Ayah: 120, Ayah: 121, Ayah: 122 & Ayah: 123

﴿ إِنَّ إِبْرَٰهِيمَ كَانَ أُمَّةً قَانِتًا لِلَّهِ حَنِيفًا وَلَمْ يَكُ مِنَ ٱلْمُشْرِكِينَ ۝ ﴾

120. Verily, Ibrâhîm (Abraham) was an Ummah (a leader having all the good righteous qualities), or a nation, obedient to Allâh, Hanîf (i.e. to worship none but Allâh), and he was not one of those who were Al-Mushrikûn (polytheists, idolaters, disbelievers in the Oneness of Allâh, and those who joined partners with Allâh).

﴿ شَاكِرًا لِّأَنْعُمِهِ ٱجْتَبَىٰهُ وَهَدَىٰهُ إِلَىٰ صِرَٰطٍ مُّسْتَقِيمٍ ۝ ﴾

121. (He was) thankful for His (Allâh's) Favors. He (Allâh) chose him (as an intimate friend) and guided him to a Straight Path (Islâmic Monotheism - neither Judaism nor Christianity).

﴿ وَءَاتَيْنَٰهُ فِى ٱلدُّنْيَا حَسَنَةً ۖ وَإِنَّهُۥ فِى ٱلْءَاخِرَةِ لَمِنَ ٱلصَّٰلِحِينَ ۝ ﴾

122. And We gave him good in this world, and in the Hereafter he shall be of the righteous.

﴿ ثُمَّ أَوْحَيْنَآ إِلَيْكَ أَنِ ٱتَّبِعْ مِلَّةَ إِبْرَٰهِيمَ حَنِيفًا ۖ وَمَا كَانَ مِنَ ٱلْمُشْرِكِينَ ۝ ﴾

123. Then, We have sent the revelation to you (O Muhammad (peace be upon him) saying): "Follow the religion of Ibrâhîm (Abraham) Hanîf (Islâmic Monotheism - to worship none but Allâh) and he was not of the Mushrikûn (polytheists, idolaters and disbelievers).

Transliteration

120. Inna ibraheema kana ommatan qanitan lillahi haneefan walam yaku mina almushrikeena 121. Shakiran li-anAAumihi ijtabahu wahadahu ila siratin mustaqeemin 122. Waataynahu fee alddunya hasanatan wa-innahu fee al-akhirati lamina alssaliheena 123. Thumma awhayna ilayka ani ittabiAA millata ibraheema haneefan wama kana mina almushrikeena

Tafsir Ibn Kathir

He selected him, as Allah says :

(And before, We indeed gave Ibrahim his integrity, and We were indeed most knowledgeable about him)(21:51). Then Allah says:

(and guided him to a straight path.) which means to worship Allah alone, without partners or associate, in the manner that He prescribed and which pleases Him.

(And We gave him good in this world,) meaning, `We granted him all that a believer may require for a good and complete life in this world.'

(and in the Hereafter he shall be of the righteous.) Concerning the Ayah: (And We gave him good in this world,) Mujahid said: "This means a truthful tongue."

(Then, We have sent the revelation to you: "Follow the religion of Ibrahim (he was a) Hanif. ..) meaning, `because of his perfection, greatness, and the soundness of his Tawhid and his way, We revealed to you, O Seal of the Messengers and Leader of the Prophets ,'

(Follow the religion of Ibrahim (he was a) Hanif and he was not of the idolaters.) This is like the Ayah in Surat Al-An`am: (Say: "Truly, my Lord has guided me to a straight path, a right religion, the religion of Ibrahim, (he was a) Hanif and he was not of the idolators.") (6:161). Then Allah rebukes the Jews,

Surah: 16 Ayah: 124

﴿ إِنَّمَا جُعِلَ ٱلسَّبْتُ عَلَى ٱلَّذِينَ ٱخْتَلَفُواْ فِيهِ ۚ وَإِنَّ رَبَّكَ لَيَحْكُمُ بَيْنَهُمْ يَوْمَ ٱلْقِيَـٰمَةِ فِيمَا كَانُواْ فِيهِ يَخْتَلِفُونَ ۝ ﴾

124. The Sabbath was only prescribed for those who differed concerning it, and verily, your Lord will judge between them on the Day of Resurrection about that wherein they used to differ.

Transliteration

124. Innama juAAila alssabtu AAala allatheena ikhtalafoo feehi wa-inna rabbaka layahkumu baynahum yawma alqiyamati feema kanoo feehi yakhtalifoona

Tafsir Ibn Kathir

The Prescription of the Sabbath for the Jews

There is no doubt that for every nation, Allah prescribed one day of the week for people to gather to worship Him. For this Ummah He prescribed Friday, because it is the sixth day, on which Allah completed and perfected His creation. On this day He gathered and completed His blessings for His servants. It was said that Allah prescribed this day for the Children of Israel through His Prophet Musa, but they changed it and chose Saturday because it was the day on which the Creator did not create anything, as He had completed His creation on Friday. Allah made observance of the Sabbath obligatory for them in the laws of the Tawrah (Torah), telling them to keep the Sabbath. At the same time, He told them to follow Muhammad when he was sent, and took their promises and covenant to that effect. Hence Allah says:

(The Sabbath was only prescribed for those who differed concerning it,) Mujahid said: "They observed the Sabbath (Saturday) and ignored Friday." Then they continued to observe Saturday until Allah sent `Isa bin Maryam. It was said that he told them to change it to Sunday, and it was also said that he did not forsake the laws of the Tawrah except for a few rulings which were abrogated, and he continued to observe the Sabbath until he was taken up (into heaven). Afterwards, the Christians at the time of Constantine were the ones who changed it to Sunday in order to be different from the Jews, and they started to pray towards the east instead of facing the Dome (i.e., Jerusalem). And Allah knows best. It was reported in the Two Sahihs that Abu Hurayrah heard the Messenger of Allah say:

Chapter 16: An-Nahl (The Bee), Verses 001-128

«نَحْنُ الْآخِرُونَ السَّابِقُونَ يَوْمَ الْقِيَامَةِ، بَيْدَ أَنَّهُمْ أُوتُوا الْكِتَابَ مِنْ قَبْلِنَا، ثُمَّ هَذَا يَوْمُهُمُ الَّذِي فَرَضَ اللهُ عَلَيْهِمْ فَاخْتَلَفُوا فِيهِ، فَهَدَانَا اللهُ لَهُ، فَالنَّاسُ لَنَا فِيهِ تَبَعٌ: الْيَهُودُ غَدًا وَالنَّصَارَى بَعْدَ غَدٍ»

(We are the last, but we will be the first on the Day of Resurrection, even though they were given the Book before us. This is the day that Allah obligated upon them, but they differed concerning it. Allah guided us to this day, and the people observe their days after us, the Jews on the following day and the Christians on the day after that.) This version was recorded by Al-Bukhari. It was reported that Abu Hurayrah and Hudhayfah said that the Messenger of Allah said:

«أَضَلَّ اللهُ عَنِ الْجُمُعَةِ مَنْ كَانَ قَبْلَنَا، فَكَانَ لِلْيَهُودِ يَوْمُ السَّبْتِ، وَكَانَ لِلنَّصَارَى يَوْمُ الْأَحَدِ، فَجَاءَ اللهُ بِنَا فَهَدَانَا اللهُ لِيَوْمِ الْجُمُعَةِ، فَجَعَلَ الْجُمُعَةَ وَالسَّبْتَ وَالْأَحَدَ، وَكَذَلِكَ هُمْ تَبَعٌ لَنَا يَوْمَ الْقِيَامَةِ نَحْنُ الْآخِرُونَ مِنْ أَهْلِ الدُّنْيَا، وَالْأَوَّلُونَ يَوْمَ الْقِيَامَةِ، وَالْمَقْضِيُّ بَيْنَهُمْ قَبْلَ الْخَلَائِقِ»

(Allah let the people who came before us stray from Friday, so the Jews had Saturday and the Christians had Sunday. Then Allah brought us and guided us to Friday. So now there are Friday, Saturday and Sunday, thus they will follow us on the Day of Resurrection. We are the last of the people of this world, but will be the first on the Day of Resurrection, and will be the first to be judged, before all of creation.) It was reported by Muslim.

Surah: 16 Ayah: 125

﴿ ادْعُ إِلَىٰ سَبِيلِ رَبِّكَ بِالْحِكْمَةِ وَالْمَوْعِظَةِ الْحَسَنَةِ ۖ وَجَادِلْهُم بِالَّتِي هِيَ أَحْسَنُ ۚ إِنَّ رَبَّكَ هُوَ أَعْلَمُ بِمَن ضَلَّ عَن سَبِيلِهِ ۖ وَهُوَ أَعْلَمُ بِالْمُهْتَدِينَ ﴾

125. Invite (mankind, O Muhammad (peace be upon him)) to the Way of your Lord (i.e. Islâm) with wisdom (i.e. with the Divine Revelation and the Qur'ân) and fair preaching, and argue with them in a way that is better. Truly, your Lord knows best who has gone astray from His Path, and He is the Best Aware of those who are guided.

Transliteration

125. OdAAu ila sabeeli rabbika bialhikmati waalmawAAithati alhasanati wajadilhum biallatee hiya ahsanu inna rabbaka huwa aAAlamu biman dalla AAan sabeelihi wahuwa aAAlamu bialmuhtadeena

Tafsir Ibn Kathir

The Command to invite people to Allah with Wisdom and Good Preaching

Allah commands His Messenger Muhammad to invite the people to Allah with Hikmah (wisdom). Ibn Jarir said: "That is what was revealed to him from the Book and the Sunnah."

(and fair preaching) meaning, with exhortation and stories of the events that happened to people that are mentioned in the Qur'an, which he is to tell them about in order to warn them of the punishment of Allah.

(and argue with them with that which is best.) meaning, if any of them want to debate and argue, then let that be in the best manner, with kindness, gentleness and good speech, as Allah says elsewhere:

(And do not argue with the People of the Book, unless it be with that which is best, except for those who purposefully do wrong.) (29:46) Allah commanded him to speak gently, as He commanded Musa and Harun to do when he sent them to Pharaoh, as He said:

(And speak to him mildly, perhaps he may accept admonition or fear (Allah))(20: 44).

(Truly, your Lord best knows who has strayed from His path,) meaning, Allah already knows who is doomed (destined for Hell) and who is blessed (destined for Paradise). This has already been written with Him and the matter is finished, so call them to Allah, but do not exhaust yourself with regret over those who go astray, for it is not your task to guide them. You are just a warner, and all you have to do is convey the Message, and it is He Who will bring them to account.

(You cannot guide whom you love) (28:56)

(It is not up to you to guide them, but Allah guides whom He wills.) (2:72)

Surah: 16 Ayah: 126, Ayah: 127 & Ayah: 128

﴿ وَإِنْ عَاقَبْتُمْ فَعَاقِبُوا۟ بِمِثْلِ مَا عُوقِبْتُم بِهِۦ ۖ وَلَئِن صَبَرْتُمْ لَهُوَ خَيْرٌ لِّلصَّٰبِرِينَ ﴾

126. And if you punish (your enemy, O you believers in the Oneness of Allâh), then punish them with the like of that with which you were afflicted. But if you endure patiently, verily, it is better for As-Sâbirûn (the patient).

$$\text{﴿ وَاصْبِرْ وَمَا صَبْرُكَ إِلَّا بِاللَّهِ ۚ وَلَا تَحْزَنْ عَلَيْهِمْ وَلَا تَكُ فِي ضَيْقٍ مِّمَّا يَمْكُرُونَ ﴾ ﴿١٢٧﴾}$$

127. And endure you patiently (O Muhammad (peace be upon him)) your patience is not but from Allâh. And grieve not over them (polytheists and pagans), and be not distressed because of what they plot.

$$\text{﴿ إِنَّ اللَّهَ مَعَ الَّذِينَ اتَّقَوا وَّالَّذِينَ هُم مُّحْسِنُونَ ﴾ ﴿١٢٨﴾}$$

128. Truly, Allâh is with those who fear Him (keep their duty unto Him), and those who are Muhsinûn (good-doers).

Transliteration

126. Wa-in AAaqabtum faAAaqiboo bimithli ma AAooqibtum bihi wala-in sabartum lahuwa khayrun lilssabireena   127. Waisbir wama sabruka illa biAllahi wala tahzan AAalayhim wala taku fee dayqin mimma yamkuroona   128. Inna Allaha maAAa allatheena ittaqaw waallatheena hum muhsinoona

Tafsir Ibn Kathir

The Command for Equality in Punishment

Allah commands justice in punishment and equity in settling the cases of rights. `Abdur-Razzaq recorded that, concerning the Ayah,

(then punish them with the like of that with which you were afflicted.) Ibn Sirin said, "If a man among you takes something from you, then you should take something similar from him." This was also the opinion of Mujahid, Ibrahim, Al-Hasan Al-Basri, and others. Ibn Jarir also favored this opinion. Ibn Zayd said: "They had been commanded to forgive the idolators, then some men became Muslim who were strong and powerful. They said, `O Messenger of Allah, if only Allah would give us permission, we would sort out these dogs!' Then this Ayah was revealed, then it was latter abrogated by the command to engage in Jihad."

(And be patient, and your patience will not be but by the help of Allah.) This emphasizes the command to be patient and tells us that patience cannot be acquired except by the will, help, decree and power of Allah. Then Allah says:

(And do not grieve over them,) meaning, those who oppose you, for Allah has decreed that this should happen.

(and do not be distressed) means do not be worried or upset.

(by their plots.) meaning; because of the efforts they are putting into opposing you and causing you harm, for Allah is protecting, helping, and supporting you, and He will cause you to prevail and defeat them.

(Truly, Allah is with those who have Taqwa, and the doers of good.) meaning; He is with them in the sense of supporting them, helping them and guiding them. This is a special kind of "being with", as Allah says elsewhere:

((Remember) when your Lord revealed to the angels, "Verily, I am with you, so support those who believe.") (8:12) And Allah said to Musa and Harun:

(Fear not, verily I am with you both, hearing and seeing.) (20:46) The Prophet said to (Abu Bakr) As-Siddiq when they were in the cave:

«لَا تَحْزَنْ إِنَّ اللهَ مَعَنَا»

(Do not worry, Allah is with us.") The general kind of "being with" some one, or something is by means of seeing, hearing and knowing, as Allah says:

(And He is with you wherever you may be. And Allah sees whatever you do.) (57:4)

(Have you not seen that Allah knows whatever is in the heavens and whatever is on the earth There is no secret counsel of three but He is their fourth, - nor of five but He is their sixth, - nor of less than that or more, but He is with them wherever they may be.) (58:7)

(You will not be in any circumstance, nor recite any portion of the Qur'an, nor having done any deeds, but We are witnessing you.) (10:61)

(those who have Taqwa) means, they keep away from that which is forbidden.

(and the doers of good.) meaning they do deeds of obedience to Allah. These are the ones whom Allah takes care of, He gives them support, and helps them to prevail over their enemies and opponents.

This is end of the Tafsir of Surat An-Nahl. To Allah be praise and blessings, and peace and blessings be upon Muhammad and his family and Companions.

www.ingramcontent.com/pod-product-compliance
Lightning Source LLC
Chambersburg PA
CBHW081113080526
44587CB00021B/3574